PRAISE FOR

The Real Pepsi C

"A well-written and well-researched story of unsung pioneers in the struggle for equality in the American workplace. A must-read for all executives looking for new ideas to diversify their organizations by learning from one of the most inspirational stories in business history."

—Patrick T. Harker, Dean, The Wharton School,
University of Pennsylvania

"A pacesetting book for emerging efforts to give long overdue credit to the historically ignored, historically neglected, and historically forgotten in the 1940s and 1950s, who through their sacrifices helped quicken the death of Jim Crow America. It reminds us how far we've come toward building an inclusive society since these pioneers paved such transformative paths—and how much work is left to do."

—John H. Stanfield II, author of *Philanthropy and Jim Crow in American Social Science*

WALL
STREET
JOURNAL
BOOKS

THE

REAL PEPSI
CHALLENGE

*How One Pioneering Company Broke Color
Barriers in 1940s American Business*

Stephanie Capparell

Wall Street Journal Books

NEW YORK · LONDON · TORONTO · SYDNEY

WALL STREET JOURNAL BOOKS

A WALL STREET JOURNAL BOOK
Published by Free Press
A Division of Simon & Schuster, Inc.
1230 Avenue of the Americas
New York, NY 10020

Copyright © 2007 by Stephanie Capparell

First Wall Street Journal Book trade paperback edition February 2008

FREE PRESS and colophon are
trademarks of Simon & Schuster, Inc.

The Wall Street Journal and The Wall Street Journal Book colophon
are trademarks of Dow Jones & Company, Inc.

For information about special discounts for bulk purchases,
please contact Simon & Schuster Special Sales: 1-800-456-6798
or business@simonandschuster.com.

Text design by Paul Dippolito

Manufactured in the United States of America

1   3   5   7   9   10   8   6   4   2

The Library of Congress has cataloged the hardcover edition as follows:

Capparell, Stephanie.
The real Pepsi challenge: the inspirational story of breaking the color barrier
in American business / Stephanie Capparell.
p.   cm.
Includes bibliographical references and index.
1. PepsiCo, inc.—Employees—Recruiting—History.   2. African American executives—
United States—History.   3. Cola drinks —United States—Marketing—History.
4. African American consumers—United States—History.   I. Title.
HD9349.S634   P462   2007
338.7'66362092396073—dc22   2006041267

ISBN-13: 978-0-7432-6571-3
ISBN-10:   0-7432-6571-8
ISBN-13: 978-0-7432-6572-0 (pbk)
ISBN-10:   0-7432-6572-6 (pbk)

For my parents,
R. Michael and Geneva Roman Capparell,
who taught their children
that everyone deserves a chance

Contents

Introduction

THE START OF THE RIVALRY BETWEEN THE PEPSI-COLA and Coca-Cola companies in the 1940s is legend in business. Less known is that a bigger, more important battle was being fought on the front lines of the cola wars at the same time: the struggle of African-Americans to gain access to white Corporate America. Underdog Pepsi-Cola—under the direction of an astute businessman with a keen sense of his role as a leader—joined forces with a group of striving African-American professionals. Their union made history, and taught American businesses a lesson in the value of a diverse workforce.

To the ranks of the unsung civil rights pioneers, add Pepsi's first special-markets sales staff. Instead of schoolrooms or lunch counters, their struggles and victories took place in offices, storefronts, and factory floors. You haven't heard the names of these men in the myriad books written about the cola wars over the decades. They were workers whose talents were hidden in plain sight because of their race; their stories played out before the civil rights revolution. Businesses were just awakening to the potential of a diverse work place and untapped markets.

The Pepsi-Cola experiment began in 1940 with the hiring of a single black man, Herman T. Smith, and was followed by the addition of two young business interns—Allen L. McKellar and Jeanette Maund.

Their mandate was to help Pepsi-Cola—then a struggling upstart— expand its consumption among African-American customers.

Some seven years before Jackie Robinson and Larry Doby integrated baseball's major leagues, these national sales representatives broke through the corporate color line. In retrospect, the Pepsi salesmen had even more of an uphill battle. Integrating sports meant creating opportunities for a few uniquely talented individuals for the sake of everyone's entertainment. Integrating business, by contrast, was a far more sweeping—and for some, threatening—proposition in white society: an invitation to the rank and file of an entire race to vie for the same jobs as everyone else in the corporate hierarchy. Yet, the business pioneers were optimistic. "Conditions are far from perfect, of course," said Maund in polite understatement during an interview at the time, "but if we can do what we have against obstacles, surely we need not be afraid of our future."

World War II interrupted the development of the special-markets department. Once the war was over, however, a renewed effort began with an even greater impetus to succeed. The victory over Hitler had encouraged social reformers in the United States to work toward making the world more just and egalitarian. It also was a time of ferment in the business world—the democratization of commerce itself. Companies were perfecting mass distribution and getting to know their consumers as individuals with particular tastes. Business leaders were beginning to see their employees as valuable contributors to their companies' success. "It was a contribution to social progress," said Edward F. Boyd, who joined the Pepsi-Cola Company in 1947 as assistant sales manager and was put in charge of selling to what was then called the Negro market. "I didn't make that much of a dollar. I wasn't paid on the basis of other executives. It was at the beginning."

Boyd was an astute judge of character, and gathered and trained a talented marketing force. Sales of the cola surged wherever the team members went; at one point they helped Pepsi outsell all its rivals in some Northern cities. It was an object lesson for other companies that were ignoring the African-American consumer and standing on the sidelines when it came to integrating their professional staffs.

On their way to nudging their country to a better place, the sales team helped define niche marketing some thirty years before it became a widespread business strategy. They gave formal talks to white driver-salesmen about their role in the company, thereby instigating some of the earliest formalized diversity training. They also helped to instill in African-Americans a unique sense of brand loyalty—to products produced by companies with a commitment to social progress as much as to product quality.

Pepsi's innovation was remarkable for its day. It took a boss with the pluck and foresight of Walter S. Mack, Jr., who led Pepsi-Cola from 1938 to 1950. He gave the team the personnel, budget, and creative freedom to explore the market on a national scale, and fully recognized its clout. "One of the truly great pleasures I have is in helping other people, giving a guy a job so that he can build himself up," he once wrote.

It didn't matter to Walter Mack that in Coke he had a rival that was linked in the American psyche with Santa Claus and the American G.I. He was the feisty, progressive New Yorker pitted against a gentleman of the Old South, Coca-Cola president Robert Woodruff, an executive known for his opposition to "racial mixing" on the job or in society at large. Mr. Woodruff did give generously to black universities, but that kind of generosity only helped prop up the system of segregation. When Mack made contributions, they were tied to opportunities and focused on individuals. It made all the difference.

This is not to say that Walter Mack was a starry-eyed do-gooder. Above all, he was motivated by the bottom line. When he looked at black, he also saw green. African-American leaders themselves had shrewdly pushed the idea to businesses that the population of fourteen million blacks in the United States represented a gold mine of pent-up consumer demand, and Mack wanted his share. None of this big picture was lost on the salesmen, who were realistic about their roles at the company. "I adored the man, but all he cared about in the end was one thing: selling Pepsi," said Boyd of his boss. "That was always foremost in his mind."

On the road, the team members became role models at a time when few Americans had ever seen a young black man with a corporate business card. But the corporate office was a lonely place for African-Americans in the 1940s. Back at headquarters, the very presence of the special-market salesmen raised touchy questions: Would black Americans fit into Pepsi-Cola's corporate culture? Could the company help develop these promising careers and keep them in the corporate family? How could management promote the men above their narrow specialty to leadership roles that guide the company as a whole?

That was the real Pepsi challenge.

The Pepsi team itself had no role models, yet somehow its members were superbly prepared for the task at hand. Working with limited resources, they crisscrossed the country to speak in black churches, women's clubs, civic centers, fraternities, campuses, and convention halls. Boyd and the Pepsi staff created advertising that was among the first to show African-Americans, and hired some of the first professional black models. Their work made a mockery of the degrading images of blacks prevalent at the time in both mainstream and black media. They dared to create ads celebrating African-Americans of achievement. Their most popular series of ads ended up as a classroom teaching tool in African-American high schools and colleges around the country. More shocking still for its day were their ad campaigns that portrayed blacks as stylish, fun-loving, middle-class citizens living the American Dream.

The Pepsi team's accomplishments were all the more impressive considering the enormous obstacles they faced in the segregated America of the day. They were traveling salesmen who had to sit in the backs of buses, ride in separate train compartments, and eat behind closed curtains in dining cars. Because many restaurants and hotels across the country didn't want their business, they often had to rely on a network of families willing to give them food and lodging in their homes while on the road.

With innate gifts of tact, humor, and sheer grit, the salesmen successfully navigated this demoralizing minefield. If their sojourn in Corporate America was often filled with disappointments, the team members rose above them. "I knew what the mission was," said Harvey C. Russell, one of Boyd's more inspired hires. "There were no other places you could get that type of job. Pepsi was really the first. They, and a couple of others, were the only ones that had these black salespeople."

In all, Boyd hired at least sixteen men during the four-plus years his team was active. At its peak in size and responsibility, Boyd had eleven men under him. The experience of these dozen men is the focus of this book. Six of them lived to tell their stories here: Edward F. Boyd, a onetime actor and singer in films, who was working for the National Urban League when he was picked to create the special-markets team; Allen L. McKellar, who first joined Pepsi as an intern in 1940 after he won a company essay contest and returned in 1950; Charles E. Wilson, a graduate of Virginia's Hampton Institute with a dream of becoming a doctor; William Simms, who was ordered by the great American thinker and human-rights advocate W. E. B. DuBois to get an education and get ahead; Jean F. Emmons, one of the few black MBAs in America; and Julian C. Nicholas, who came from a family of businessmen—and especially businesswomen—with a drive to succeed. Shortly after the publication of this book, Edward Boyd died at age 92.

Two more—Harvey C. Russell and Richard L. Hurt—were interviewed for my 1997 *Wall Street Journal* column on the Pepsi team, but have since died. Other team members whose contributions are greatly missed include David F. Watson, H. Floyd Britton, Harold W. Woodruff, Alexander L. Jackson, Frank L. Smith, Winston C. Wright, Paul D. Davis, and William E. Payne.

After the breakup of the team, most of the men went on to remarkable second careers in international business, politics, journalism, medicine, and education. One, Harvey Russell, became a vice president at Pepsi-Cola in 1962, the first African-American to earn that title at a major corporation.

The life stories of the Pepsi salesmen connect us to the depth and complexity of the African-American experience in the twentieth century. Lest their stories seem a musty glimpse of a shameful bygone era, know that after I first told this story in the 1997 article, I received repeated calls from a Ku Klux Klan member who tried unsuccessfully to get an interview for the Grand Wizard. The article had mentioned a long-ago, Klan-led boycott of Pepsi, and the woman wanted to defend the Klan's side of the story.

My research for this book began with interviews of the team members. They were in their eighties and nineties. I was counting on recollections of each person's path to success despite adversity. Among the most moving stories told to me were those about the support given by their families and communities to prepare them for life's struggles. But before long it was clear I was among business royalty, the likes of which I had rarely seen during fifteen years of writing and editing for the *Journal*.

That they were ahead of their time is evidenced by the fact that it wasn't until 1952, a year after the team was disbanded, that *The Wall Street Journal* first addressed in a major article the so-called Negro market. The story valued the black population's total income at fifteen billion dollars, a 50 percent increase over estimates made elsewhere just five years earlier. Ever since then, newspapers have reported consistently on "the increasing importance of the expanding market" represented by African-Americans.

My first book, *Shackleton's Way,* was about the lessons learned from a hair-raising tale of survival of a crew shipwrecked in the savage nature of Antarctica. This is another tale of survival, in the uncharted waters of social progress, and it seems that manmade disasters can be every bit as harrowing. The lessons learned from the Pepsi men are how to strive for personal excellence even when the rewards seem distant. From their corporate leaders we see how a business can thrive only where diversity thrives; that the roadblocks to social progress are the same as those that hamper economic success.

To help document their experiences, team members saved an impressive sampling of their workaday correspondence, photographs, and newspaper clippings, and generously offered them for research on this book. Extensive research was done to corroborate their recollections where possible. Long-forgotten ad campaigns by various creative talents subsequently were unearthed. Where practical, articles and letters are generously quoted here to capture the language of the times. *Negro* was the accepted word for African-Americans at mid-twentieth century, and African-Americans had to fight just to ensure it was always capitalized in print and properly pronounced. The term *special markets* is used interchangeably with *Negro market* to describe the Pepsi-Cola campaign, even though the sales team was in the process of redefining its meaning.

It is a challenge to recount in brief African-American history of this period. I read through a dozen years of black weekly newspapers on microfilm and, thanks to modern search engines, more than one hundred years of major dailies on specific topics. The description of the events of the day—in turns shocking and joyful—as told by African-American journalists at the weeklies was overwhelming, and I am indebted to my colleagues of yesteryear for their diligent reporting of the background of this story.

The famous dates in history, the landmark court cases, the new laws, the successful marches, the worthy black heroes, the enlightened white leaders—all grabbed the spotlight for a time, but they tell only part of the story. Progress came in almost imperceptible increments, with changes repeatedly written in sand before they became a concrete gain. The Pepsi team members worked at a time when the African-American population encouraged many Rosa Parkses before *the* Rosa Parks refused to take a back seat on a bus. These foot soldiers tirelessly staged protests and walkouts and won scores of smaller court victories over a brutal system of segregation under the so-called Jim Crow laws.

These leaders were stalwarts of what has been dubbed the Greatest Generation, the ones who translated a wartime victory over white supremacy overseas into a peacetime struggle for equality at home. They were living among aging former slaves and self-made millionaires—and some who were both. Most of their neighbors may have worn workers' overalls, but they were able to envision themselves in the highest echelons of business and government. That they never doubted their eventual success was a remarkable show of faith in America.

The marketing team's endeavor was in many ways a resounding success: a study in how determination, focus, and a sense of purpose on the part of employees, combined with enlightened leadership, can enhance the bottom line while offering social benefits beyond the walls of the corporation. Jean Emmons, who joined the team in 1950, one day pulled out a newspaper clipping he kept in his pocket, dated in the late 1990s, that listed "major U.S. companies where blacks wield the most clout." It started with Kenneth I. Chenault, CEO of American Express, and ended with Oprah Winfrey, chairman and CEO of Harpo Incorporated. "I'm proud I helped make that possible," said Emmons, who left Pepsi to earn a PhD in education. "There's no way in the world that in 1950 anyone outside of God would have said this result today was possible."

The result ultimately included the promotion in August 2006 of Indra K. Nooyi, a fifty-year-old woman born in India, to the post of chief executive officer of PepsiCo Incorporated, just months after another "unthinkable" had happened: PepsiCo had surpassed the Coca-Cola Company in terms of market capitalization, roughly $105.4 billion to $103 billion.

The project's failures were more complicated. In short, Pepsi-Cola's early foray into diversifying its workforce, while a gigantic leap for its day, was seen by some of its managers as a limited task rather than the seeds of a permanent transformation of a modern corporation. In the end, the team was broken up without any meaningful plan for the continued hiring and promoting of minority applicants.

Many issues about race and opportunity that surfaced then have not yet been resolved in the business world. Managers today aren't so much thinking about how to keep minorities out, as they aren't thinking about minorities at all. But maintaining diversity is an ongoing task, said Frank Wu, dean of Wayne State University Law School, not an assignment to be completed and checked off a list. "Diversity, like democracy, is a process; it never ends," he said. "If you're an optimist, you should never want it to end. No one ever says, 'I can't believe I'm here voting again.' The goal is to participate in something larger than yourself and to keep inviting more people to participate."

When looking at discrimination, our society has come to rely on a useful cliché: We've come a long way, but we still have a long way to go. It's critical that we pause sometimes to get an honest measure of the distance traveled, to refocus on the goal of fairness and equality, and to recommit to making that end a reality.

The real coward, W. E. B. DuBois observed, is the one who dares not to know.

THE
REAL PEPSI
CHALLENGE

— Chapter One —

The High Road to Profit

IT WAS TIME TO "SUGAR UP" THE AUDIENCE.

Walter S. Mack, the dapper president of the Pepsi-Cola Company whose name was synonymous with Pepsi in the 1940s, liked to use that expression instead of "butter up" when he was cheerleading for his company. His obsession with sugar started during World War II, when strict sugar rationing nearly killed his soft-drink company in its infancy. It survived only because Mack became an expert in sugaring up in the literal sense, risking government fines to scavenge the precious commodity anywhere in the hemisphere he could find it.

That evening in 1949, he was wining and dining some of the company's five hundred bottlers and their spouses in the Grand Ballroom of the Waldorf-Astoria Hotel in New York City. They were not in a good mood. Even after a heat wave in the summer of 1948 brought a surge in Pepsi's sales, net income for the full year had plunged to $3.15 million, less than half of what it had been the year before. In 1949, "Pepsi-Cola Co. stood as close to the brink of bankruptcy as it could and still function," *Business Week* reported. Profits were being squeezed by rising production costs.

As the decade was drawing to a close, healthy companies finally were beginning to see a real postwar revival. Americans were in the mood to enjoy themselves again, spending money on luxury items that were just becoming available to the mass market: long-playing records, televisions, kitchen appliances, fashionable clothes. Mack was thinking he had to smarten up the image of Pepsi to fit the changing times. Pepsi was no longer strictly a five-cent bottle, but it still had the bargain-drink image that had made it a hit during the Depression, and was a continuing favorite among laborers, young people, and African-Americans.

Mack walked up to the podium. He cut a fine figure. He was tall and, at fifty-three years of age, still slender, with dark, slicked-back hair. He exuded charm and a practiced elegance, but he was not a polished public speaker, describing himself as "more of a behind-the-scenes kind of guy." He awkwardly welcomed the crowd.

Edward F. Boyd, assistant national sales manager in charge of the so-called Negro-market team, listened from the front row. He had been with Pepsi for about two years and was moving ahead with plans to expand his staff of African-American salesmen to an even dozen, himself included. That would make it the largest national Negro-market sales team in the United States, where a mere forty or so men and women worked in the field, according to a 1948 *Ebony* magazine article, and not all of them worked full-time or on a national level.

The five men on Boyd's Pepsi sales team—Richard L. Hurt, Charles E. Wilson, David F. Watson, Harold W. Woodruff, and H. Floyd Britton—were scattered around the room, as Boyd had instructed. He wanted the bottlers, all white men and mostly from the South, to see his salesmen and to feel comfortable around them. He told his men to strike up conversations. Socializing over drinks in a classy Northern hotel was a way to prepare for doing business over the following months in the bottlers' home territories, never an easy assignment.

One of the salesmen sat next to Boyd: David Watson, his first hire. Watson was a Morehouse College graduate who had just married into a prominent black family. Ed Boyd liked "Watty," as his colleagues called him. Everyone did. Watson was a good salesman. He had an easy laugh and a Southerner's love of a good story. He also knew how to deflect trouble, even though, as the darkest-complexioned man on the team, he was often a lightning rod for the endless problems the men faced when they traveled across the country. It surprised no one that he ended up spending his entire career at Pepsi; it seemed a good fit from the start.

Mack was droning on about the increase in sales of cases of Pepsi and giving his improbably rosy forecast. When he was nearly finished, he told the audience about his long-term plans for the company. "We're going to have to give Pepsi a little more status, a little more class—in other words, we're going to have to develop a way whereby it will no longer be known as a nigger drink," the salesmen recalled him saying.

Boyd was stunned. Wasn't the whole purpose of his sales team to win loyalty in the black community? Hadn't his men helped build the Pepsi franchise on the black consumer's dollar? How could Boyd and his team demand the respect of the most intransigent white bottlers when the famously liberal head of the company resorted to such a vulgar slur?

Boyd turned to Watson. He could see the anger and disappointment on his face. "Keep your seat," he told him. "I have to leave." He knew Watson would want to follow him, but he didn't want him to jeopardize his job, too. Boyd stood up straight, walked to the center aisle between the rows of folding chairs, and made his way to the back of the room and through the door. "That was the longest walk of my life," he said later. He remembered feeling like one of the representatives at the newly formed United Nations who would walk out of the general assembly to protest a vote.

He walked into the foyer outside the ballroom and had a seat. The speech was soon over and Boyd immediately was surrounded by his staff. The men were hot over the matter, but he calmed them down.

Some bottlers also came by to say hello, without mentioning the walk-out. Before long, Boyd's wife, Edith, arrived to offer her support, as she always did. She had just left work at *Time* magazine, where she was a librarian. That night, she had just a few blocks to walk from Rockefeller Center, but no matter where Boyd went in the country for these bottler conventions, she would join him for the main dinner. "White men were always thinking that black men were after their women, so I made sure I was never at dinner alone," Boyd explained. "That way they couldn't accuse me of approaching their wives."

The next day, Boyd went to see his boss. He told Mack that he found the word "nigger" offensive and that it should never have been used, in any context. Mack was taken aback, and quick with an apology. "Ed, you know I would never do anything to hurt you," he told Boyd, and thanked him for bringing it to his attention.

Boyd decided not to hold it against Mack, but he never forgot the incident.

The special-marketing staff—even those hired long after the incident—would tell that story again and again over the years. "If that's what they said in front of hundreds of people, what did they say behind closed doors?" asked Jean F. Emmons, who joined the team in 1950. "It was just the times. It's a wonder Boyd didn't go nuts; he was under such pressure."

The anecdote reminded the salesmen of just how difficult their jobs were. Selling various products to the black community was easy compared with selling the black consumer to the corporations that made those products. It never ceased to amaze them how even the most enlightened corporate leader could be so clueless about their most basic concerns. "Mack did try to help. But when I say Mack was liberal, I mean he was politically liberal. But that really only went so far," team member Harvey C. Russell said.

The "N word," as the men referred to it, was sometimes used in the vernacular of those times to mean the opposite of luxury. But to hear Mack casually use it at a public business meeting was a shock. Mack had long battled just that sort of racist stereotyping in the white corporate world, most visibly by creating Pepsi's Negro-market department back in 1940. Beyond the language used, was Mack having a change of heart about his special-markets team? Or was he just seeing the writing on the wall? Over the past decade, the black sales team and the company itself had been seared by war, racism, and seismic shifts in American business. The company and the country were headed in a new direction.

———

The decade had begun with such promise. In 1940, Mack was at the top of his game. In just over a year at the helm of the company, he had solidified his leadership and become a one-man show. The man who was already known as a corporate turnaround wizard had quickly built a whole new reputation as a genius at promotion. Always trying to reinvent conventional business models, he made his boldest move of all in March 1940, when he hired Herman T. Smith, a twenty-eight-year-old African-American newspaper adman, to launch a campaign to pump up sales of Pepsi in black communities. Rare as it was, the hiring of Smith merited a mere thirty-four words in the March 18, 1940, edition of *The New York Times.* It read: "Herman T. Smith, who is active in the Negro newspaper field, has been hired for a special sales promotion position at Pepsi-Cola. Smith will plan and carry out sales promotion in the Negro market."

To the black press, the hiring was big news. Reporters from those papers crowded into Pepsi's offices at the company's Long Island City headquarters and plant in Queens to hear the announcement. Smith called his position "one of the most important held by a Negro in private industry today," according to *The Pittsburgh Courier*, where Smith had been working.

"The Pepsi-Cola Company has shown a great deal of respect and confidence in the Race by his appointment," added the *Chicago Defender*, paraphrasing the new director.

During the news conference, Smith unveiled an ambitious plan: to create "interesting promotional campaigns" in every Negro community in the forty-eight states then in the union. The program would be launched in Birmingham, Alabama, and move first across the South. "The drink is headed for an all-time high in the Negro market this year," Smith said. That was not so much a prediction as it was a promise to make it happen.

Smith, a native of Norfolk, Virginia, had begun his career as an assistant circulation manager of the respected Norfolk *Journal and Guide*, a black weekly newspaper, and went on to become circulation manager of the *Washington Tribune*, special representative for the Blue Coal Company, field representative for *The Pittsburgh Courier*, and sales promotion man for Gooderham & Worts Whiskeys. He seemed to have worked at least a couple of those jobs simultaneously. He attended Virginia Union University in Richmond and Temple University in Philadelphia, as well as the New York University School of Commerce.

In the *Courier*, the coverage of the Smith hiring was sandwiched between two other items that showed both the problems and the promise of the relationship between the black community and corporations. At the top of the page, a banner headline claimed, "NEGROES ENLIST BECAUSE OF CIVILIAN JOB SHORTAGE." The story took issue with a War Department statement suggesting that blacks "were happy with conditions in the service." Instead, a black veteran complained that given "the failure of private industry to absorb colored labor, it is the lesser of two evils to remain in the army." A remarkable 80 percent of blacks reenlisted in the army in 1939, compared with 38 percent of whites, it stated. Yet, there were just 4,316 black soldiers versus 223,000 white, and only 4 commissioned black officers compared with 13,996 white officers in the segregated forces. The article contended that the army should be 10 percent black because 10 percent of the population was black—and paying taxes, too.

At the bottom of the page was an ad for Vaseline, just one of the big companies—including Conoco, Chevrolet, St. Joseph aspirin, Beech-Nut gum, Vicks, Ex-Lax, and Pepsi-Cola—that were beginning to tiptoe into the Negro press. Some had ordered up specially designed campaigns for the readership, showing African-American faces above the product.

Herman Smith took credit for convincing Walter Mack that he needed to pursue more black customers, and that he was the man to do it. It's unclear whether Pepsi beat Coke in total sales nationwide in the black population, but Pepsi-Cola found perhaps its strongest per capita consumption in that market. Just the week before his appointment made news, the New York *Amsterdam News* had run a story under the headline "Negro Market Study Urged," that quoted the new president of the Hampton Association of New York telling his group, "Big business ought to know more about today's Negro market and its potential development." His other message to American employers was: "Equip our largest minority with the means of increasing their purchasing power and we create a better prosperity for the nation as a whole."

The hiring of salesmen such as Smith, then, was a sign of a deeper commitment: a willingness to put corporate salaries into the hands of African-Americans, as well as to take their consumer dollar. What was thrilling to the black press about Pepsi's venture was that it hired a black man for a national campaign to sell a common product to the general public. African-American salesmen had been relegated mostly to peddling "vice" products such as alcohol and cigarettes—and even then mostly to local and regional markets. Not long after Smith was hired, the *Courier* announced the "second race man to become a national beverage representative." He was John W. Roy, working for the American Brewing Company, a Houston-based maker of Regal beer. He had already worked on the city and state levels. Now it was announced that he would be going "about his business over the nation"—and his wife would be joining him.

Just how unfamiliar and insensitive American business, in general, was to the black population is suggested by the following, which passed for humor in The *Wall Street Journal*'s lighthearted feature "Pepper and Salt":

WETS VS. DRYS

A Negro Baptist was exhorting: "Now breddren and sistern, come up to de altar and have yo' sins washed away."

All came up but one man.

"Why, Brudder Jones, don't yo' want yo' sins washed away?"

"I done had my sins washed away."

"Yo' has? Where yo' had yo' sins washed away?"

"Over at de church across de road."

"Ah, Brudder Jones, yo' ain't been washed; yo' jes' been dry cleaned."

It wasn't unusual for whites or blacks to use dialect in humor. What infuriated African-Americans was that the mainstream media portrayed them almost exclusively in demeaning stereotypes. Before the war, the white press also gave limited attention to critical problems within the black population.

Business first fully grasped the concept of a Negro market about a decade earlier, when the Depression forced desperate manufacturers, despite their prejudices, to seek new buyers for their products. Management strategist Peter F. Drucker credited the identification of a Negro market with saving the Cadillac. General Motors was on the verge of shutting down the division when Nick Dreystadt, the German-born service manager at Cadillac, persuaded the company to try promoting its cars to Negroes, Drucker wrote in his 1979 book, *Adventures of a Bystander.* "It was company policy not to sell Cadillacs to Negroes," he said, because it wanted the "prestige" buyer. But affluent white customers were disappearing as the economy sank. Dreystadt knew the car was already doing well among wealthy Negroes, mostly entertainers, boxers, doctors, or Realtors, who often had to have a white friend or manager buy the car for them, and persuaded his bosses to actively court the African-American consumer. The company ended up selling enough cars "to make the Cadillac division break even by 1934," Drucker wrote.

That same year, the Esso Standard Oil Company hired a black man to sell its products to the new black-operated gas stations opening mainly on the East Coast. If there is one African-American considered the dean of the black Negro-market salesmen, it is James A. "Billboard" Jackson. He got his nickname not from his corporate advertising work but from his stint as an actor and a theatrical press agent whose work often appeared in *Billboard* magazine. After he started his new sales career at age fifty-five, he began calling himself "the Esso man." Around the time Jackson was hired, Abbott Laboratories hired African-American pharmacist Richard B. Alphran to promote its products. By the end of the 1930s, popular Cleveland salesman William Graham hit the jackpot when he got the black Elks Club to make Pabst its official beer, and soon moved to New York to open his own ad agency in Times Square.

Otherwise, companies tended to hire white men to lead their first forays into the market. After he wrote a 1932 book titled *The Southern Urban Negro as a Consumer,* Paul K. Edwards, a white professor teaching at black Fisk University in Nashville, Tennessee, landed a job with the Rumford baking-powder company as "director of sales promotion in Negro markets."

The experiment with so-called race salesmen had gone well enough that in 1939, the Afro American Company in Baltimore, which owned the black weekly in that city, felt it was time to publish a booklet called "A Survey of the Negro Market." It was the start of what would become a concerted effort by a unified African-American press to attract ad dollars from large white-owned advertisers and manufacturers.

Pepsi also survived the Depression by appealing to Negro consumers, except no one had actively courted the market. Charles Guth, who bought the rights to Pepsi in 1932, had decided to sell the drink for five cents, the same price as those of its rivals, but sold it in used twelve-ounce beer bottles, which were readily available and relatively inexpensive. This gave Pepsi an instant advantage over the six-ounce bottle of market leader Coca-Cola, or Nehi's nine-ounce bottle, for example. "People who didn't have much money, and very few blacks had much money, took to Pepsi," observed Harvey Russell, who joined the team in 1950. "Pepsi was very, very strong among Negroes, but not when considering class. If you were striving, as we say, you'd serve Pepsi in the kitchen, but you'd serve Coke in the living room, when you had guests."

As soon as Mack joined Pepsi in 1938 he vowed to cement the drink's hold on its traditional customer base: laborers, blacks, young people. "I am a great guy for liking the masses," Mack wrote in his 1982 autobiography, *No Time Lost,* published when he was eighty-seven years old. (He died at age ninety-four.) "They're my people. I was brought up with them, I know them, I like them, and I appreciate their judgment."

Mack had come to live a very different life from his childhood days among "the masses." He socialized with the most famous writers of his day, including Dorothy Parker and playwright George S. Kaufman. He aspired to imitate their naughty, sophisticated humor in his appeals to customers. Mack used cartoons individually tailored to the readership of whatever magazine they ran in: Robert Day's cartoon with a Kremlin theme for the news magazines, Peter Arno's risqué drawings for *The New Yorker,* and Otto Soglow's simple sketches for mass-appeal magazines like *Popular Mechanics* and *Collier's.* Pepsi-Cola once sponsored a contest in humor magazines for "he-she" jokes. The copy that ran in *Puck,* for example, had Mack's voice: "If you're not a he or a she, don't bother."

Mack even envisioned the cartoon character Popeye downing Pepsi instead of spinach, but he couldn't afford the rights. Instead, he settled for a cartoon featuring the roly-poly cops Pepsi and Pete. "One important spur to Mack's advertising ingenuity was poverty," *Fortune* magazine observed. In 1939, Pepsi had a $600,000 ad budget, compared with Coca-Cola's $20 million. "Pepsi's dollars had to bring in more than their share of customers, and the only way to do that [was] to strike off in a new direction."

Mack did just that. Above all, he knew how to make a good idea a great one, appropriating the suggestions of those around him with the declaration: "That's exactly what I'm talking about!" For example, Mack had inherited from his predecessor Charles Guth, who left Pepsi in April 1939, an exclusive agreement with the Skywriting Corporation of America for use of its patented skywriting planes. Mack made a deal with the pilot Sid Pike to write PEPSI-COLA in smoke all across America. Pike would be paid only if the weather allowed the words to hang in the air at least three minutes. Pike started in Florida and moved west. PEPSI-COLA dotted the skies all over the country, to the delight of the public. The company got years of mileage out of the gimmick, and Mack allowed few other companies to use the patent.

Later in 1939, two men—a couple of screwballs, to use that wonderful thirties' term—dropped by Mack's office in Queens. The comics Bradley Kent and Austen Herbert Croom, dressed in white shoes and open shirts, set up a Victrola and played a lengthy commercial they had written that included a fifteen-second ditty borrowed from an English hunting tune. It went:

> Pepsi-Cola hits the spot,
> Twelve full ounces, that's a lot,
> Twice as much for a nickel, too,
> Pepsi-Cola is the drink for you.

Mack offered them five hundred dollars on the spot and said he'd give them fifteen hundred more if it worked. He turned it over to his new ad agency, Newell-Emmett, with an order—"Clean away the spinach!"—to cut to the jingle. Mack hated the five-minute radio commercials typical then, calling them "bathroom breaks." But he couldn't get NBC, CBS, or any other radio station to sell him thirty-second or even sixty-second spots. His own ad agency warned him that no new product with such tough competition could be sold without explaining it to the consumer. Mack wouldn't hear it. "You've got to know more about your advertising than the agency does," he insisted.

He got his way, and the agency finally found some small stations in New Jersey that were hungry for ad dollars. A small Newark station aired it first. Within two weeks, it was a sensation. That's how Walter Mack invented the commercial jingle. "It's surprising what you can get into a thirty-second spot, but up until that time nobody had thought of it," boasted Mack in his book.

CBS and NBC came crawling back to him to sell airtime in whatever segments he wanted. By 1941, the jingle had been broadcast 296,426 times on 469 stations. That was the year the Pepsi-Cola Company was first traded on the New York Stock Exchange. The following year, Mack had the "Nickel Nickel" jingle orchestrated, and handed out one hundred thousand copies on vinyl records. Various musicians interpreted it as a march, a waltz, and a rumba. It became an international hit, translated into fifty-five languages.

Mack wasn't just selling a cola, he was writing the book on how to sell a fun, hip image to a national audience. Everything he did seemed pitch-perfect. The folks at Coca-Cola couldn't believe they suddenly had a real rival. Mind you, Pepsi was still a pip-squeak compared with the international powerhouse. Pepsi's sales for 1939 were $4.87 million, compared with Coca-Cola's $128 million, which represented more than half of the U.S. carbonated-drinks market. And Coca-Cola was still the undisputed king of the soda fountain. But Pepsi was selling one-third as many bottles of cola as Coke did. Frustrated Coca-Cola deliverymen started to pull down Pepsi signs in stores, Mack said, and to bury its bottles under Coke displays. Mack responded by disguising some of his workers in A&P uniforms to take pictures of the vandalism and showed them to the local Coke bottlers, with a threat to take legal action. It stopped.

The cola wars were on.

Mack relished being the scrappy David to the Goliath that was Coca-Cola. And the potential for growth seemed huge. Americans were hooked on soft drinks. Cola, once marketed as an elixir, was starting to be seen as a potential problem by some health professionals, who worried that children were beginning to reject milk and water.

The curious thing about Pepsi's surging sales was that they didn't seem to be making a dent in Coke's figures. Mack was getting new cola drinkers. That fact spurred him to have even more fun with his ads, because, he figured, there was no way he was going to change anyone's taste in drinks. He had the general population figured out: 65 percent were cola drinkers; 12 percent were lemon-and-lime drinkers; 5 percent orange; 5 percent root beer; 4 percent ginger ale, and all the other flavors made up the rest. He insisted to the end of his life that no amount of advertising could significantly change those proportions. It was a matter of taste.

Building deeper brand loyalty among the already Pepsi-friendly African-American consumers was a pragmatic decision, but Mack had other motivations as well. He was going to take the high road to profit—and wind up just as rich as the next guy. "I am an unrepentant capitalist and a liberal," he declared in his book. "The two have always lived comfortably within my personal philosophy."

Mack the capitalist also was good at selling Mack the political liberal. He did it the same way he sold his cola: using the power of radio and a fresh idea. As much as he disliked public speaking, Mack was comfortable on the radio, where he sometimes editorialized on the state of industry. He saw an opportunity to raise his political profile during the 1940 elections.

Although Mack was active in the New York Republican Party and had been its candidate for the state Senate, he refused to help his party defeat Franklin D. Roosevelt in the 1932 and 1936 presidential races. He admired FDR and believed he headed off "a bloody revolution" after the Great Depression left thirty-four million Americans with no means of support. But after two administrations, Mack saw a viable alternative to FDR in Wendell L. Willkie of Ohio, "a brilliant lawyer," an internationalist, and a recent defector to the Republican Party. Mack agreed with Willkie's philosophy that the world's problems could be solved through the cooperation of the great powers. He also knew personally his party's favored candidate, New York Governor Thomas Dewey, and didn't like him.

When Mack arrived as a delegate to the 1940 Republican Party convention in Philadelphia, he went to work behind the scenes. No candidate had emerged after two rounds of voting, although Dewey seemed certain to get the nod on the third round. But just as the New

York delegates were about to cast their votes as a bloc, as was the tradition, Mack interrupted. His was the voice heard across America, as he bellowed his demand that each individual delegate be polled. Then, for state after state, other delegates he had prompted also asked for a head count. The hall went wild! People were booing and shouting down the vote. It was perfectly legal, Mack said, but no one had done it before. Willkie won the nomination, and Mack began to counsel him on campaign strategy.

But the Pepsi chief was used to selling products, not personalities, and he tangled with the obstinate Willkie. "He began to believe he was as great as they all were telling him he was," Mack said of the candidate's budding "messiah" complex. "That's the worst thing that can happen to anybody, and especially to a candidate for office."

Roosevelt won his third term. Mack—and Pepsi—soon had a financial reason to regret Willkie's defeat as well as a political one: Coca-Cola used its ties to the Democrats to win big favors from the Roosevelt administration during the war.

When Herman Smith arrived at Pepsi in the spring of 1940, he was the company's first black professional employee. If that achievement didn't get the publicity it deserved, Mack decided to make sure his next business innovation would. In July, Mack orchestrated an event worthy of his new kingmaker status. Again, the effort involved putting a new twist on an old convention—in this case, hiring and training new college graduates.

He created the Job Awards for American Youth, giving thirteen college graduates a chance to work. Under the program, each of the graduates would get a one-year assignment in the department of their choice at Pepsi-Cola, at an annual salary of thirteen hundred dollars, a livable wage for those times. After one year, they would be given either permanent employment or help finding other work in their chosen fields. The jobs—open to men and women of all races—would be newly created for the program, and rotated to new interns every subsequent year.

This time, the major daily newspapers gave full coverage to the news. *The Wall Street Journal* wrote that it was "understood to be the first specific step of its kind in industry." *The New York Times* echoed: "The awards represent Mr. Mack's pioneer measure to develop jobs for young college people knocking at the door of the business world."

Mack took credit for inventing the business internship as it is known today. Before his idea, he claimed, the method for hiring graduates was "haphazard, discouraging."

Always looking for a fun angle, Mack decided to pick the candidates by holding an essay contest. The topic was How American Youth Faces Its Future. Some 330 men and women from 254 colleges in forty-five states entered, all recommended by their college presidents as the ones who "were likely to succeed in life." Mack believed in identifying "leadership potential" in young applicants, not just brains. The student essays were to be judged by a panel of educators, followed by personal interviews. Black colleges were specifically included in the contest and co-ed schools had to present one male and one female entrant. Allen L. McKellar was working in the office of the president of South Carolina State Colored Agricultural and Mechanical College in Orangeburg when the head of the school asked him if he would be interested in the contest.

He was.

The twenty-one-year-old McKellar, called Sweet Pea by his fellow students as much for his disposition as his slender five-foot-three-inch frame, jumped at the opportunity. Any student would have been happy for such a chance, but for a black American graduate at the time, it was something incredible. Although statistics vary widely, *The Wall Street*

Journal estimated at the time that in 1941, a banner year, just eighteen hundred Negroes, out of a U.S. population of twelve million, earned a college degree, almost all from segregated universities. Of those, some 80 percent got jobs in direct service to the black community, according to a United Negro College Fund survey from the 1940s. Schools like McKellar's typically steered graduates toward teaching posts, or into graduate school to become doctors, lawyers, and other professionals with their own businesses. It wasn't wise to plan to work for a major corporation.

Even entering a "mixed" contest was unusual. The black press of the day was filled with stories about raffles in which the winning ticket was drawn, an African-American claimed the prize, and the ticket was thrown back into the pool until the drawing produced a white winner. This was usually followed by local protests, a public outcry if it got enough publicity, a lawsuit, and some sort of compromise. The *Pittsburgh Courier* wrote about one Cleveland high-school student who entered a business-sponsored art contest. The young man won second prize in the national competition and got a half-year scholarship to attend Kansas City (Missouri) Art Institute and School of Design. He was set to go to the school when he got a second letter saying it had been "discovered that he was a Negro" and that his acceptance had been withdrawn. Panicked, the young artist asked for the money instead, but the Kansas City business donors said no. The student then wrote to the National Association for the Advancement of Colored People, which negotiated giving him the equivalent in cash—$112.50—to be used to attend another school. While the white-owned media treated similar travesties as unjust, many reporters couldn't resist chastising the black American for being foolish enough to attempt the impossible.

To Allen McKellar, the Pepsi-Cola contest seemed "a bit rushed," coming as it did right before graduation. But he did it. His winning essay was filled with worries over the war in Europe, declarations of his patriotism, and confidence in his potential. "The great hosts of American youth, just emerging from school and college, must face a very uncertain future," McKellar wrote. He went on to ask: "Are all of those things on which we have built the foundations of our lives about to be replaced or destroyed by dogmas, isms and war? . . . Shall we find a job in which and from which we may build a life?" He answered at the end: "There is still a sign, 'Men Wanted,' for men who can do the job better than anyone else. Efficient work is still the law of life, and the one sure way to meet the challenge of an unbalanced world. We can still face the future with courage, with hope and with unbounded gratitude because America offers its youth an opportunity to face the dawn."

McKellar had already arrived in Atlantic City to begin his summer job as a waiter and hotel clerk when a telegram arrived at his home in Abbeville, South Carolina, on July 1, 1940, notifying him that he was one of twenty-five finalists in the Pepsi contest. A lengthy congratulatory letter followed, fraught with patriotic symbolism. It informed McKellar that he would receive a train ticket for the Fourth of July, a check for five dollars to cover incidentals, and accommodations at the George Washington Hotel in Manhattan. All contestants would stay from Friday to Monday. The final selection of interns would be made on Sunday at a Waldorf-Astoria banquet. McKellar rushed to New York from Atlantic City for the competition. When the winners finally were announced, they formed an impressive group: Seven of the thirteen were female and two were African-American. Along with McKellar, the judges had chosen Jeanette Maund, a brainy twenty-nine-year-old from Worcester, Massachusetts, who was a graduate of Hampton Institute, a black college in Virginia.

The celebratory luncheon, held the following Monday at LaGuardia Field in Queens, was "almost as carefully planned as the invasion of Normandy," *Fortune* magazine quipped, with guest invitations divided among thirty-nine celebrity categories, such as Society;

Old Guard, Grade A & B; and Café Society, Grade A & B. New York City Mayor Fiorello H. LaGuardia, a close friend of Walter Mack, was a guest speaker. First Lady Eleanor Roosevelt delivered the keynote address. Some three hundred business, labor, and education leaders attended, including David Rockefeller and William Randolph Hearst, Jr. Mack threw down a challenge. "If all business organizations take up the plan, it will go a long way toward solving the job situation facing college graduates each year," he told them. Without specifically addressing the democratic makeup of his intern group, he asked the business leaders to follow his example.

McKellar remembered Mack congratulating each of the winners, and he has a photo of himself with the corporate chief. "How are you doing, young fellow?" Mack asked McKellar, and continued to call him "young fellow" whenever the budding salesman took a rare break from the road and returned to headquarters. "I thanked Mr. Mack for the opportunity, and told him I would prove to him that I could do a good job," McKellar said. "Then, I went out and did likewise."

Of course, many corporate leaders helped African-Americans, supporting schools, orphanages, hospitals, and the like: Robert Woodruff of the Coca-Cola Company, David Rockefeller of the Rockefeller Foundation, and Josiah Rosenwald of Sears, Roebuck and Company, to name but a few. Their charity work earned accolades in the black communities, but the biggest need and desire was for jobs. By 1940, the steady flow of blacks moving from the South to the North had swelled. The identity of a typical African-American was about to change from rural Southerner to urban Northerner. There was not nearly enough employment, or housing, to meet the new demand. Blacks were hired for the lowest-level jobs. It was rare to see a black man working in anything but a janitor's overalls, the uniform of a bellhop or an elevator operator, or the starched whites of a cook. Most black women in the cities were employed as maids.

So when McKellar and Maund won their internships, many African-Americans nationwide cheered, and they became instant celebrities in the black press. A Nashville paper wrote: "They are intelligent, conscientious young people, and are winning friends for their company and themselves." The *Weekly Review* of New Albany, Indiana, ran a large photo of the two, saluting them as "America's Two Smartest Graduates." The Pepsi internships marked "a forward step by a business in giving qualified Negro youths a break," the article said. McKellar, still unaccustomed to the attention he was getting, scribbled modestly over the headline: "Please don't show to anyone."

McKellar's first assignment, which started in September that year, was in Dallas. Texas, he said, had always been considered somewhat more hospitable to blacks than the rest of the South, but he knew he was on new ground. "Imagine in 1940, when we came out to work the marketplace. Inconceivable! But there we were, representatives, in a shirt and tie—clean, walking tall, and meeting people. They were flabbergasted, and thrilled, and happy—the black population was."

The news that the pair might win permanent jobs if they did their work well spurred many African-Americans to help their young business envoys succeed. That was fortunate, because Pepsi gave them little by way of training or tools to reach new black customers. If the overall ad budget was tight, funds earmarked for Negro marketing were minuscule. There were no Pepsi ads in print featuring black Americans back then. The team was lucky to get any marketing materials other than their business cards. "You had to be innovative and come up with concepts that would be beneficial to a bottler," McKellar said.

The interns looked to Herman Smith, who was experienced in the field, such as it was. Smith told *Ebony* magazine in an interview some years later that he used to give wallets with five-dollar bills in them to black dining-car waiters to push Pepsi to the country's white railroad passengers—and to win the waiters' loyalty to the brand.

Smith liked to tell a story about his first assignment for Pepsi-Cola in Birmingham. He said he got the cold shoulder by the white plant owners, who asked to meet with him one night. "You are not wanted here," the meeting chairman said brusquely, "and you can't do us any good because nobody would buy from you." Smith said the man gave an example of a local African-American businesswoman who wouldn't buy ice from the black-owned company next door to her "because she actually believes the white man's ice is colder."

Smith responded: "The white man just did a better job of salesmanship."

"It was a bulls-eye," reported Alfred Smith relating the tale in his "Adventures in Race Relations" column for the *Defender.* "The whites all relaxed, grinned and said: 'OK bub, you win, you'll do. What can we do to help you?' "

Regardless of the veracity of the story, Smith used it to illustrate for his new interns the uphill battles they faced at every turn—and how they could always find a way to handle them.

The goal of the new African-American marketing team was, of course, to build up the enthusiasm for Pepsi in the areas they visited, sometimes staying for two weeks or more at a time. The team members did that by meeting as many people as possible, introducing them to the drink, and spreading the word about what Pepsi was doing to benefit the black community. First, they'd go to the local bottler to get the locations of every outlet where Pepsi was sold. Then they would head for the nearest newspaper office, not only to get publicity but as an entrée into the local communities.

There wasn't an outlet or a group too small to visit. The typical outlet the team targeted in the 1940s was a mom-and-pop store, although it could be a school or a skating rink, or anywhere else Pepsi was sold. McKellar remembered his pitch: "I'm Allen McKellar from Pepsi-Cola of New York. I'm your national sales representative. I just wanted to come into the marketplace to meet you, Mr. Jones, and give you an indication of what is changing in this country. I think you may be aware that Pepsi is one of the companies in the United States that have decided to utilize the services of the blacks to get some business from the black community."

They hit every outlet they could during the day, then booked a talk for every civic, social, educational, or religious gathering they could find, often working evenings. The audience found the Pepsi special-markets representatives infinitely more interesting than the free samples of the product they were handing out. The hard sell consisted mainly of the three telling their life stories and how they got their jobs. They started out working together, but demand for them was so high, they each eventually developed separate territories.

The white bottlers, on the other hand, didn't quite know what to make of the new special-markets team. "We told *them* what we proposed to do," McKellar said. "Most bottlers couldn't pronounce *Negro*. We had to teach them that."

The one thing McKellar always refused to do was to ride with the Pepsi deliverymen. "That was a no-no. We weren't about to be on a truck with a white driver," he added. "He would want you to assist him lifting cases. We didn't want to do that, and let them know immediately."

Because Jeanette was eight years older than McKellar, she became a big-sister figure to him. He, in turn, helped her overcome the emotional turmoil of traveling in the South for the first time. "She was shocked," McKellar recalled. "She couldn't understand why there were segregated fountains—'colored' and 'white'—restrooms—'colored' or 'Negro' or whatever they called them—it was crazy. . . . Nothing was integrated in the South. Nothing. I had to teach her about that."

It was a painful education. At about the time the pair joined Pepsi, the black press reported that the NAACP was challenging a survey that claimed no lynchings had occurred in the United States in the first half of 1940. The press warned that "streamlined" lynchings, involving fewer people and guns, rather than the traditional huge mobs and hangings, were beginning to go unreported as racial crimes. The NAACP, in fact, lost one of its own workers. Everett Williams, age thirty-two, was murdered in Brownsville, Tennessee, after ignoring death threats to continue his work registering black voters. He was drowned in a river.

McKellar said he kept his cool about the murders. "I knew it could happen, but I was never too fearful because I understood these people; I grew up with them," he said. "If I started getting involved in racial matters, the whole program would have failed."

To avoid confrontations, the salespeople were told to ride in Pullmans so that they could dine and sleep by themselves. But even their traveling in the special, high-priced sleeping cars offended some people. "The conductor would come and pull down the shades so the whites couldn't see blacks," McKellar said.

McKellar had learned from his father at a tender age about the danger of doing business with whites. When he was a child, Allen, Sr., told him about one lynching he had witnessed in 1916 of a local black man—Anthony Crawford, a successful cotton farmer in the community—by hundreds of white residents. "He had a business encounter with some whites, and you know the words used," McKellar recalled his father saying. "They got together and lynched him."

(Some eighty-nine years later, Doria Dee Johnson, Crawford's great-great-granddaughter, was on the floor of the U.S. Senate when it voted, on June 13, 2005, to apologize for its failure to pass any of the myriad antilynching bills introduced in the first half of the twentieth century. Without a federal law, lynchings often were not investigated, and the murderers rarely were brought to justice.)

"Abbeville, South Carolina, was a strange little place at that time," McKellar said, known as the number-one lynching town. The competition for that title was fierce. Even before the resurgence of the Ku Klux Klan in the 1920s, more than three thousand blacks had been lynched in the South. The violence became so entrenched in U.S. culture that RCA Records once produced copies of KKK theme songs. Immigrants were also such frequent targets that in the early twentieth century, the U.S. State Department paid reparations to China, Italy, and Mexico on behalf of victims.

Any number of reasons—or no reason at all—could provoke the murder of African-Americans. A 1940 article in the black press went so far as to tie lynchings to cotton prices. When cotton prices fell, lynchings went up, according to an authority on lynching at the Carnegie Foundation. "This violence wasn't random or private," said Dr. john a powell (punctuation his), professor of law at the Moritz College of Law, the Ohio State University in a 2004 interview. "Lynching and other violence by whites against blacks during this period was designed to define the boundary where blacks were excluded. Competition with whites for jobs, status, or business simply was not allowed."

———

Allen Lee McKellar, the eldest son in a family of seven children, was born on January 8, 1920, in Abbeville. As far as McKellar knows, neither side of his family had ever been slaves. His mother, Essie Watt, was the daughter of a successful blacksmith and a particularly strong-willed woman who did laundry for white families. With their hard work, Robert and Sally Watt saved enough money to buy land in the town's center. They were the talk—and envy—of the town, which had about two thousand residents, almost one-third black, McKellar recalled. Essie Watt vowed to go to her grave without giving up a single acre of her family's estate, and she did.

McKellar's father came from a family of druggists and dentists.

Allen, Sr., could pass for white, and his ability to circulate unnoticed outside his hometown allowed him to be privy to actions and conversations many blacks wouldn't hear. It was often an advantage to the family, and neighbors sometimes asked him to do their bidding in the white world. But it was also a curse. "He saw it all," McKellar said, "and he carried that very heavily."

In an attempt to shield his family from insult and harm, the elder McKellar limited the business dealings between local whites and his darker-skinned wife and children. If his wife wanted to buy shoes, for example, Allen, Sr., would bring home samples from the store, let her make her selection, and then take the others back. Although she had some junior-college education, Essie McKellar's mother was not permitted to work, only to teach piano in her home. Allen, Sr., also put a stop to his young son's entrepreneurship when he got a job picking cotton after school. "My father found out and I got a whooping. I never picked cotton again in my life," McKellar said. "I didn't make but a nickel for the amount that I picked. I was only four or five, but I was gung-ho—any way to make money."

Unwilling to let his son stoop to work in the fields, Allen, Sr., paid him to shine family members' shoes for a dime, and do other chores around the eight-room house—such as tending the garden, caring for the livestock, and working in the family's smokehouse. The work discipline was strict: The McKellar children got home from school, did their chores, ate dinner at 5 PM, then studied.

Despite all the rules, McKellar remembered his home as a gentle one. His father taught the children not to perpetuate hatred. "Daddy said to walk tall, treat everyone with respect, and don't try to integrate, don't even think about it," McKellar remembered. "He never taught racism. He just said to keep your eyes on the bad people."

Although his father wasn't a churchgoer, his mother was religious and encouraged her children to be the same. Essie McKellar had a deep belief that whatever was wrong in this life would be 180 degrees the other way in the afterlife. She didn't permit work on Sundays; the children could only go to church. There, McKellar sang while his mother played the piano. She also filled their home with music.

Allen, Sr., was the maître d'hotel at the Eureka Hotel. He supervised the staff and oversaw the dining room. This job had its advantages. "When people would eat half a steak, we got the rest," McKellar said. He was also "allowed to operate," as McKellar put it, a horse-and-wagon hauling operation. Many of his neighbors worked in the local textile mills, where employees were segregated. The more able-bodied tried to get jobs at the local railroad turnstile. There were black firemen on the engines, and blacks shoveled coal into the train's furnace. Otherwise, the local residents worked in the cotton fields. "There weren't many black professionals in Abbeville; it was too small," McKellar said.

In the South, McKellar said, blacks and whites tended to be in closer contact than up North. He had many white friends as a child, although the fraternization stopped at the school doors. McKellar went to one school for blacks through the eighth grade, the Abbeville County Training School, or ACTS. He went to another for high school.

When McKellar started traveling to the North, he found that the races were often more segregated than in the South, though not by law. Nevertheless, "you felt a degree of freedom when you were on that side of the Mason-Dixon line," he said. For one, jobs weren't so race-specific up North, and they paid better. When McKellar visited his grandmother's family in Evanston, Illinois, his brother-in-law got him a job washing walls in hotels, at seventy-five cents an hour, which the youth considered big money.

In Evanston, a wider world opened up. McKellar began to think about his surroundings. "When you're in the middle of that muddle you don't pay much attention to it. When I went to Evanston and saw the difference in people and things and [then] went back to Abbeville,

I began to analyze all aspects of it: segregation and racism. It affects every black person's way of life—then and today."

Before the Depression hit, McKellar's father had been warned by one of the hotel owners to take his money out of the bank, but he didn't listen. "Daddy came home one day and took me down by the barnyard and told me he lost all his money. And he cried," said McKellar, himself crying at the memory.

His father, then in his thirties, told McKellar he would try to recover financially, but it would be tough going. McKellar promised his father that he would see that all his siblings were educated. He kept that promise.

From that day on, the young McKellar worried about how to make money for himself and his siblings to attend school. The Depression loosened the family rules for working outside the home. McKellar got a paper route and began to accompany a wealthy acquaintance of the family, the hardware-store owner, to Myrtle Beach to fish, handling his bait and equipment. Because the man was white, McKellar could stay in hotels that were otherwise closed to him. McKellar also got a job on a delivery truck, keeping track of inventory. "That job made a little businessman out of me," he said.

In high school, McKellar sold apples in the fall after they arrived by truck. Through all his jobs, his father taught him how to budget and save. He also taught his son to put the value of money in perspective: "After he lost his money, Daddy kept moving forward," McKellar said. "I didn't see that he was depressed." His father became McKellar's role model and mentor.

Still, the cost of college would be considerable for the family. When McKellar graduated from high school at age fifteen, his father talked to the governor of the state, Olin D. Johnston, who dined occasionally in the hotel, to see if he'd be willing to help with a scholarship. The governor did. His influence also landed McKellar a job in the office of the college president. McKellar did everything he could to prove that he deserved the scholarship. "Everything they needed, I got," he said. He drove the campus car for the president and his visitors.

Always ambitious, McKellar also became an entrepreneur. Noticing that many offices and organizations on campus were always ordering flowers, he set up a deal with some florists to get a 20 percent commission on all the orders he brought in.

Working in the top office on campus was life-changing. McKellar met many well-known people in the small black community of higher education. "If there was any silver lining to Jim Crow, it was the closeness, the brush with greatness," McKellar said. Among those early encounters was his meeting with Benjamin E. Mays, head of Morehouse College, who was later considered a spiritual mentor of Dr. Martin Luther King, Jr.

So, McKellar wasn't intimidated when, as an intern at Pepsi-Cola, he had to approach, for example, the controversial and flamboyant evangelist Daddy Grace, who was living large and buying up real estate for his House of Prayer, based in Philadelphia. A clipping in McKellar's thick scrapbook shows Daddy Grace and the announcement of one of McKellar's early victories: "Pepsi-Cola is used each year exclusively at House of Prayer convocations."

McKellar wasn't afraid, either, to chase after the biggest catch in the Negro market: the African-American Elks Club, made up of about half a million working-class men and women. These groups were already boosting sales of some brewing companies. The South didn't have many bars open to blacks in the early 1940s, so the only public places blacks could go to drink were the Elks Lodges, which had permits for alcohol. "That was a ball on weekends," McKellar said.

McKellar had to figure out how to push a more wholesome drink. He'd cram the trunk of a company car with ice chests filled with Pepsi and hand out bottles to members entering the hall. "Sometimes they'd say, 'Hey, young fellow, do you have anything to go with it?'" McKellar said, affecting a deep voice. He obliged. A line item on one of his early expense reports reads: "bottle of gin, $2." "McKellar has done much to make this nationally known group realize the importance of patronizing Pepsi-Cola," one paper later said about McKellar's work with the Elks.

By the end of their first eight months, McKellar and Maund had traveled through twenty-one states and over thousands of miles by car, train, and bus, selling Pepsi. With such a record, they had no trouble becoming permanent employees after their one-year internship. And as promised, Mack hired two more African-Americans to take their vacated posts: Philip Kane, twenty-two, of Baltimore, a graduate of Morgan State College, in the same city; and Marion O. Bond, twenty-one, of Kansas City, Kansas, a graduate of Land College, in Jackson, Tennessee.

Pepsi-Cola was growing fast, and the Negro-marketing team was more than keeping pace. "It is gratifying," wrote the *Echo*, a weekly, on its front page, "how Mr. McKellar, in a businesslike way, is doing a creditable piece of work for his firm and his race, in that he is probing what may be done by all ambitious youth, regardless of race or color."

Reporters and others frequently asked Jeanette Maund and Allen McKellar to define their contributions to the greater good. The two tried to convey their feelings about their work in a radio interview (there were only a handful of stations in the United States geared toward black audiences at that time) conducted at a Denver hotel, with a journalist identified only as Mr. Durr. He asked McKellar to talk about what their jobs meant in terms of opportunities for young blacks at corporations. "Our experience and those of others have shown that Negroes can work in the South and be successful," he replied. "The Negro market has been neglected, because big business was not aware of the tremendous buying power of the Negro group. Big business now recognizes this, and all efforts are being made to attract this buying power to the individual product or products of each organization, and due to the awakening interest of the Negro in his own kind, he has made it almost a necessity that Negro representatives and other workers be used."

Maund, a Northerner, tried to explain her view of the South. Her responses were thoughtful, but, despite a sincere optimism, they betrayed a despair about what she had seen. "I see no reason why the Negro should apologize for his group in the South," she said. "We need to respect ourselves more; to become conscious of our potentialities [sic], to make the other group feel the need of us, and realize that no one can succeed without the support of all. We all need to know this truth."

Jeanette Maund soon asked to stop working in the South. Her tactful public comments were too much at odds with the hard reality of her experiences.

By then, America was at war. The nation's war footing had an immediate and profound effect on African-Americans—boosting the urgency of civil rights legislation because of a labor shortage. In 1941, the Fair Employment Act prohibited racial discrimination by private employers. In return, civil rights activists A. Philip Randolph and Bayard Rustin called off a march on Washington. Also, public construction contracts had to stipulate that Negroes be hired in proportion to local population. In October 1942, *The Wall Street Journal* predicted that such aggressive equal-rights legislation was leading to a social revolution. "This war may give the dark-skinned people something the Civil War did not: assured economic position," said Dr. Robert C. Weaver, African-American son of a postal clerk and chief of the Negro Manpower Service under the War Manpower Commissioner. He had two suggestions for industry: refrain from making blacks start out in custodial work and fire any white worker who objected to integration.

(Weaver went on to become the first black in a presidential cabinet when, in 1966, President Johnson appointed him secretary of the newly created Department of Housing and Urban Development.)

With companies generally desperate for workers, many business leaders proved more open-minded about changes in the workforce than their employees. To head off trouble, Lockheed had Joe Louis, the heavyweight boxing champion, escort the one hundredth new Negro worker into its aircraft plant in Burbank, California. Many labor leaders also found themselves caught in the middle between angry white workers and newly hired black employees.

Color lines rarely had been crossed before the war. In June 1940, for example, aeronautical engineer Joseph Dunning, of MIT and Stanford, was employed by the Douglas Aircraft Company to work in its stress-analysis department—probably the first black in the industry, one paper speculated. By late 1942, average black workers were crossing barriers in large numbers. Aircraft factories reported going from having a handful of blacks on the payroll to having twelve thousand in just two years. The federal government sent out pamphlets to thirty thousand industrialists demanding that they hire an estimated one million black men and women who were unemployed or underemployed. Washington used the specter of Hitler as a tool against the more intransigent racists. The government barred the practice of pay differentials between workers of different races by declaring: "Economic and political discrimination on account of race or creed is in line with the Nazi program."

The wave of new African-American hires had some unexpected consequences. In Mississippi and Connecticut, angry homemakers complained that their domestics were leaving for factory work, some recruited by the husbands of the household. *The Wall Street Journal* reported that "the FBI has investigated very seriously a rumor spread through many cities to the effect that colored women were forming 'Eleanor clubs' to avoid housework." One version of the rumor held that every maid would quit her job on the same day. Unable to track down a single club member, officials blamed enemy agents for the rumor. Already, the paper reported, Japanese propagandists were broadcasting daily appeals by shortwave radio to American Negroes, who were seen as potential anti-American sympathizers.

On the contrary, African-Americans felt a deep commitment to America's role in the war. For them, the war against Hitler was a fight against a despised white supremacist, and they drew a distinct parallel to their domestic struggle. In 1942, *The Pittsburgh Courier* initiated the Double V Campaign: "Victory at home, Victory abroad." The movement began with a letter to the editor by James G. Thompson, a twenty-six-year-old black man. His letter had the mix of anger, hope, and patriotism that fueled his generation. He asked: "Would it be demanding too much to demand full citizenship rights in exchange for the sacrificing of my life?" He continued: "The V for victory sign is being displayed prominently in all so-called democratic countries which are fighting for victory over aggression, slavery and tyranny. If this V sign means that to those now engaged in this great conflict, then let we Colored Americans adopt the double V for a double victory. The first V for victory over our enemies from without, the second V for victory over our enemies from within. For surely those who perpetuate these ugly prejudices here are seeking to destroy our democratic form of government just as surely as the Axis forces.

"I might say that there is no doubt that this country is worth defending; things will be different for the next generation; Colored Americans will come into their own, and America will eventually become the true democracy it was designed to be. These things will become a reality in time, but not through any relaxation of the efforts to secure them. . . . I love America and am willing to die for the America I know will someday become a reality."

McKellar was an enthusiastic supporter of the Double V Campaign.

A photo shows him among fans of the renowned jazz vibraphonist Lionel Hampton, one of the most active of the black entertainers and one willing to help him promote Pepsi. Everyone in the audience is posing for the picture by making V signs with both hands. The message resounded through the war and beyond.

McKellar and Smith did their best to shape their promotional efforts to the war effort. They papered the black sections of cities with notices to children: "Save your Pepsi-Cola Crowns" and "Join the Get-Hep Club." They gave the youngsters prizes for filling barrels with the valuable bottle caps, as government rations of metal for industries were kept to 70 percent of their 1941 volume. The cork used to seal the caps was also in short supply.

During this period, Pepsi's Walter Mack became active in the war effort for the New York area. He started a campaign to gather scrap metal, held a fund-raiser in Madison Square Garden, and gave checks to the Red Cross. He also set up four Pepsi-Cola Junior Clubs in Queens and Harlem to help teens facing wartime losses and the subsequent strains on their families. Mack insisted that the centers, open in the evenings for recreation, be run by the teenagers themselves, working through house councils and directed by adults from the neighborhoods. Two were still open by the end of the decade. He also started a square-dance program in Brooklyn's Prospect Park, and continued to support it even though the concessions wouldn't sell Pepsi to the crowds, which sometimes swelled to ten thousand. In spring 1945, he chaired the committee that planned the VE Day celebrations in Central Park, and later he cohosted with the Officers Service Committee a gala navy ball for twenty-five hundred officers and their families at the Ritz-Carlton Hotel.

Most important to African-Americans, Mack opened three big canteens for service personnel in Washington, San Francisco, and New York. All were open to all races. Departing soldiers got a place to relax, shower, shave, have their uniforms pressed, and get a free Pepsi and a nickel hamburger. They also got to make a free recording of their voices to send home. If they couldn't come up with a message, they could pick one of sixteen that Pepsi provided. Mack's favorite: "Let me tell you, Uncle Sam is doing a good job keeping me in the pink of condition for you, honey, so don't be worrying about me."

"Today it looks a little corny," Mack wrote in 1982, "but we didn't worry about being corny during that war. National cynicism was still a generation away."

Some twenty-nine million servicemen used Pepsi's canteens during the war years and immediately after. That they were integrated was no small thing. The government's canteens—like the army itself—were segregated. Racial tensions in the service were such that a black newspaper reported that black and white soldiers once took up arms against each other in Italy. The problem, as was typical, stemmed from some white officers' anger over black soldiers' fraternization with local women.

Mack's biggest wartime charity was to his struggling bottlers. The federal government had restricted use of sugar to 80 percent of a company's 1941 level. For an established company like Coca-Cola, rationing was manageable. But many Pepsi bottlers hadn't operated for the full year in 1941, so the effective deficit was much greater than 20 percent. Even worse for Pepsi, the government selected a Coca-Cola vice president to be in charge of rationing.

Mack admitted in his autobiography that he thought the sugar shortage was mostly phony, but was afraid he'd be called unpatriotic if he said so. Officials suggested that anyway, once he started complaining. One unidentified official was quoted in *Fortune:* "You'd have a lot of trouble appealing to him on any other grounds than profit. He just wouldn't understand you. He's in business, period."

But Mack was fighting for the life of his company, using his self-professed talent for working behind the scenes. He got the Mexican government's permission to make fully sugared syrup there and export it to the United States. He bought up all that country's surplus sugar for three years at a price far above market value. Mack got past both Mexico's export and America's import restrictions. The whole scheme eventually fell apart, but it had worked when needed most.

In 1943, when rations fell to 60 percent of 1941 sales, Mack went to Cuba to buy a sugar plantation. He also made a deal to buy Louisiana sugarcane juice. He made twelve million pounds of sugar equivalent available to his bottlers before he was caught and fined. Another Cuban deal, for molasses, got him fined as well. In the end, Mack could boast that he didn't lose a single bottler in the war.

But he did lose the battle with the president's administration. James A. Farley, president of Coca-Cola Export, was FDR's former campaign manager and an ex–postmaster general. Farley made a deal that wherever the troops went they would have Coke available, supposedly to boost morale. If World War I troops needed tobacco as much as bullets to win the war, as General John Pershing said, then World War II soldiers needed cola. General Dwight D. Eisenhower himself demanded that his troops get ample supply of the beverage after a survey showed that more of his men preferred it to beer. Plants were set up in Italy, France, and Germany, all built by the government. The joke at the time was that the Coke arrived at the front lines before the ammunition.

Mack quoted the president as saying that he didn't want the sugar shortage "to prevent people from drinking soft drinks because this was a part of their civilization." In the end, Coca-Cola got sixty-three plants operated overseas with army assistance and an exemption from sugar restrictions. Pepsi got none until the navy finally allowed a single plant in Guam. Back home, Mack went to work selling Pepsi as a way to help the war effort in the factories. One ad portrayed Pepsi as a good workingman's drink because it had so many energy-giving calories. (An asterisk pointed to an explanation of the term *calorie*.)

Considering all the obstacles Pepsi faced during the war, black customers' loyalty to the brand was invaluable. A black newspaper in Alabama, covering a visit by McKellar, encouraged its readers to keep drinking Pepsi. The August 1942 article stated that "since sugar is being rationed throughout the U.S., the company can't put on any sale promotion. The only thing that can be done is the company national representative can visit each city on Good-Will tours. The tours are only to remind our good many customers and friends about the goodness that is still in Pepsi-Cola."

The *Defender* cheerfully reported soon after that "in spite of the war and general business curtailment, Smith's work in the company has increased and additional Negroes have been employed by the parent Pepsi-Cola Company and its independent bottlers."

In "the white collar bracket" the newspaper counted eight, the four former interns—McKellar, Maund, Bond, and Kane—plus four people doing "special work in army camps of a morale-building nature" sponsored by the company. Of the four working with soldiers—Thomas C. Richter of Howard University; Thomas Livingston of Lincoln (Pa.) University; Joseph Christian, former ad manager of the *Amsterdam Star-News* and the *People's Voice;* and Ed Dudley, a former assistant New York State Attorney General—two were in the army themselves, Livingston and Kane. Another twenty-three "Negro salesmen" were employed by Pepsi-Cola bottlers around the country, and several hundred blacks did other work in the plants nationwide, the paper added.

The efforts of the Pepsi salesmen and others in their field were beginning to draw attention in the mainstream press as well, with the help of eager black publishers. When the American Marketing Association met in New York at the end of 1942, *The New York Times* covered its panel on the Negro market, which included representatives of the *Amsterdam Star-News* and the *People's Voice*, among other black newspapers. "The buying power of the Negro population of this country amounts to $7 billion to $10 billion annually," the *Times* reported. "The marketing men were told that a new racial loyalty is developing steadily among the Negro people, which therefore makes it advisable for manufacturers to employ Negro salesmen when seeking to tap the Negro market."

In its push for more ads, representatives of the black press pointed out:

- Negroes are very brand conscious.
- Sixty-eight percent in the New York market listen to the radio.
- The total circulation of the four hundred Negro papers is about 2.5 million.
- Negro papers give more detailed and comprehensive merchandising assistance to manufacturers than other papers.
- Seventeen percent of the nation's drugstore business is done with blacks even though they represent just ten percent of the U.S. population.

The Pepsi effort was proof to industry that these were the building blocks of success. Despite the wartime hardships, and partly because of them, Pepsi's profits rose to $6.44 million in 1943, compared with $6.27 million the year before.

McKellar himself coaxed thousands of people a week to make Pepsi their soft drink. One of his more fortunate stops was in 1942, on the campus of Fisk University, where he spoke to the entire student body. In the audience that day was Ernestine Jones, daughter of Chicago surgeon Henry Clay Jones. "I knew this person from Pepsi was going to be in chapel that day," she said. "All the students were saying, 'Let's go!'" The two met through friends after his talk and eventually were married.

Every two weeks on the road, McKellar submitted an expense account and waited to pick up reimbursement at a local bottler. The white workers in the home office could hardly imagine what their black colleagues were facing on the road under the segregation practiced in virtually every state, including those that rigidly enforced Jim Crow laws, a legal system named for a minstrel character. "Some dummies at the office who had never been in the South would ask us for a hotel receipt," McKellar recalled. "I'd say, 'We can't stay in a hotel!' "

Here is a snapshot of one week's feverish activity, as outlined on McKellar's expense report for the start of 1943:

Jan. 12: Addressed 32 at Johnson Business School. Met with Junior Chamber of Commerce group of 28. Served drinks [Pepsi]. Made contacts with 13 outlets (mostly mom and pop stores in black neighborhoods). Taxi & bus fares, $3.50.

Jan. 13: Spoke before group of 700 at Ballroom. Gave 10 cartons to jitterbug couples. Addressed 41 at Franklin Beauty School. Made contacts with personnel at Houston Hospital. Contacted 9 spots. Taxi & bus fares, $3.35.

Jan. 14: Spoke before Eveready Club of 19 and visited Negro labor union. Also contacted Crawford Girls school & visited housing project. Contacted 15 outlets. Taxi & bus fares, $2.85.

Jan. 15: Addressed group of 65 at USO center. Spoke before Senior Negro Chamber of Commerce group of 108. Contacted 12 outlets & made individual contacts. Taxi & bus fares, $3.20.

Jan. 16: Addressed Minister group of 54. Spoke before Excelsior Club group of 12. Contacted 26 outlets, including nightspots. Taxi fare, $2.75.

Jan. 17: Spoke before church group of 90, also before social group of 150. Made donation of 1.00 to church. Visited fraternal house & 6 spots. Took head of USO out for lunch. ($2.85). Taxi & bus fare, $1.55.

Jan. 18: Addressed waiters club of 58. Served drinks & also spoke before school group of 160. Contacted 14 outlets & visited newspaper office. Taxi & bus fares, $1.80.

The total of the above, plus other of his week's expenses, was $71.42 for meeting more than one thousand people. That was a lot of return on a small ad budget.

McKellar didn't stay on at Pepsi-Cola much longer, as the marketing team began to feel the impact of the war economy. Jeanette Maund, too, quit the company and entered graduate school. She was grateful for one particularly happy result at her stint with Pepsi-Cola: she was reunited with her little brother. Maund was born in Harlem, but her father died when she was three years old. Her mother, unable to care for her four children, had sent Maund and two of her siblings to the local Colored Orphan Asylum while her infant son was taken in by a friend. Nearly four years later, Maund's aunt in Worchester rescued the three from the orphanage and raised them as her own. They never saw their little brother again until he spotted Maund in a local newspaper and introduced himself to her at one of her appearances.

McKellar, who had been looking for a better-paying job, was drafted into the army. Before he left, however, he again asked Governor Olin D. Johnston to write a letter of recommendation for him. Dated November 30, 1942, it read:

To Whom It May Concern: This is to certify that I have known Allen L. McKellar, Jr., for several years. During my first administration (1936), I secured a scholarship for him at the State College (colored), Orangeburg, South Carolina. This young man is as worthy as any young man of his race. His character is above reproach. He is very able and has a splendid personality. He is worthy of any confidence that may be placed in him.

— Chapter Two —

Black, White, and Green

RIGHT FROM THE START AT PEPSI-COLA, MACK KNEW THAT race would be a significant front in the cola wars—and a highly risky one. He wrote about arriving at the company in 1938 to find that its plants had no blacks on its ten production lines and blamed the unions for keeping them out. The new president set up two more lines, staffed entirely by African-Americans, forcing the affiliated unions to accept their membership. Mack was apologetic in later years that his solution involved a segregated arrangement, but he saw it as the best he could do at the time. "I was not noble but fair," he once said of his efforts.

But in those days, just being fair could seem a noble act. By the end of the war, Mack had built a reputation for being a "businessman of conscience," as one magazine put it, in both the black and the white communities. "We definitely thought of Pepsi as the liberal, Northern drink," Harvey Russell said.

Fortune magazine wrote bluntly about how being positioned as a bargain drink meant Pepsi was at a disadvantage, "especially in the South. There, large size and low price often make a product popular among Negroes, with the result that many southern whites shun it." For that reason, the article continued, Mack knew "when to suppress publicity for the good of the company," as one friend told the reporter. Mack's caution would help explain why so little was written about Pepsi's special-markets group in the mainstream press, and no reference was made in Mack's autobiography.

Shunning was a powerful weapon against corporations and individuals who did business with blacks. The suicide of a South Carolina lawyer, "the one white man in this area who had championed the cause of the Negro . . . against the Ku Klux Klan terrorism," made headlines in the black press in 1940. Friends said the man's depression stemmed from his ostracism by his community after he defended an African-American in court. As a countermeasure, African-Americans began to widen the use of the boycott against hostile whites. But beyond getting a small restaurant or business to shut down, their actions could hardly match the power of a boycott organized by white segregationists.

The competition for jobs aggravated racial tensions. Throughout World War II, as industry managers discussed the hiring of women and African-Americans to bolster wartime production, they worried about what would happen after the war, when the latecomers lost their jobs to returning veterans, and when black veterans would be denied equal privileges. It was one of the issues that preoccupied postwar America, particularly its literati. In the six months from September 1945 to March 1946, *The Wall Street Journal* reviewed no fewer than five Broadway plays about the return of the black veteran and his unjust treatment. Although the reviews were mixed, the critic, writing about director Elia Kazan's hugely popular play *Deep Are the Roots,* said: "The case for the Negro seems in for a real hearing around these parts."

Many playwrights, artists, journalists, politicians, and business leaders joined forces to make sure that such a hearing would take place. There was a sense of purpose and optimism after the war, and many people in the United States and worldwide pledged to do their part to improve their societies. Some saw racial intolerance as a relic of the older generation's lifestyle. "Liberal forces are on the march," an enthusiastic Dr. Margaret Mead wrote in 1945, compared with five years earlier, when the famous anthropologist had declared that the fight against race prejudice had been "characterized by devotion and zeal and a singular lack of success."

Adam Clayton Powell, in his 1946 book *Marching Blacks,* urged all blacks to leave the South to get access to better schools, hospitals, and housing, but most of all, to have "the opportunity to participate in the non-violent bloodless revolution of ballot and boycott that the New Negro and the new white man are carrying out."

The idea of a so-called New Negro was a theme revisited by each generation of African-Americans at least since Harlem Renaissance writer Alain Locke most famously used the term in 1925 to describe a real move away from slave culture, as well as from the myth of the Old Negro. The participation that the New York congressman demanded was already impressive. At times it seemed that nearly every African-American had become a foot soldier in the struggle for equality. If a slur was heard on the radio, for example, a station might get dozens of calls in seconds, including some from editors in the black press demanding an apology. If a black person was denied a room in a hotel, a black bellhop might call in the local NAACP representative before the customer could even be shown the door. Racism, they said, was un-American, and a remnant of Nazism, which Americans had paid so dearly to defeat. But as the momentum for change grew, so did the reaction against it, and lynchings rose after the war.

The black media did a remarkable job of teaching everyone the same message, saying, in effect: We are pouring our money into banks, spending our money in retail stores, and paying taxes, so we shouldn't be shut out of jobs on any level in those banks, stores, and government. "Money is green, not white or black," Essie Robeson, wife of the famous actor-activist Paul Robeson, once said in a lecture after the war. "We are 100 percent American—or less than that—only according to democratic or undemocratic behavior."

Many black weekly newspapers published a version of the honor roll that the *Chicago Defender* ran at the start of each year, listing the progressive whites who could be counted on to support equal rights. Actors Orson Welles, Rita Hayworth, and Arthur Godfrey made the list, to name a few, plus jazz producer Norm Ganz, bandleader Benny Goodman, broadcasting pioneer William Paley, and publisher Henry Luce. Frank Sinatra was at the top of one postwar list for the hundreds of talks he gave in schools against prejudice. "We called Sinatra a *Negrophile*," said Julian Nicholas, a future Pepsi team member. "We always had a story to tell about him: 'Did you hear Frankie beat up a guy because of what he said about us?' "

Many others used their celebrity clout to support fair treatment of blacks. When the District of Columbia suddenly enforced segregation in its recreation parks, actor Gene Kelly, who had been playing mixed doubles with young blacks and whites, joined the protests. He dared police to arrest him, saying that to be told whom he should have as friends "usurps the idea of democracy." In another case where several African-Americans were unfairly rounded up after a skirmish, letters of protest were sent to authorities by film director David O. Selznick, Eleanor Roosevelt, and Albert Einstein, among others.

Mack was among those who were determined to do their share. After the war, he set out to reestablish his footing in the business and civic communities. His educational scholarships—open to all races— became the centerpiece. One magazine reported that he walked out of a segregated hotel that refused to serve one of the prestigious black educators who sat on his scholarship board.

Mack wrote in his old age about how he came to be committed to black causes: "I went through Harvard, the navy, and my early years seeing blacks primarily as entertainers, athletes, or laborers, yet once my consciousness was awakened, once I was made aware of my own blindness, I worked to correct society's blind spots through my work with the unions and the scholarships at Pepsi, and on the anti-discrimination councils in the state of New York. . . . We grow, we learn, and we use what we have learned through growth to help our fellow man."

Through the Pepsi Scholarship Program, Mack again hoped to spot leaders, not just scholars. Every graduating class in participating high schools voted for the five "most likely to succeed" to take an exam. From there, each state chose two winning students; segregated states got to add two more African-Americans. In addition to the full scholarships, another ten students or so from each state won fifty-dollar stipends when they entered a university.

About five hundred men and women were sent to universities on full scholarships in the eight years that the program was active, and many more got the stipends. Mack estimated the program cost Pepsi six hundred thousand dollars in 1945, its first year. He claimed later that his program was the model for the National Merit Scholarship Program backed by private industry that started in 1955.

Pepsi-Cola's charities were seen as Mack's "calculated attempt to build slowly, for the long pull, the public impression that Pepsi-Cola is a company with a much broader interest in the public than merely making a dollar out of it," *Fortune* wrote of Mack. Not everyone could see the value of this strategy. Some Pepsi employees, and many shareholders, thought too much money was being spent on "that strange agglomeration of activities that Mack likes to call his community services," as the magazine described them. Of an advertising budget that reached a record high in 1946 of $4.5 million, Pepsi-Cola spent about $2.2 million on national print and radio ads, $1 million on point-of-purchase ads that the bottlers had to match dollar-for-dollar, and

$1 million on the charitable programs. "I'd rather have my community services than Frank Sinatra," Mack snapped at one reporter.

———————

Mack's generosity and sense of community were not learned in his parents' home. He hated his father's obsessive saving and stinginess. "He went without money so he could have it," was how Mack put it. His father disliked anyone who was rich and felt that anyone who had a lot of money must have gotten it dishonestly. His own textile business was up-again, down-again.

Walter Mack's autobiography is a tale of a curious, smart, successful, energetic, and, above all, a life-loving man who was determined not to live in anonymity. He felt deeply that he was part of the lifeblood of his promising young country and could grow and improve with it, with a little guts and vision. "I don't think of myself as a particularly unusual man. I'm not all that much smarter than the next fellow, but I have been luckier, that's for sure," he said.

The lucky part was not so much false modesty—although Mack was often accused of that—but a sincere acknowledgment of the fact that he was born to circumstances that put success within his reach.

"How did Mack strike me?" asked Julian Nicholas, who joined the special-markets team in 1951, under a new regime. "New York, New York. Slick New York. Like someone in the movies."

If Mack appeared the quintessential New Yorker, he liked to think he had some of his Texan grandfather in him. Gustave Ranger emigrated from England to Texas just before the Civil War, then cornered the cotton market with his brother by breaking the wartime blockades and running cotton to the Northeast from around the tip of Florida. The town of Ranger, Texas, Mack said, was his grandfather's namesake. "They were merchants, to be sure, but more important, they were adventurers," he said of his mother's father and her uncle. "I think I inherited some of [my grandfather's] spirit of adventure and daring."

Mack didn't know exactly how his parents had met, but they married and settled on Manhattan's Upper West Side. Walter Staunton Mack was born on October 19, 1895—the year the Coca-Cola Company announced it finally was available in every state in the union. His friends and neighbors were especially important in his life because they taught him how to live—how to enjoy being a New Yorker, taking advantage of its museums and shows in a way his father wouldn't.

Outside his home, on the New York City streets, Mack quickly learned something of his place and privilege in the world. Just to get to school every day, he had to fight his way through a tough Puerto Rican neighborhood, he recalled, forming a defensive line with ten other boys. When he didn't have his friends with him, he found a way to avoid a confrontation. "Those early lessons stayed with me over the years and served me well in business," he wrote, "where you can have everything in your favor on paper, but if you haven't got the street smarts and you haven't got the stomach, then you really haven't got it."

The fighting didn't stop in the streets. In high school, the same two factions fought it out in the stairwells. When Frank Doty, "a large Irishman who was head of the athletic department," put Mack in charge of forming a team of hall monitors dubbed the Doty Squad, Mack didn't ask his friends to join, but went to the toughest of the bullies. "People who don't really have any responsibility, people who have nothing to do, resent the position they're in, so that often when you give them a position with some importance it changes their whole attitude," Mack wrote. "This may not always work, but over the years I've found that it's almost always worth a try."

Mack didn't consider himself an exceptional student, but he did well on his college entrance exams and was one of just two students selected from New York City to go to Harvard. Harvard students at that time weren't merely elite, white, and Protestant, he noted, but also mostly from Boston, and even then mostly from the same neighborhood. Mack can sound naïve writing about his life between the two wars, but he claimed never to have experienced prejudice—even though as a Jew he lived through a period of widespread anti-Semitism. "Perhaps it was there," he said of prejudice, "but if so I simply ignored it and it disappeared."

Instead, Mack relished being different from his classmates, he said. He found that many people liked having someone unique around them. Mack was good-looking and outgoing. People are basically shy, he said, so he decided he would always be "the icebreaker."

Harvard was easy after the rigors of New York City public schools, Mack said. He joined all manner of clubs and teams, whether he had a lick of talent for what they were doing or not. "I started out in the freshman crew, until they figured out what was wrong with the freshman crew," he joked.

He learned a lot at Harvard, but not from books. He learned how to organize, how to budget his time, and where to go for answers and information. He also learned about money and the people who had plenty of it. They appeared priggish in public but were wild behind closed doors, he said. In addition to attending countless parties, he and his fellow students, with their overnight dates, spent most mornings skinny-dipping in the campus indoor pools before the start of class, drying off in front of the huge fireplaces at poolside.

In general, he found his elite friends and their circle to be lascivious, lazy, parochial, and not terribly bright for people who basically ran everything. In other words, he found them to be what they often accused the working class and ethnics of being. But Mack admired their sense of fun and adventure—and their confidence. When it came to the point where his classmates started asking him for jobs, however, he couldn't bring himself to hire more than a couple. "They didn't know enough types of people, or have enough varied experience, to be able to function in the world," he explained.

When World War I interrupted his fourth year of college, Mack was the only student in his class who got his regular degree, having completed his required classes by the end of his third year. The rest of his class got war-deferred degrees, he recalled.

In the army, he found again that the best "on paper" didn't always get the job done. He was a commissioned officer on ships that transported up to six thousand soldiers at a time across the Atlantic. They had highly trained spotters using state-of the-art binoculars to search the horizon for the periscopes of German submarines. Those men never spotted anything, according to Mack. It seemed to him that every single periscope was spotted by some poor guy who happened to be throwing up over the side of the ship.

When the war was over, Mack headed off his anxiety about reentering society by getting involved in charities and politics. It saved him from the banality of civilian life, just as it would later rescue him from the banality of wealth. "I feel we can't just take out, we have to put something back in; we have to keep feeding ourselves," he wrote of his charity work.

In 1922, Mack married, going from unhappy home to unhappy home. His wife was Marion Reckford, a member of the wealthy Lewisohn family. Although he described a troubled marriage, Mack was fond of his wife's grandfather, Adolph Lewisohn, a philanthropist who built a fortune with his Amalgamated Copper Company. Marrying into that family gave Mack the luxury of not having to worry about money. When his father retired, Mack liquidated his textile business—which was going south in every sense of the word—gave him all the money, and left to seek his own fortune. He wrote about tearing up his first paycheck, a sizable one, from a new Cleveland-based brokerage firm because he had to sell securities when he wanted to build businesses. He left to join a friend's small investment firm, specializing in discount-store and supermarket chains, which proved later to be relatively Depression-proof. Mack had already learned during a brief stint in his father's business that he was good at sales and at fixing what was wrong with a company.

The Prohibition years suited Mack just fine, not because he was against alcohol but because in the Roaring Twenties he was young, rich, and well connected—a frequent visitor to the riotous speakeasies. For the first time, more Americans lived in the cities than in the country, and all walks of life, all races, socialized together in those illegal drinking establishments. Anyone with twenty-five dollars for a fifth of bootleg whiskey was welcome. Mack remembered one man who opened the door with a democratic "Hello, sucker" to all comers.

Mack was introduced to the bohemian life after he rented his wife's Manhattan townhouse to the Pulitzer Prize–winning playwright George F. Kaufman. Mack would get drunk with him and with his friends—Dorothy Parker and her Round Table cohorts Robert Benchley, Heywood Broun, and Alexander Woollcott—at the Fifty-second Street hangouts. He thought the writers were fun and whip-smart, but realized after a while how carefully crafted their jokes seemed. "True charm," he reasoned, "is always premeditated."

Mack wanted his own high-profile life and decided to make his mark in public office. In the politics of the day, he felt he could have been either a conservative Democrat or a liberal Republican. He went where there seemed to be a future, he said. As usual, it also was where he would be the different one. He ended up running the Silk Stocking Club of affluent Republicans in New York City, and in 1932 he became the Republican candidate for state senate. His district included some of the wealthiest and some of the poorest neighborhoods in the city. Mack liked to tell the story of how the mobster Dutch Schultz, the district's rumrunner, told him he would deliver votes for a fee of five thousand dollars. Mack refused, certain of victory. When Election Day came and Mack saw long lines in the poorest districts, he knew the voting had been rigged. Mostly Spanish-speaking voters were prevented from casting ballots. If anyone did make it inside a booth, a thug would jump in and vote against Mack, he wrote. He lost by eighteen hundred votes.

Mack was livid. The next morning, he took two of his secretaries and went door-to-door to take statements about what happened. He had the papers notarized on the spot. He brought all the affidavits to the authorities to challenge the election results, but eventually he dropped his bid, settling instead to join a bigger fight against corruption, as it grew under Prohibition. Then-prosecutor Thomas Dewey took over the investigation—and the credit for it. For that reason, Mack disliked him and supported Willkie for president in 1940.

As far as Mack was concerned, the only people who had the guts to confront the issue, and the mob, head-on were the poor people whose votes had been discounted. Many were beaten in their homes after speaking to Mack, he said. But there they would be the next morning, faces and bodies bruised, to testify before the grand jury that had been convened. Mack was in awe, and he never forgot their bravery.

That was Mack's last race. "If I had won that election, I'd probably be senator from New York today instead of president of Pepsi-Cola," he told a reporter years later. Mack fancied himself a leader of people and was convinced that he could run anything. He remained president of the Silk Stocking Club, but, ever the contrarian, he also became the only Republican member of the Jackson Club, a group of powerful Democrats who met near Annapolis, Maryland. He particularly liked to play poker with Harry Truman, who would begin a game by yelling to the others, "Let's take this goddamn Republican's money."

In 1933, the year following the election, Mack joined Chicagoan Wallace Groves to form the Phoenix Securities Company. The firm, named for the mythical bird that rose from its own ashes, bought up controlling shares in Depression-crippled businesses, fixed them up, and sold them at a profit. With Mack as president, Phoenix became the fastest-growing investment company in the United States. "I got to the point where I could walk through a factory and tell whether or not that factory was operating satisfactorily just by the tempo of the men, their attitude, what they were doing, and how enthusiastic they were about their work," Mack wrote.

He preferred dealing with concerns that had a potential mass market. He worked with a cigarette and cigar dealer, a wallboard maker, a sugar producer, a metals company, a roofing-material maker, and an auto and truck maker. The toughest business, he thought, was department stores because of their big, constantly changing inventories. The easiest, he decided, was the soft-drink industry, because it's not seasonal, doesn't change in style, is a cash business with no accounts receivable, has inventory with an almost indefinite shelf life, and has a potential return on capital investment that "is out of this world."

———————

Pepsi was invented in 1898 by Caleb Bradham, a New Bern, North Carolina, druggist. He added pepsin, a digestive enzyme, along with sugar and seltzer, to a kola-nut brew and sold it as a stomach tonic, Pepsin Cola. It was popular enough that in 1902, he founded the Pepsi-Cola Company. By 1920, however, the company was in bankruptcy. It was liquidated in 1931, and the formula and trademark were bought for fourteen thousand dollars by Charles Guth, president of the candy-store chain Loft, Inc. He sold the drink only at Loft's counters until 1932, when he started a bottling business. When he left Loft three years later, in the middle of a strike, he took with him 91 percent of Pepsi's stock.

That's when Loft came to Mack's attention. In late 1936, with the company unable to meet its payroll, Guth's successor, James Cartner, asked Phoenix to help sue Guth for his shares, arguing that he had used Loft's resources to operate the business. Mack did his usual due diligence and went to the company's factory in Queens. "I'm a great one for fundamentals," he said. Based on his findings, Phoenix endorsed $800,000 in notes and got options of $1.50 to $2.00 a share on 400,000 shares of Loft's unauthorized but issued stock, *Fortune* reported.

Mack saw the factory as a good source for a five-cent candy bar. He also met some talented chemists in its lab, and thought that Pepsi tasted better than Coke. "Coke is spicy, Pepsi is citrusy," explained Thomas Elmezzi, one of the two main chemists who perfected the flavor of Pepsi. Elmezzi, ninety-one years old, was interviewed in 2005 in the office of the Jeanne and Thomas Elmezzi Private Foundation, in Queens, where he continued to report to work daily until his death in October of that year. He was the last surviving member of the original Pepsi staff.

Elmezzi, who joined Loft at age sixteen in 1929, and his senior lab partner, John Ritchie, took out the pepsin in the original Pepsi formula and gave the cola the taste it became famous for in the 1940s. Elmezzi was the son of poor Italian immigrants who lived near the original candy factory. He remembered Guth as a disagreeable man, a diabetic with a weakness for everything that was bad for his health. He wanted Pepsi to be sweet. To save the Pepsi formula from being undrinkable, Elmezzi and Ritchie would bring Guth a sample cola to taste. When Guth inevitably said to make it sweeter, they would leave the room and return with the exact same sample. "Better," Guth would say.

Once, Guth fired Elmezzi. "He hated Italians," Elmezzi claimed. But the invaluable young chemist was soon rehired. For decades afterward, he said, he kept the Pepsi formula in his head, jetting around the world to set up plants. No one ever asked Elmezzi, who became a vice president, to write it down or tell anyone else, and he never did, according to his biography, *The Man Who Kept the Secret*.

Loft's lawsuit against Guth was argued in Wilmington, Delaware, where Pepsi-Cola was registered. On September 17, 1938, the chancellor of Delaware ruled that Guth had to give Loft all his Pepsi-Cola shares. Guth appealed the ruling. Until a decision was reached, Mack was named president of Pepsi-Cola. Guth remained in charge of the plant, however, and was so hostile to Mack's presence that he refused to give him a pencil, a pen, or a piece of paper from the office, and made Mack ask him for the key to the men's room. In April 1939, Guth lost his appeal and relinquished his Pepsi holdings, except for a Baltimore franchise that he had purchased with his own money.

After the cases were settled, Pepsi shares soared. Loft shareholders then sued Phoenix for illegal speculation. Mack settled out of court and Phoenix grudgingly gave one million dollars in cash to Loft. The shareholders' attorneys got eighty thousand dollars. Mack was furious about the loss and railed against the lawyers, Ben and Jacob Javits. "[Jacob] is, as I am, a liberal Republican, so our paths have crossed frequently over the past forty years, but neither of us will ever forget our first bitter meeting," Mack wrote in his book.

When Mack became sole head of Pepsi in early 1939, he and Groves liquidated Phoenix and Mack turned his full attention to the cola business. It wasn't long until Mack was involved in more legal battles, this time defending the company against Coca-Cola. Mack estimated that Pepsi-Cola was one of some 240 trademark-infringement lawsuits started by Coca-Cola against its rivals.

Coca-Cola's president, Robert Woodruff, cut the Pepsi trial short by inviting Mack to meet with him in his Manhattan apartment. Mack said Woodruff wrote a simple sentence as they downed martinis: "I, Robert Woodruff, executive officer and president of Coca-Cola Company, hereby agree to recognize Pepsi-Cola's trademark in the United

States and will never attack it." Woodruff signed it and that was the end of the case—until 1942, when the two companies fought their final trademark case in the United Kingdom.

The first thing Mack did once he could breathe freely was set up a bottling franchise system. Coca-Cola had 1,150 franchises in the United States, no territory larger than what its original red, horse-drawn wagons could drive across and return with empties each day. Mack maintained 370 bottlers in territories no larger than what a motor truck could drive to and from for a day's delivery. He took control with a flurry of decisions: a new bottle, new labels, and a new method for quality control. Consistency and cleanliness were the biggest and most persistent problems in the bottling plants.

Initially, Mack let his bottlers use secondhand beer bottles. The glass bottles came in green, white, brown, and various other hues, and all required a two-cent deposit from the stores on delivery, giving bottlers some extra cash to play with. Mack added a paper label and a crimped bottle cap, called the crown. These were the bottles that Smith, McKellar, and Maund had to work with. They made a mess when they got wet in coolers and the labels gummed up and slipped off, McKellar complained.

After the bottlers tore through the secondhand inventory, Mack hired J. Gordon Carr, who designed the interior of Tiffany's Fifth Avenue store, to come up with a new bottle with a baked-in label. This was around 1941. The Depression was loosening its grip, but Mack kept the popular twelve-ounce bottle and the nickel price. Cost factors were not that much greater per bottle for the bigger drink, he reasoned. What difference there was, came out of the bottlers' pockets, however, and it was a burden. Coke syrup was sold to the bottlers ready to mix. Pepsi bottlers not only needed more formula, but the concentrate required the bottlers to provide almost 80 percent of the sugar themselves. A Coca-Cola bottler got fifteen to twenty cents per case profit, compared with as little as seven cents for Pepsi, making the franchise a hard sell. "You might say Pepsi got the second tier of bottlers," future special-markets team member Charles E. Wilson said.

Mack's responsibility was to make sure there was enough sugar to buy. When sugar prices jumped in 1939, he bought a big sugar plantation in Cuba. He was horrified to see that the workers lived in abject poverty, cutting sugarcane by hand for four months, then sinking into debt during the remaining idle months of the year as they bought from company stores. Mack decided to help them raise crops, chickens, cattle, and pigs to sell in the markets year round. He sent animals, seed, and feed to Cuba, plus some engineers to dig four wells. The community farm was going so well, other communities began to ask for the same, Mack said.

Two months later, Mack said, the Cuban government hit Pepsi with a tax bill of nine million dollars and promised to find more "back taxes" owed. Mack sold the plantation to some politicians and never went back. That left Pepsi-Cola without its supply buffer when sugar rationing went into effect. As Mack told it, "a strong capitalist company by the name of Pepsi-Cola had gone into Cuba and set up Cuba's first communist commune." He believed the community farms might have eliminated the need for a revolution. As it was, he said, had he been a Cuban, he would have followed Castro in 1959. Seeing firsthand the class divisions around the world, with the wealthy elite living behind walls topped by barbed wire, made Mack sympathetic to the poor. "I'd be on the other side of the fence ready to rip it apart along with the society that put me there," he said.

———————

If Mack could see himself leading a mob through the barricades, his rival at the helm of Coca-Cola, Robert Woodruff, enjoyed life on the other side. Robert Winship Woodruff, born in Columbus, Georgia, in 1889, was a shy, outdoorsy Southern gentleman. The title of Mack's autobiography, written with Peter Buckley, is *No Time Lost.* Woodruff's biography, by Charles Newton Elliott, is *Mr. Anonymous.* Unlike Thomas J. Watson of IBM, "whose press department issues a release nearly every time he goes to the elevator, Woodruff has issued few ... for he hates to see his name in print," joked *Fortune* magazine in a May 1945 profile of Woodruff. His press agent, Steve Hannagan, seemingly was hired to keep his boss's name *out* of the papers.

That was a difficult task. By the end of World War II, Coca-Cola had become the global symbol of the American soldier, and of American culture as a whole. "Coke might be the most widely distributed mass-produced product in the world," *Fortune* wrote. "The U.S. consumes nearly 100 drinks of it per capita annually."

The cola drink has its roots in Africa, where natives used green kola nuts as a water purifier, love potion, and hangover cure. In the mid-nineteenth century, the British noticed how it pushed the endurance of local workers. The nuts were taken back to England, where a chemist wrote about them in a journal, read by Atlanta druggist John S. Pemberton. Pemberton brewed a tea using the nuts, sugar, and coca leaves, containing cocaine, imported from South America. His "esteemed brain tonic and intellectual beverage" was peddled as a hangover cure. He then added carbonated water and began selling the drink at the fountains in his pharmacy as Coca-Cola on May 8, 1886. Pemberton ran into trouble, however, when he overspent on advertising. In 1891, he sold off most of the company to Asa Candler for the grand sum of twenty-three hundred dollars.

Candler marketed Coke as a popular drink and sold the syrup to druggists in every state. It did so well that he opened a bottling plant in Chattanooga, Tennessee, in 1899. The U.S. government made the company remove the cocaine from the formula in 1912. By then, it was the preferred drink over root beer, sarsaparilla, and all the other popular drinks. In 1919, Ernest Woodruff bought it for twenty-five million dollars.

Ernest Woodruff might have been smart enough to spot a great opportunity, but his son, Robert W., was given credit for the company's further success. He was the talented day-to-day manager and salesman, admired by local big shots, such as Georgia Governor Eugene Talmadge. If Woodruff got any unwanted press, it was because of his ties to such controversial political figures as the Talmadge family, all staunch segregationists. No one actually knew Woodruff's personal politics, and he saw no need to define himself politically or to carve out a civic role in society at large. Rather, he focused on personal relationships. He was famous for remembering hundreds of people's birthdays with cards or small gifts. "His appetite for human companionship is insatiable," one friend told a reporter. Even at the Coca-Cola Company, he got his information through personal conversations, and welcomed frank opinions. Yet, Woodruff was quick to cut to the chase and make a decision.

If Mack's seemingly quintessential New York sensibilities were shaped in part by his Texan grandfather, so Woodruff's good-ol'-boy persona hid his New England roots. His paternal grandfather was a Connecticut entrepreneur who invested in Southern flour mills. His mother, Emily, was a Winship, a prominent family from Massachusetts. Ernest Woodruff made a fortune by grabbing up businesses, but was so frugal that he collected hotel soap. When he bought Coca-Cola, he issued half a million shares, many bought up by friends and banks. Coke made many stockholders, managers, retailers, employees, and bottlers rich.

Like Mack, Woodruff was a born salesman with boundless energy.

Unlike Mack, a lot of it was spent worrying. "The world belongs to the discontented," Woodruff liked to say. "Things you worry about don't happen if you worry enough."

That rule served him well in troubleshooting at the company. In 1922, Coca-Cola nearly went broke under the volatility of sugar prices. After Robert stepped in, sales between 1923 and 1930 rose from twenty-four million dollars to thirty-five million, with net profit surging from five million dollars to thirteen million. He spent millions on advertising, favoring billboards and institutional ads. Coke's market leadership was never threatened, but by 1942, the year the company lost its trademark-infringement suit against Pepsi-Cola in the United Kingdom, Coca-Cola's phenomenal growth had begun to level off. Sales of rivals Pepsi, Dr Pepper, and Royal Crown Cola were all rising faster than those of Coke, with Pepsi's popularity bolstered by its winning ad campaigns. "People say Pepsi's radio ads are successful and Coke's are not because Coke's reflect Bobby's own taste," *Fortune* stated.

Woodruff responded by buying up more Coke bottlers for the parent company. Then, he dreamed up the plan to convince the government that soldiers needed Coke to maintain morale. Military consumption of the drink was twice the civilian average, and the sugar for it was exempted from rationing. It was expensive to set up the bottling plants overseas, and often unprofitable, but the move secured Coke as the number-one soft drink in Europe for decades to come. And the soldiers kept drinking Coke when they returned home.

Unlike his father, Robert knew how to enjoy his wealth. Among his homes, he owned a mansion in the exclusive Buckhead section of Atlanta, but his great pride and pleasure was his plantation, Ichauway, situated on some forty-seven thousand acres four hours from Atlanta. Visitors described the plantation as a vast game preserve, comprised of a group of homes, stables, and kennels surrounding a grassy circle shaded by magnolia trees. It was run by a staff of about three hundred workers, mostly black sharecroppers. The plantation manifested Woodruff's famous innate resistance to change. According to the *Fortune* article, the black servants wore white porter's coats and called Woodruff "Colonel Bob" or "Mista Bob," reflecting the sensibilities of the day. On Saturdays after dinner, the staff sang spirituals for guests, trained by Woodruff's wife, Nell.

In his way, Woodruff was charitable to his African-American employees. At Christmastime, for example, everyone on the staff, plus family members, got new outfits down to underwear. He also supplied the uniforms for the Ichauway Crackers, a black baseball team that played in the Georgia-Florida semi-pro league. In 1933, four years after Woodruff opened Ichauway, when someone was lynched outside the plantation's general store, Woodruff hired Pinkerton detectives to work undercover as farmers. The culprits were never found, but the violence stopped. And when a black sharecropper contracted malaria, Woodruff got Emory University to work on the problem. "Within five years there was not an active case in the county," wrote Frederick Allen in *Secret Formula.* He also once rebuilt a tiny black church that had burned down on the plantation, but insisted he not be publicly thanked. Woodruff gave generously to Emory University and to black colleges. But Woodruff also had the reputation of being highly controlling in his philanthropy, carefully directing how every dollar was spent.

Eventually, Woodruff came to realize his own blindness to race causes, as Mack might put it, and became "mindful of the toxic effect racial unrest could have on his business and his city," wrote Constance L. Hays, author of *The Real Thing: Truth and Power at the Coca-Cola Company.* But it was a long time coming. "The people who packaged and sold and advertised Coca-Cola were nearly always white," she wrote. Blacks were hired, but "few made it past entry-level jobs during the sixty years that Woodruff was in charge."

Part of Woodruff's reluctance was that Coca-Cola was a very visible

Southern institution, which made it a more likely target for white boycotts. Just how deep the potential threat was from even average Americans was shown in a survey on race published in the *Chicago Defender*. The September 1946 poll by the National Opinion Research Center found just 53 percent of whites thought blacks were as intelligent as whites when given equal educations, but that was up from 44 percent in a 1944 poll. Divided by region, 61 percent of Northerners—double the number of Southern whites—believed in the races' equality. Even more disturbing was that of all those surveyed who believed blacks were as intelligent as whites, a mere 35 percent felt they should have the same job opportunities. But generations of subjugation failed to change how African-Americans saw themselves. In both the 1944 and 1946 surveys, 92 percent of African-Americans believed they were as intelligent as whites.

Training for the war had put many Northern African-American men in contact with poor, rural white Southerners for the first time, and it was an awakening. The *Chicago Defender* published a letter home from one local soldier to his mother, Mrs. E. M. Cunningham, from Camp Claiborne, "down in the Louisiana Swamps." In the letter, forwarded to the paper in January 1944, the soldier wrote: "You can't imagine how these white people live. One-room shacks with the telephone booths [outhouses] in the back yards. The front door hanging on one hinge so you can see through the house from the road. Chickens roosting on the rafters, hogs and barefoot children wandering about the house."

For businesses, the survey that mattered most was the 1945 census showing that of the total U.S. population of 139.6 million, nonwhites accounted for 14.6 million. They were interested in the 10 percent of the population that was African-American with dollars to spend.

The war slowed the progress of the special-markets experiment at Pepsi-Cola and ended the internship program. After the departure of McKellar and Maund, Herman Smith stayed on until after the war, then went to work for the Schenley Distiller Corporation, at a reported huge salary increase to ten thousand dollars, plus expenses. Alfred Smith of the *Defender* wrote another admiring column about how the salesman dazzled his new white colleagues by walking into a liquor store in Washington, D.C., and having the owner immediately welcome him. "I haven't been taking your stuff because I don't like the manners of that cracker salesman you send up here telling mammy jokes and all. But if you are with 'em now, Herman, I'll take a few cases to start because I know you'll straighten 'em out," the owner was quoted as saying.

"The white sales executive and salesmen got an education," the columnist concluded. "But not being born colored, they still can't figure out how Herman does it."

Even as the Negro-market staff at Pepsi-Cola headquarters dwindled away in Smith's final years, the company continued to place ads in black newspapers—at a time when other advertisements still implored the postwar public, "Keep Turning in Your Used Fats!" Pepsi-Cola was alone in 1946 in sponsoring several large, creative, and increasingly political ads on behalf of the United Negro College Fund. Other businesses, however, helped efforts to raise $1.55 million for scholarships. Two years before, Walter Hoving, president of Lord & Taylor, was named the national campaign chairman of the fund in what was hailed as the "first cooperative nationwide effort between whites and Negroes to establish an academic community chest for the benefit of Negroes." David Rockefeller was another big contributor.

"Must Their Service End?" a February Pepsi ad asked, showing pictures of four black professionals. The copy read: "Thousands of Negro service men and women are daily becoming civilians, leaving behind them a proud record of service to their country. Must their service end when they doff their uniforms? The answer can be a resounding 'No!' . . . Be big. Give generously to those who have fought for you."

That same month, another Pepsi ad for the fund showed a smiling young boy and asked, "Doctor? Lawyer? Merchant? Chief? It's up to YOU!"

The most frequently run ad started in June, showing a picture of a black soldier putting on a cap and gown over his uniform: "I'm stepping *into* character. . . . I was fighting for this chance before I put on a uniform. All my life I have worked to go to college. Now I can, thanks to the G.I. Bill of Rights."

The campaign got bolder. By November, a headline screamed "KEEP 'EM MARCHING!" "Here are our leaders," the copy read, "our doctors, lawyers, and professional men. Here, and in other graduating classes, are our hopes. Don't sell them short. . . ."

Companies, such as Lysol, Vaseline, St. Joseph aspirin, and Gerber, bought small ads for their products using the faces of black models. But there, too, Pepsi-Cola was ready to make a bold leap forward, with the help of another group of innovators. In July 1946, Brandford Models, Inc., of New York City, became the first all-black modeling agency in the country, promising proper contracts for its professionals. Some 200 hopefuls rushed to apply. Actor Canada Lee, appearing at the agency's first fashion show, called the company's opening "the beginning of something we Negroes have known should have existed for a long time," wrote trade magazine *Advertising Age.*

Pepsi-Cola, the agency later bragged, would lead the way by "showing Negro and white teenagers enjoying a soft drink together." It isn't clear whether such a photo ever made it into an advertising piece. But the agency was getting more businesses to rethink their marketing strategies.

"Organized to sell the idea of using Negro models in advertising aimed at the Negro market, which annually spends a billion and a third dollars on clothing and cosmetics alone, the Brandford Agency found that it must persuade advertisers to change the slant of their ads," the

Chicago Defender wrote in a November article. The agency apparently had persuaded several brands to use its services. Pet Milk, for one, put its models on its new billboards. Smaller companies, such as American School Thread, also hired Brandford models.

The three founders of Brandford Models were Edward Brandford, a commercial artist; Barbara Watson, who had run a public-service program for the government and had produced a local radio show; and a white woman, Mary Louise Yabro, a former department-store stylist. As spokesman for the firm, Yabro outlined the agency's plan to train models in makeup, posture, and grooming, and its philosophy. "We will not release an 'Aunt Jemina' or 'Uncle Tom' type because we believe this is not a true picture of the colored people," she told the *Afro American*. They also planned to fight manufacturers who were "foisting cheap, shoddy garments on Harlem." And the firm vowed to stop ads in the black papers for skin-whitening creams that pushed white standards of beauty. "This is humiliating to the race," Yabro said, "and is also poor advertising."

As if to prove the point, just under the *Defender*'s agency story ran a two-column ad from a Tennessee company selling face cream. In the illustration, a woman asks a nurse: "Why don't men like me?"

The reply: "Your skin is too dark, suntanned. Try White's face cream."

The move into the Negro market wasn't going to be easy for any side. If Mack was ready to jump-start his special-markets campaign, his new effort had to go far beyond hiring goodwill ambassadors. He had to create a black sales department of equal status to his general one. Always on the lookout for leadership talent, Mack would start building a new Negro-market division from the top.

— Chapter Three —

How Big Is Your Negro Market?

WALTER MACK WAS HAVING LUNCH AT THE ALGONQUIN Hotel on West Forty-fourth Street one afternoon at the end of the summer of 1947. His Round Table friends had long since disbanded, but the restaurant was still a hangout for journalists and playwrights, and African-Americans were welcome, which was not always the case in the better Manhattan establishments.

The regular customers, like Mack, knew one another and circulated among the tables when they weren't eating. Leonard Lyons was looking for scraps of celebrity news for his daily column, "The Lyons Den," in the *New York Post.* Mack had gotten Lyons and his family to pose for his ad series, Pepsi's Album of Real American Families. The columnist stopped to chat with Norman Cousins, the editor of the *Saturday Review of Literature,* who was dining with his publisher and a distinguished-looking young African-American. Cousins was famous for his work in the world peace movement and in improving race relations, and also gathered information at these lunches. He was well connected in certain circles, but he had nothing for Lyons.

After Lyons moved on, Mack approached. Cousins greeted him and then gestured to his young lunch guest. "You should know this guy," he told Mack.

The "guy" was Edward F. Boyd, thirty-three years old and a recent arrival to New York City. A native of California, he had left his beloved San Francisco to work for the National Urban League in New York on a project that sought to alleviate racial tensions in selected American cities. He was briefing Cousins on the program. Boyd's expertise was housing, and his first year on the job had been eye-opening. He was organizing community services in ways that challenged the entrenched policies of city officials, many of them determined to disrupt any chance of peaceful integration.

Boyd was six-foot-two, slender and well dressed, with a thin, neatly trimmed Hollywood-style mustache. He'd had voice training, which save him a sonorous, carefully articulated way of speaking. It had landed him jobs singing and acting in bit parts in some big movies. He had a serious, no-nonsense demeanor, and wasn't quick to laugh, but when he did smile he showed dimples. He felt comfortable at the Algonquin.

Mack, always at ease socially, stood at the table and engaged Boyd in conversation. "Nothing was said about a job," Boyd said, "but Mack was always thinking about how to sell Pepsi, so within a couple of weeks, I got a call."

Boyd made the long commute from his new apartment in Harlem to an interview in September at the isolated Pepsi headquarters and plant in Long Island City, in Queens. The commute involved two subway trains and a bus and took well over an hour. The bus dropped him a long walk away from the factory on the edge of the East River, where boats from Cuba delivered sugarcane. The plant and storage facilities were on the ground floor of the building, with the executives on the second floor. Boyd made his way to the upper floor;

the offices lined the windowed walls of the building, surrounding an open area where salesmen could find a desk whenever they were in town. The sugary smell of the cooking cola syrup permeated the plant. "It wasn't an unpleasant smell, but it wasn't that pleasant, either," Boyd recalled.

Around the time Mack interviewed Boyd, the Pepsi president was being interviewed by *Fortune* magazine for a long profile. Photos taken for the article show exactly what Boyd would have seen on his first visit to the company: Mack dressed in a fine dark suit with a white shirt and white pocket handkerchief, sitting up straight at his desk, holding a cigarette. He looks comfortable, but not exactly relaxed. Everywhere are large metal signs of Pepsi bottle caps and the famous nickel bottle, which was then being phased out by some profit-starved retailers. The desk is chock-full of papers and Pepsi paraphernalia, yet doesn't look messy. "Mr. Mack was a meticulous man," Boyd said.

Mack, the reporter wrote, always offered visitors a glass of Pepsi, but was gracious enough to tell them they didn't have to drink it. *Fortune* was writing about Pepsi-Cola's "brilliantly fertile merchandising program that has put it where it is today despite war, rationing, and Coca-Cola." The article sang the praises of Mack's marketing genius in a field that was overcrowded and in turmoil over production costs and pricing. The reporter described Mack, at fifty-two, as "tan, healthy, and fit, and his fast, restless mind emits ideas of its own as rapidly as it seizes and appropriates the ideas of others."

Boyd found Mack to be more genteel than the reporter had described him. But then, the reporter probably knew the old Mack. By the time Boyd met him, Walter Mack was a changed man. He was happily married to his second wife, Ruth, and had a baby daughter, who was being raised with the elder son and daughter he had adopted in an unsuccessful attempt to save his first marriage. After thirty-plus years as a philanderer, he had become a faithful husband and doting father, committed to taking one month off each year to spend only with his family. In answer to a TV interviewer's question late in his life, Mack said that his second wife had the greatest influence on him of anyone because she changed his habits overnight. His life, he explained, took on "an emotional dimension" it never had before. No one seemed more amazed than Mack himself that he could have an engaging home life to complement his hectic business and political careers. He put his new wife in charge of his other passion, his community services.

The *Fortune* reporter didn't mention Mack's very public, very messy divorce two years earlier. Mack had decided he was in love with his longtime secretary, Ruth J. Watkins, who had become good friends with Mack's mother over the years. When Mack's wife refused to grant him a divorce, Mack went to Reno, Nevada, for a quick settlement, setting up "a branch office" in Carson City in the meantime, Mack wrote in his autobiography. He married his secretary moments after the divorce was final—on Valentine's Day, 1945. It was a second marriage for her as well. They left Nevada together, but because New York didn't recognize the divorce, Mack was at risk of being arrested for bigamy. He set up another branch office in Newark, New Jersey, and asked Pepsi's executives to take trains there for meetings. They complied.

By August of that year, his first wife relented and was granted a divorce on the grounds of desertion. Mack later wrote grudgingly about their $50,000-a-year alimony agreement.

So, when Boyd met Mack, he actually was as reserved as he seemed, although maybe not so much changed as retired after years of the high life. In his public and business lives, however, he was no less flamboyant than before his marriage. Mack continued to be in the news, whether it was for battling authorities of every sort or for accepting an award for good works. In 1947 alone, he won the Horatio Alger Award, selected from a nationwide college poll for "symbolizing the American tradition of starting from scratch"; received a "clean environment" award for raising funds to benefit the Outdoor Cleanliness Association; joined celebrities in supporting a New York home for needy children of all races; and donated his Times Square canteen to the city to use as a telephone information center.

Fortune found Mack "hooked" on his own quirky sales gimmicks, incapable of conventional business strategies. Instead, his old ideas just kept getting bigger. Mack got six skywriters together for an exhibition of the new Pepsi ad. Flying together in formation, each letter in P-E-P-S-I was made by sets of two planes, working in sequence. The finished message was 1.5 miles high and 15 miles long and visible for up to 20 miles. The skywriters "all . . . have distinguished war records," the press stated.

Another Mack stunt grew far beyond its intended scope. By 1947, Mack's seventh annual art contest had put Pepsi calendars into 720,000 homes and businesses across the country. The contest had begun when bottlers asked Mack to make a promotional calendar like the ones every other business had. Mack hated the "cheesecake and schmaltz" typical of calendar art then, and instead decided to use contemporary American art that would generate some interest. It did, and the contest grew steadily even through the war years. More than five thousand canvases were entered in the 1947 contest, twenty of which were selected for the calendar. Mack himself was one of the final judges, as well as a frequent buyer of the works. It cost Pepsi-Cola two hundred thousand dollars a year.

Mack's biggest splash in 1947 was a publicity-grabbing innovation on a most unlikely stage: Pepsi-Cola's April shareholders' meeting. "I instituted something else that apparently no one had ever thought about before: I opened up my stockholders' meetings to the stockholders," Mack stated sarcastically in his book. Such meetings, of course, were always open, but company executives never cared much who came.

How Big Is Your Negro Market?

Mack did. He threw five big parties: two in New York and one each in Los Angeles, Chicago, and Jacksonville, Florida. Of some twenty-five thousand stockholders, eight thousand attended, "and had a whale of a time," Mack recalled. "As a result we thereafter had eight thousand new Pepsi rooters and salesmen to spread out across America, which is no small number for a growing company."

He couldn't have bought better advertising. *Life* magazine gave the event three pages of coverage with lots of big photographs: There was Mack shaking hands with old ladies in fine hats; Mack in front of hundreds of empty bottles of Pepsi he joked that he drank in two days; and Mack standing with four clearly self-conscious Pepsi executives gathered to sing the famous "Nickel Nickel" jingle. The parties cost Pepsi-Cola an estimated twenty thousand dollars. Mack prodded his audience to "ask your very worst questions." The worst, *Life* reported, came from a little girl in New York who wanted to know why certain stores charged more for a Pepsi than the advertised price of six cents. "Mr. Mack," the magazine stated, "endeavored to explain the delicate problem of chiselers in a sellers' market."

"It takes a rare touch to turn a stockholders' meeting into a well-publicized party, harness the American art world to the making of a calendar and transform a routine personnel activity into a public service," *Fortune* said admiringly of Mack, the latter a reference to his pioneering the hiring of interns seven years before.

Pepsi's five hundred bottlers were less impressed. They were growing impatient with what they viewed as Mack's superfluous spending. They wanted help with the surging production costs, particularly the rising sugar prices, and they saw Mack as unsympathetic and unwilling to locate cheaper sugar supplies. Instead, he was busy lobbying Congress

– 69 –

in 1947 to end sugar rationing, which he saw as the key to stabilizing the industry. He appeared before the Senate Banking Subcommittee, asking for limits on hoarding rather than strict rations. In June, he testified at a hearing on a bill proposing immediate decontrol of sugar supplies. The bill was offered by Joseph R. McCarthy, the Republican senator from Wisconsin, who was still some four years away from the start of the anticommunist histrionics that would bear his name.

Mack was publicly backing President Truman's efforts to keep prices down during postwar readjustment. The cost of living had soared 52 percent since 1941, and American households were feeling squeezed. But the price of a Pepsi was inching higher. In the spring of 1947, Mack placed an ad in both black-owned and white-owned newspapers to assure the public. The copy read:

A DEMOCRATIC PRESIDENT AND A REPUBLICAN CONGRESS AGREE . . . Whenever a really vital issue confronts the people of America, we set aside our political differences and present a united front in the public interest. And so, Pepsi-Cola applauds the combined efforts of our government in working together to keep down the cost of living . . . America's No. 1 problem in 1947. In the soft drink industry, Pepsi-Cola is leading the field in our drive to help the American people reduce their actual living expenses. You can buy Pepsi-Cola today in retail grocery stores across the nation at not over a half-cent an ounce. Compare that price with the cost of other nationally advertised soft drinks.

If Mack's actions seemed unreasonably optimistic amid economic strains and internal dissent, it was because that spring Pepsi had posted a 22 percent increase in net income for 1946, to $6.29 million, over the previous year. Industrywide, annual soft-drink consumption had soared to eighteen billion bottles. Mack was also hopeful about selling

Evervess mineral water. He wanted to push it as a health benefit, but the postwar public was more interested in using bottled water to mix with cocktails.

More good news followed. On July 28, 1947, strict sugar rationing was lifted. Mack said Pepsi-Cola would use all the sugar it could get. He then felt secure enough about the future of his business to begin planning a move of the executive offices from Queens to Manhattan. He also began delegating more of the daily operations to his vice presidents, leaving his weekends free for his family at home in Connecticut.

Pepsi, *Fortune* noted, was no longer a "one-man show." The most conspicuous addition was a new executive vice president, and later board member, the salty Bryan Houston, a former Young & Rubicam advertising executive who had previously worked in the War Department in Washington. He was big, loud, and had the same sort of slicked-back raven hair as Mack had, except on him it looked less debonair. Unlike the typical executive of his day, Houston's publicity photos showed him smiling, rather than looking stern. He had a somewhat different take on Mack's idea that consumers just needed a little "nudging" to choose Pepsi. "Hell," Houston told a reporter, "you're not going to get leprosy if you drink Pepsi-Cola, or if you drink Coca-Cola, or if you don't drink anything at all."

After interviewing Boyd, Mack invited Houston into his office to help give a picture of the company's latest sales efforts. "He was the opposite of Mack. He was a little crude—a hard-boiled, hard-bitten Texan—and we hit it off immediately," Boyd said. Houston was Boyd's opposite, too, but it turned out that his work in Washington had put him in touch with some of the black professionals whom Boyd knew. His friendliness and ease around Boyd, as well as the way he brought Boyd into his inner circle in the months to come, made him a close colleague.

Mack and Houston painted a bleak picture of Pepsi's Negro-market campaign. Bills had piled up from before Herman Smith's departure in

July, and the program had become a patchwork of local efforts by individual bottlers, with no cohesive national strategy. One event that summer in Chicago was typical of the sort of costly efforts bottlers made to build brand awareness in black neighborhoods. Bold headlines in the *Chicago Defender* touted the local bottler's generosity: "14,400 CUPS OF COLD DRINKS FOR KIDDIES," the newspaper promised, supplied by Pepsi free of charge for the eighteenth annual Bud Billiken Club picnic and parade, named for a comic character.

The arranger of these events was Louis C. Turner, district representative for Pepsi-Cola and the Evervess Company of Chicago. Turner was an African-American war veteran who in three years with the Chicago bottler had worked his way up from maintenance man. He promised that "workers in full uniform" would distribute cold Pepsi-Cola and Evervess mineral water. Photos in the *Chicago Defender* show five alluring black women standing behind posters of Pepsi bottle caps. Another shows him handing Lionel Hampton bottles of Pepsi and Evervess. Turner also introduced to the crowd the latest winners of Pepsi's *Amateur Hour* radio talent contest, which was cohosted by three young adults from the neighborhood.

The fact that Pepsi hired men like Turner, who in turn hired so many local youths, was more important than any promotional event. The *Defender,* for one, could always be counted on to give full coverage to the company's hires. The same was true for the educational giveaways. In 1947, Pepsi awarded scholarships to 23 Negro students of the 126 given nationwide. Not only did the grants help students enter college, they supported graduate education for students who showed real ability.

During their September interview, Mack told Boyd of all the good deeds Pepsi-Cola did in black communities, and stressed that making this work known should be part of any sales pitch to African-American consumers. Boyd was only vaguely aware of the Pepsi scholarships, but he knew very well the servicemen's canteen in San Francisco. He wasn't a veteran, but amid the racial strife that he had dealt with daily, the service center seemed to him remarkably sensible and pragmatic. "It was a wonderful canteen, near the point of embarkation," Boyd recalled. "Soldiers would go and socialize before shipping out. And it was open to all."

Mack told Boyd that he realized the strength of the Negro market and wanted to capture it. He asked Boyd for his ideas. "I said he should treat the market as a market and not just try to do the obvious thing of getting celebrity advertising," Boyd recalled. "I suggested to Mack that a whole department would have to be developed. I wanted a program that would include people carrying the banner for Pepsi in different parts of the country—and not just to go out and shake hands, but to take orders."

Boyd was a man with big ideas, and Mack liked people who had ideas that made a difference. Nor could it have hurt that Boyd had Hollywood experience, for Mack favored big productions. Boyd knew he had the job before he left the building. He was to start at the end of the month. Boyd was promised a department of twelve salesmen, plus a secretary, with a mandate to groom them into the most influential national Negro sales staff in the country.

The hoopla that greeted Boyd's hiring suggests what a rarity black corporate professionals still were years after Smith, McKellar, and Maund were hired. Pepsi didn't hesitate to capitalize on its enlightened policy. Publicist Ruth Meier offered reporters a lengthy biography of Boyd, and the complete history of Pepsi's charitable efforts on behalf of African-Americans. "Pepsi-Cola has a firm and established policy of encouraging opportunities for Negroes in all of its business activities and related endeavors," Mack stated. "Besides the direct employment of Negroes as well as white people in its own organization, the company has always insisted that its community projects be for the benefit of all, without regard to race, creed, or color." The black press eagerly ran with the story:

"ED BOYD, GRANDSON OF CALIFORNIA PIONEERS, GETS BIG JOB WITH PEPSI-COLA CO.," exulted the *Los Angeles Tribune.*

"NEGRO STAFF TO BE INTEGRATED IN PEPSI-COLA FIELD ORGANIZATION," said the Norfolk *Journal and Guide.*

"PEPSI-COLA CO. APPOINTS MAN TO HIGH SALES POST," wrote the *Chicago Defender.*

"PEPSI-COLA PLANS NEGRO FIELD STAFF: EDWARD F. BOYD IS NAMED ASSISTANT SALES MANAGER," said *The Pittsburgh Courier.*

As much as anything, Boyd's hiring was a heady victory for the black press. It had taken years of effort for the newspapers to awaken manufacturers to their message that a multibillion-dollar black-consumer market was ripe for the picking. How national advertisers were forced to recognize black consumers before and after World War II illustrates the almost unimaginable racial divide that existed in America then. Blacks populated a parallel and almost invisible universe from society. Many whites, if they thought about African-Americans at all, fit them into various stereotypes—all different from themselves in every way.

That first major push for recognition in the late 1930s, when the Baltimore *Afro American* newspaper published its booklet on the Negro market, continued throughout the 1940s. *Ebony's* debut in 1945 helped build momentum. The new, slick magazine sponsored frequent promotional campaigns to lure advertisers and carried stories showing black Americans as ordinary, middle-class citizens. Finally, a long postwar effort painted a picture of the Negro market's potential that few companies could afford to ignore.

A major turning point in the campaign for white ad dollars came in the spring of 1946, when the American Marketing Association again held a luncheon featuring a panel on the growing Negro market. Unlike the one held four years earlier, this one centered on discussion of a proper survey, "one of the most comprehensive ever conducted on the Negro market," according to a *New York Times* story. The Research Company of America had questioned one thousand families in the Philadelphia-Baltimore-Washington area, turning up what was news to many: that blacks held middle-class values and wanted to buy the same things as everyone else. The survey revealed that Negro families "are volume and quality buyers with brand preferences and shopping habits similar to white families." What's more, their educational aspirations were "extremely high." Their first priority for spending wartime savings was their children's education, followed by purchasing a home and making home repairs, the study found.

The researchers concluded that "the influence of the Negro market in our national economy is greatly underrated and manufacturers are losing sales as a result."

Black publishers seized the moment. The trade group Interstate United Newspapers, Inc., representing 158 Negro newspapers—all weeklies or semiweeklies except for the *Atlanta World* daily—hired the Research Company to conduct the first nationwide study of the Negro market, the size of which was estimated to have reached ten billion dollars for a black population of about fourteen million. Simultaneously, the National Negro Publishers Association, aiming to halt criticism from potential advertisers, embarked on a concerted effort to improve the journalistic quality of its member newspapers. The group gathered in June 1946 to recommend reforms. Already, the group assured the public, "the day of the part-time Negro reporter, sometimes a minister, sometimes an insurance collector—but rarely a journalist—has gone," resulting in fewer errors in stories. Committee chief P. L. Prattis, managing editor of *The Pittsburgh Courier,* credited the role of black war correspondents with lifting press standards. The golden age of the black press had begun.

The NNPA got President Truman to telegraph the conference with his support. Truman wrote: "I have been particularly struck by a sentence from the Negro publishers' creed which some of your papers reprint regularly: 'All are hurt so long as anyone is held back.' This seems to me sound philosophy. The provision of equal opportunity and the protection of equal rights should be the goal of government and of all of us. I wish you every success in your sessions and through the years."

Yet another step was taken the following year, when the NNPA decided during a meeting in Detroit to form advertising and editorial societies. This time, conference participants included some big-business representatives: George H. Cushing, of the Automobile Manufacturers Association, and Charles S. Scott, general manager of the International Business Machines Corporation for the Detroit area, who addressed the meeting on advertising in the Negro press.

Ted Le Berthon, writing in his "White Man's View" column for *The Pittsburgh Courier,* chided white-owned businesses for their lack of interest in the black press. In a critique that was not entirely tongue-in-cheek, he tied the lack of advertising to a fear in white society of black subversion. He wrote: "The suspicion may arise that dark skin and lack of buying power go together, or that the skin color is the cause of the lack. This exclusion is what makes rebels, especially Communists." Advertising in the black press, he concluded, "would break down that not-wanted feeling" and isolation within black society, and "would do much to foster interracial good."

White manufacturers and white-owned media, in turn, blamed the paucity of mainstream advertisements on the shortcomings of the black press itself. The most persistent complaint was the papers' news content. At best, these weeklies printed what one white author termed "items generally not of interest to whites"; at worst, they were called sensationalist and hostile to whites. Adrian Hirschborn, a white student who went on to a fifty-year career in advertising, studied the budding Negro market for his 1949 MBA thesis at City College of New York. He found that the black publishers were caught in a bind, with manufacturers objecting to the papers' dependency on ads for questionable products such as patent medicines, charms, and skin lighteners, yet denying them the business needed to turn others away.

Cost was another deterrent. Not only was advertising more costly per line in black weeklies than in white-owned dailies, but advertisers had to create separate campaigns, with black models and writers, if they chose to tailor the ads to the black readership. Many advertisers failed to see the need for the extra expense, presuming that everyone read the local dailies.

What white advertisers and readers derided as sensational journalism, however, was partly just a reflection of the times. The papers covered a population regularly subjected to rape, lynching, and bloody clashes over such routine acts as attempting to vote, to use public transportation, to see movies, to use restrooms, to drink from water fountains, or simply to go out at night. Reporters sometimes became emotional or angry. "TRIAL DATE SET FOR 31 LYNCHERS," read one April 26, 1947, headline about the largest mass lynch trial held in the South, in Greenville, South Carolina. It concerned the murder of a twenty-four-year-old African-American named Willie Earle the morning after he was arrested on charges of attacking a white cabdriver. What's more, the black press was limited in what it could cover. The White House didn't allow an African-American in its press conferences until 1941, for example.

If black papers carried lurid and opinionated news coverage, they also frequently tackled complicated issues in a more thoughtful and comprehensive fashion than did the mainstream press, and provided a forum for some of the most fertile minds of the day. Imagine opening up the weekly local newspaper and reading the essays of scholar and activist W. E. B. DuBois, poet Langston Hughes, or the leaders at the front lines of the equal-rights movement, such as Walter White of the NAACP or Lester Granger of the National Urban League. It might have been useful for the general public to read the black weeklies' unique perspectives on some of the issues of the day. One reporter, covering the new United Nations and its promise to address world conflict, wrote about how shocked he was that the one problem central to peace was never at the top of the agenda for major powers: the eradication of racism worldwide.

These papers were surely the only place readers could find stories on the small, but significant, rights campaigns, such as pressuring white newspapers to capitalize the *N* in *Negro,* or outlawing the use of race descriptions in newspaper crime stories. In those pages, too, was the only consistent public record of black accomplishments: an item on a black woman going off to the University of Paris to get her PhD in French, or a black graduate student in the music department of Columbia University completing a folk operetta for Negro youth. This is not to say that the biggest newspapers in America ignored the nation's ongoing racial strife. But instances of distinguished reportage were often sullied by the white-owned media's persistence in stereotyping.

By the time Boyd went to work for Pepsi-Cola, major advertisers could no longer ignore the numbers being dangled before them. "Wearier than a U.N. conferee on Palestine is the notion that American Negroes are a fringe group marketing-wise, and hardly worth any concentrated selling effort," the trade magazine *Modern Industry* wrote in an article titled "How Big Is Your Negro Market?" The piece added: "When should anyone sneeze at an estimated $8 [billion] to $10 billion in buying power?" It identified African-Americans as the highest per capita purchasers of drugs, cosmetics, and toiletries, and big buyers of farm equipment, electrical appliances, and construction materials. The thriving black-owned banking and insurances companies, it added, bought plenty of office supplies, cars, and trucks. What's more, most major cities had a black newspaper, and they claimed readerships as high as 98 percent of the local populations. Looking at the major black weekly newspapers over the year 1947, it's easy to track the upward trajectory of advertising linage. Early in the year, the established, mainstream advertisers, such as Vaseline and Lysol, frequently were running small ads, gearing some to the black readership by simply inserting a photo or drawing of a black face into a standard layout. Vaseline ads, for example, showed a black Boy Scout's smiling face warning: "Be Prepared."

But as the year progressed, more and larger ads were running. The Philip Morris Company announced in April the launch of its first big national campaign in the black press. The *Chicago Defender* noted that the ads would feature "the well-known midget, Johnny." The story referred to real-life bellboy Johnny Roventini of Brooklyn, who was discovered in 1933 by adman Milton Biow at the New Yorker Hotel in Manhattan. The story goes that Biow heard Roventini alerting customers to telephone calls and liked his style. He asked him to page "Philip Morris." The bellboy roamed the lobby yelling, "Call for Philip Moorreeeeaaaasssss," and that slogan went on to become an advertising sensation.

Biow's ad agency saw no need to try to come up with an African-American replacement for Johnny. A May 31 ad shows a large image of Roventini holding in his white-gloved hands a pack of cigarettes half as big as he is. The company's only appeal to African-Americans was in its news article about the campaign, in which the *Defender* gave details about Philip Morris's record of hiring blacks. It employed one thousand Negroes in its factories, it said. But the story, in describing improvements made, unwittingly hinted at the probable reason for their strong representation: historically deplorable working conditions. "Sickness and accident, one of America's industrial handicaps, had to be overcome. So free, modern factory hospital facilities as well as sanitary eating and washing conditions were provided. To prevent accidents, equipment was improved and safety precautions were taken. Relief and rest periods were made part of company policy. Many Negroes now wear with pride their five, ten, and more years of service pins given by this company; a pride built up by the security of a yearly paid two weeks' vacation, group insurance, old-age pension plan, hospitalization insurance, and seniority rights—a pride that carries into their community life to make them better citizens."

Philip Morris's announcement was soon followed by big, flashy Chesterfield ads specially designed for the weeklies. They featured boxing champion Joe Louis, photographed in boxer trunks and in a suit. The Liggett & Myers Tobacco Company said in an accompanying story that reproductions of oil paintings of the champ "in various fighting stances" would be available to retail outlets. "Heavyweight Champion of the World, Joe Louis will lead a galaxy of Negro athletes in the Chesterfield cigarette advertisement series," the *Chicago Defender* reported. But Liggett & Myers had to run a disclaimer stressing that "the Brown Bomber is not a smoker himself," and that Louis was merely recommending Chesterfields for use by fans who did smoke.

In midsummer, just as sugar rationing ended, Pepsi rival Royal Crown Cola unveiled its own elaborate ad campaign: an "RC tastes best!" taste-test series that ran frequently over several months. RC enlisted endorsements from a host of black entertainers, all photographed in a professional pose in front of a line of glasses marked

"X, Y, and Z" for the taste test. RC, of course, was always the winner, as in the first ad of the series, featuring jazz trumpeter Oran "Hot Lips" Page: "My blues just blew away," he says, "when I found RC! I took the famous taste-test—tried leading colas in paper cups. RC won in a breeze!"

African-American musicians, as well as professional models, were suddenly sought after by advertisers. Jazz trumpet ace Erskine Hawkins reportedly was pursued by three unnamed tobacco companies that wanted to make his the first "name" black band to do a "transcription," as they called commercials, for a national company, although it isn't clear whether he ever signed an agreement. *Ebony* garnered full-page ads from white-owned and black-owned businesses alike, including black cosmetics maker Rose Meta Cosmetics of Harlem, Kotex feminine products, and the Chesterfield ads with Joe Louis. Ex-Lax created ads showing an African-American mother and daughter. For all its success, however, *Ebony* still took ads that played to stereotypes, such as: "Don't be Wire-Haired Willie, the man nobody loves . . . Let Snow White help you have smooth, richly gleaming hair." Ads for knickknacks abounded, such as an ashtray fashioned so that cigarettes could be stubbed out in the mouth of a black figurine.

With this fresh push to sell to the Negro market, Mack suddenly found Pepsi-Cola lagging behind some big, innovative manufacturers. Pepsi's philanthropy, progressive hiring practices, and community outreach had been groundbreaking, but the company was now missing opportunities for print campaigns. Of course, Mack could afford to be patient. Pepsi was still gaining sales among African-Americans. In Baltimore, one of the few markets where African-American consumption was measured, Pepsi had captured 45 percent of the cola market among blacks, according to a 1946 survey by the Research Company of America, compared with 36 percent for Coke and 16 percent for RC.

It was unusual for Mack to follow the pack on creative promotions and community activities. He would make up for it by plotting a bigger, better, and bolder ad campaign than those of his rivals. It would be up to Boyd to put Pepsi-Cola in the lead again.

———————

Boyd took an office down the hall from Mack's, next to the boss's former classmate, Talbot "Toby" Freeman, one of the "sharp-penciled little bastards from Harvard," as Houston liked to call the office MBAs. Freeman managed a traveling team that sold equipment to bottlers. Boyd liked Freeman, who treated him well and became a friend.

Far from feeling intimidated by his first job in the private sector, Boyd's first impression of the big-league corporate world was how "unenlightened" many of his colleagues were. And Mack claimed he had already screened out the most parochial among them. Like Walter Mack, Boyd was surprised that privileged people would choose to lead such sheltered lives.

It didn't take long for Boyd to find out where he stood with his new co-workers. "Mack was warmer to me than anyone else there," Boyd said of his staunchest ally. Others in the office weren't so much hostile as they were indifferent. "In those days, there were white people and there were White People," he said.

Boyd had learned from his parents early in life how to deal with the White People. "My mother said they don't have to like you, but they have to respect you. If they don't like you, you just do what's right."

Respect, his mother reasoned, followed people who were educated, did excellent work, had dignity, and treated themselves and others with respect. And it helped if you could fight. Boyd learned all this, but he also learned to limit his dreams. He grew up wanting to be "the world's greatest diplomat," but was told that black envoys were sent only to Haiti and Liberia. When his good looks and vocal talent landed him jobs in Hollywood, he was given insulting roles. "One of the hardest things I've had to do in my life is not to become embittered," he said, "because if I did, I'd lose my objectivity and become nonfunctional."

———————

Edward Francis Boyd was born on June 27, 1914, the third son of a family of three boys and a girl; one older brother died shortly after Boyd was born. He grew up in Riverside, California, in one of the few black middle-class families in the area. His paternal grandfather, Robert Boyd, was the son of a white plantation owner in the Raleigh-Durham area of North Carolina, who had fallen in love with Mattie, the daughter of a house slave. The young lovers were, of course, forbidden by law to marry and so fled via the Underground Railroad to Toledo, Ohio. Once there, they married and had a son, Robert James Boyd. When the son was still a child, his father fell ill and died. Mattie then married a black man and moved the family to McKeesport, Pennsylvania. The young man, however, wasn't comfortable in his new home. "Dad's stepfather wasn't nice to him, so he went back to Toledo, Ohio, alone," Boyd said. There, the youth developed a lifelong friendship with Edmond Locke, a son of the family that published *The Toledo Blade,* then known as the voice of the local Republican Party. "The Lockes were an old, established family and the newspaper was thriving then," Boyd added. The white family took the young man under their wing, developing a warm, long-term relationship.

Robert grew up to become a successful barber, with an almost unheard-of twelve chairs in a prime downtown office building. "At that time, gentlemen didn't shave themselves, so they were at the barbers every day," Boyd explained. "Close relationships developed. The white customers had the ear of their barbers, and vice versa. Many black men at the time became prominent businessmen after a start as a barber, like the man who founded Atlanta Life Insurance [former slave Alonzo Franklin Herndon]."

Robert married, divorced, then moved to Los Angeles, where he opened another large barbershop in the downtown area. There, he met and married his second wife, Emma Barrett, Edward Boyd's mother. His friend Edmond Locke followed, and built for himself and his new wife one of the first mansions in Beverly Hills. As Emma began bearing children, her doctor recommended she seek a better climate for her health, and she moved to Riverside in 1910. All along, her husband ran successful barbershops, but once in Riverside, she founded Boyd & Boyd Real Estate as a second family business. Emma was the driving force in the company, although her husband, fourteen years her senior, shared some of the work until he was in his eighties. Enterprising African-Americans found a measure of success in the real-estate markets in the first half of the twentieth century, working with a vengeance to put land into the hands of their people, who had given so many lives to working the earth only for the benefit of others. Emma Boyd's family was particularly adamant about land ownership. When Emma became an adult, she and her mother, saving money from work as domestics, built a home together in Los Angeles; so, when the daughter married, her husband simply bought out his mother-in-law's share.

The Boyds raised their children in Riverside, then a mix of white, Mexican, and black residents. His mother bought and sold property without regard to color, and so became the target of local racists. One day, the family awoke to find KKK painted across the front of their house. Boyd remembered clearly his mother's side of the conversation when she telephoned the chief of police, a Mexican-American, who was a friend of hers. She described the vandalism and ended the conversation matter-of-factly: "I'm not calling to ask you for protection. I'm just letting you know what happened in case you get another call from me to pick up some bodies."

It wasn't the first time Boyd had heard his mother battle on the telephone. Whenever she received a threatening call because of her color-blind policies, she would chide the caller: "I'm ready for you; come on over."

"Our house was a small arsenal," Boyd explained. "My father was a hunter, but the weapons were not only for hunting purposes." All the children in the Boyd family knew how to use a gun, and were told never to hesitate to use one to protect themselves. "My mother was a fighter. She was vocal and very active. Everyone in town knew where Mrs. Boyd stood on things," Boyd said. "My father had strong feelings about race issues, but he was less vocal."

Emma Boyd's strength, confidence, and sense of place were rooted in her family's long history in California. Emma Boyd was the granddaughter, on her father's side, of a tough-minded pioneer who joined the California Gold Rush of 1849 in a covered wagon after he was widowed. Her grandfather, William Barrett, ended up ranching and operating one of the area's earliest vineyards, acquiring several hundred acres by homesteading in and around what is now the city of Stockton.

Emma Boyd wanted her children to lead refined lives and carefully chose their company. "I can remember as a child falling asleep on her lap on the way back to Riverside from Los Angeles, where she had brought my sister and brother to a dance or party," Boyd said. "She kept fully involved in the city's social scene there. If any young girl started to get what we called 'a reputation,' my sister would be forbidden to see her."

Edward Boyd didn't need much prodding to get involved in the arts, in politics, or in good living. He sang in the high-school choir for his class of 1932 and continued as a bass baritone when he went to Riverside Junior College. Riverside had its own small opera company and he was able to sing and continue private lessons there. Boyd was employed for a time as a soloist in the town's most famous institution, the Mission Inn, run by Frank Miller, a friend of the Boyd family. The elegant hotel took up more than a block and lured presidents, European royalty, and writers to its doors. Miller had become involved in the international peace movement through Andrew Carnegie, and he helped found a local chapter of the NAACP after he became indignant over three young black girls being barred from a local public pool on a graduation-day picnic, Boyd recalled. The inn gave free space to students, and Boyd started and led an international-relations club that met there. When he went on to study for a bachelor's degree at the University of California at Los Angeles, Boyd majored in international relations, and public and personnel administration. He also remained active in the area. He joined a group that filled station wagons with food, clothing, and books to bring to the desperate Okies fleeing to California from the Dust Bowl. He learned then that no one race had a monopoly on poverty or despair. "These were people who probably otherwise would never choose to have anything to do with me or anyone of my race," said Boyd. "But I was very much concerned."

While at UCLA, Boyd got further training in voice and acting. He made extra money singing on recordings for Hollywood movies, and he won some small roles. He hated the demeaning characters he was forced to play. He was put in blackface to make himself darker, and played ignorant, shuffling slaves. He worked on *Jezebel,* starring Bette Davis, and on other major films, but his insignificant roles often ended up on the cutting-room floor. He was grateful for that. Later in life, he declined to name any of his films. "If I had it to do over again, I would never put on that makeup to sing those 'darkie' songs—never!" he said. "I wouldn't do it for anything."

Boyd continued: "At the time, we all felt terrible doing it, but we just made jokes about it on the set." One friend of Boyd's who tried to use humor to deflect controversy was Hattie McDaniel. His plan to escort her to the Academy Awards in 1939 fell through. That night, she became the first African-American ever to win an Oscar, for her supporting role as Mammy in *Gone With the Wind*. When critics chastised her for taking the role of a slave, she snapped back, "Did you think I was going to play Scarlett O'Hara?" Boyd recalled, laughing.

The final straw for Boyd was when he sang for the movie *Top of the Town*. A British makeup director, testing costumes for a shoot, took one look at Boyd with his green eyes peering out of his blackface and said, "I thought they were sending me a Negro."

Not long after that, singer-actor-activist Paul Robeson said he would never appear in a film again until Hollywood stopped its degradation of black actors. It wasn't just that they were cast almost exclusively as maids and slaves, but that the characters lacked any realism—any human or intellectual dimension. Even sympathetic directors tended to fall back on cartoonish stereotypes.

Boyd's bit parts and singing assignments, however, allowed him to join the Junior Screen Actors Guild, where he sometimes rubbed elbows with some of the top screen artists of the day. He was on the Hollywood lots when Judy Garland and Bob Hope did their first movies. In Junior SAG, the black membership encouraged Boyd to run for a seat on the board of directors. His campaign was successful, and he won enough votes to get a two-year term. The experience taught him how to make a pitch in front of a critical audience. SAG had some prominent leftist members then, Boyd recalled, although he was a moderate. He was particularly put off by one left-leaning firebrand— an actor named Ronald Reagan.

After graduating in 1938, Boyd stayed two years with SAG's personnel department then moved to a similar job with the Federal National Youth Administration. From 1942 to 1945, he worked in California for government war-housing programs. That put him at the center of one of the biggest racial controversies of his day: relocating black and white workers, mostly from the South, to new jobs along the West Coast for the war effort. The work gave Boyd a draft deferment. He first went to work for the Los Angeles City Housing Authority to supervise a six-hundred-unit project, then to a fourteen-thousand-unit project for the Housing Authority for the City of Vallejo.

In Vallejo, a new dormitory for single men was segregated but not separate enough for the white laborers. The housing group had to face down hostility from all sides: white workers, their unions, and local citizens who resented living and working alongside the new black residents. The local NAACP had to sue the metalworkers' union to get it to integrate. When the *San Francisco Chronicle* interviewed Boyd for a story, he gave a scathing indictment of racist policies on every level. The story created a stir. "He almost got us both fired," said Boyd of the reporter. Boyd left to take a number-two position in the Civil Service Commission in San Francisco, becoming the first black professional to work there. His job was to coordinate the classifications and pay scales for the personnel of the city's major utility projects.

Boyd fell in love with the city, becoming active on many levels of life there. He supported Presbyterian minister Dr. Albert Fisk in founding an interracial church. They appointed prominent African-American theologian Dr. Howard Thurmond to the role of church leader. "The Fellowship Church set San Francisco on fire for a while," Boyd said, because of Dr. Thurmond's charismatic preaching and work toward racial harmony.

In 1944, Boyd married his girlfriend, Edith Jones of Los Angeles. Edith's father, Clarence A. Jones, was an attorney, one of the first African-Americans to graduate from Ohio State Law School. Her mother was also a graduate of Ohio State, where she majored in Greek and Latin. Edith Jones knew Boyd from family connections and also from the big screen. "Ah, yes!" she remembered. "I was sitting in the theater with a date watching an old Bette Davis film when a black guy on screen walks up to a boy in a tree, reaches up, and taps his foot. I

said, 'That's Ed Boyd tapping that foot!' " The unflattering role nevertheless piqued her interest in Boyd.

The couple hadn't been married long when Boyd was contacted by
Eugene Kinckle Jones, founding director of the National Urban
League. He told Boyd of a thirteen-city project the league was cospon-
soring with the Rockefeller Foundation. Boyd, with his background,
was hired as a housing specialist. "It was a three-year project based in
New York, after which I planned to go back to my beloved San Francisco," Boyd said.

Fate would have him take another route, and he settled in New York
City. The Community Relations Project aimed to ease racial tension in
medium-size cities around the country by targeting five sectors—
employment, public health, family services, recreation, and housing.
Once cities were identified as needing help, Boyd and the team of sector specialists would meet with local officials, gathering firsthand
information about the area. Usually, Boyd's task force recommended
more public housing and suggested federal programs to finance it. He
also recommended management changes that would allow blacks to be
included in decision making. "We mostly had to get people to understand that people are people, no matter their race," Boyd said.

The work helped Boyd hone his ability to work with those who
might not like him but had to respect him. It also gave him his first
experience traveling around the country on business. He had to
learn the varied laws from state to state and how to avoid trouble.
While he traveled, he'd stay with black families and arrange for his
team's lodging and meals, because there were few decent hotels for
blacks, and they never knew when they might be denied restaurant
service.

Boyd's wife, Edith, meanwhile, got a job at *Time* magazine in Manhattan as a librarian. The couple landed in New York City during its
postwar housing crisis and first had to stay with a family. Before long,

they used connections to get an apartment in one of Harlem's choice addresses: 409 Edgecombe. The Harlem high-rise was home to W. E. B. DuBois, Walter White, and Roy Wilkins. "They used to say, if a bomb were dropped on 409 Edgecombe, the black leadership of the country would be gone," said Edith Boyd. "There was a variety of opinion, from communist to Republican, sometimes in the same family, but there was an acceptance of everyone."

America was at a crossroads in 1947, culturally as well as politically, where race was concerned. "White America is more conscious of its guilt in the Negro question, having more understanding of the darker brother than in any other era of history," *Ebony* wrote at the start of the year. The magazine listed all the good news African-Americans could celebrate, even if that list was short on hard figures: a higher standard of living, records of achievement in every field, more employed and at better jobs, more registered to vote, more enrolled in schools, a higher birth rate.

In publishing, New York companies were still "frantically grabbing at any and all manuscripts which touch on the Negro," as *Ebony* had reported. The magazine gave an award to white author Sinclair Lewis for his *Kingsblood Royal,* about a banker who learns he is biracial. James A. Michener published *Tales of the South Pacific,* which later won the Pulitzer Prize, about a woman who couldn't love a man who had biracial children. Langston Hughes published *Fields of Wonder,* his only poetry collection not about race.

In academia, only some twenty-five colleges employed more than sixty black faculty members, but many drew packed lecture rooms.

In film, Elia Kazan won an Oscar for best director and Gregory Peck for best actor in *Gentleman's Agreement,* based on a book by

Laura Z. Hobson about a journalist who poses as a Jew to expose anti-Semitism.

In the theater, Hilda Simms, wife of future Pepsi team member William Simms, became one of the first black Broadway stars after her lead role in the surprise hit *Anna Lucasta,* originated by the American Negro Theater. It was the first all-black production with a nonracial theme. *Finian's Rainbow,* by E. Y. Harburg, was a popular musical about an Irishman who comes to America to bury a pot of gold. In the play, a racist is turned black to realize his errors.

In journalism, antisegregation crusader Stetson Kennedy, a Florida native, did a groundbreaking investigative piece on the Ku Klux Klan after infiltrating a chapter in Georgia. He exposed secret rituals and a membership roster that included one local mayor. In one story, he described how thirty-five carloads of hooded Klansmen in Elberton, Georgia, rode through black neighborhoods "blowing horns and shouting threats." Terrified black truck drivers refused to make deliveries, putting pressure on businesses.

In 1947, black papers first noted the thrilling prospect of Hawaii becoming America's first nonwhite state. The population of the forty-ninth state would be less than one-quarter white, with Japanese making up the biggest sector at 37.3 percent, the *Defender* wrote.

Those most fed up with the status quo tried to erase the color divide altogether. *Ebony* asserted that of fourteen million African-Americans in the United States, about five million were passing for white. One white minister in Minnesota declared that from that day forward, he would consider himself black. A black man later responded that, inspired by the minister, he was going to declare himself white. A white jazz musician, Milton Mezzrow, wrote a book, *Really the Blues,* in which he contended that he was "psychologically a black man" and would live his life as such. He even managed to get his draft card changed to read "Negro."

The optimistic tone was set, in part, by a bizarre twist of fate. Predictions of a liberalization of the South had been dashed in November 1946, when Southern voters returned to office two of the region's most vocal and vicious racists: Mississippi Senator Theodore Bilbo and Georgia Governor Eugene Talmadge. One *Ebony* writer had predicted "a bloody postwar era of rioting that would exceed the dire days of 1919, the worst year of racial violence in all U.S. history."

But neither man took office. Talmadge died of a heart attack before the year's end. Bilbo got cancer of the mouth and died some months later. The black press could hardly hide its glee, especially in its coverage of the senator's demise. Langston Hughes wrote in the *Defender:* "Within a few hours after the news of his death came over the radio, I saw gaily colored streamers pasted across mirrors of a Harlem Italian-owned bar announcing in holiday mood: BILBO IS DEAD! I gathered that at least two American minorities had teamed up to rejoice."

On other fronts, one simple protest created headlines for weeks, and became a catchphrase for a generation. In June 1947, A. Philip Randolph of the Pullman porters' union was testifying at a fair-employment hearing of the U.S. Senate when he took Louisiana Senator Allen J. Ellender to task for calling him "Randolph" during questioning. "Call me Mr. Randolph!" was the protest heard round the country.

Most of all, it was a year notable for gains by African-Americans in the workforce. The National Urban League claimed to have placed twenty-five thousand blacks in white-collar jobs during 1947. The black press recorded a dizzying number of firsts for African-Americans. Below are just some of the news snippets from the year. (The reference to fifty-odd years refers to the 1896 Supreme Court ruling on *Plessy v. Ferguson* that established the separate-but-equal doctrine, killing off any vestiges of Reconstruction's equal-rights gains.)

First Negro admitted to Chicago Journeymen Plumbers Union local 130.

First Negro elected to the Ohio Senate in fifty-five years.

First Negro woman accepted by Gary [Indiana] Real Estate Board.

First Negro-owned department store in Buffalo.

First mixed jury in Arkansas in more than fifty years.

First Negro member of the California Knights of Columbus.

First Negro candidate for city council in Wheeling, West Virginia.

First time Negro and white members of all branches of labor—the CIO, the AFL, and the Independent Railroad Brotherhood—marched together.

First Negro-written, -acted, and -sponsored commercial radio show.

First Negro switchboard operators for Illinois Bell Telephone.

First Negro woman in training to be a large-scale buyer at Macy's.

First Negro enrolled in nurse's training at Rockland State Hospital, New York.

In November, a three-day ceremony heralded one of the most cele-brated firsts: Charles Johnson became the first Negro president of Fisk, the prestigious eighty-one-year-old black college in Nashville, Ten-nessee.

But the first among firsts that captured the imagination of the nation was when Jackie Robinson broke the color line in Major League Baseball. On April 10, 1947, Branch Rickey called Robinson up from the Montreal Royals farm team to play for the Dodgers at Ebbets Field in Brooklyn. Robinson became a hero of both races, particularly those active in the integration movement, and integration was the battle cry of that generation of African-Americans.

The outpouring of goodwill toward Robinson was so great that within a month, Rickey was scolding African-Americans for burying the ballplayer under at least five thousand invitations to every type of event across the country. "They treat Robinson as if he were a freak and not a ballplayer of ability," Rickey said. "He needs rest—and he needs time to eat his meals. . . . It would be best for all these people to let Robinson alone."

But his fans couldn't leave him alone. Their support countered the relentless threats Robinson faced daily by racists who were riled by his success. The fans won out. By October, a radio poll listed Robinson as the third most popular American after Bing Crosby and Frank Sinatra. He beat out Eleanor Roosevelt, General Dwight Eisenhower, and President Truman. Three months after Robinson's move, there was only slightly less fanfare when the Cleveland Indians signed Larry Doby, star infielder of the Newark Eagles, as the first African-American in the American League.

It was amid that euphoria that Mack, and other business leaders, began reviewing their own organizations. Mack went on to make a more substantial effort toward integrating his workplace. His efforts didn't go unnoticed in the African-American population. When the *Chicago Defender* released its Honor Roll for 1947, Walter Mack was one of the top five of a long list of advocates for improved race relations, just under the revered Jackie Robinson.

Robinson was the consummate gentleman athlete. *Ebony* wrote: "With his quiet, modest, yet assured manner [he] is winning many, many friends and proving himself the exact opposite of all the stereotypes about ballplayers and about Negroes." He and his wife, Rachel, didn't drink, smoke, or go to clubs, and modestly shared an apartment in Brooklyn with another couple during baseball season and lived with Rachel's mother in Los Angeles in the off-season.

Robinson's squeaky-clean image had advertisers scrambling to get his endorsements on everything from hats to cigarettes. In the fall of 1947, Old Gold cigarettes began an eye-catching ad campaign in the black press featuring a series of photos of Robinson in action. No disclaimer on smoking was necessary.

The ads that Robinson, and Joe Louis before him, did for the cigarette companies were typical of the high-powered Negro-market pitches. Owners of stores and bars would put copies of the most popular ads in their storefronts. Boyd was determined not to follow their lead. "It offended me to promote products by having photos of black celebrities in a window," he said. "It had no meaning." He made newspaper ads a priority as soon as he set up his office. Working closely with Pepsi-Cola's in-house adman, Al Goetz, Boyd set up meetings with the Newell-Emmett advertising agency. He spent the remainder of the year writing proposals and budgets, and getting to know the operations and the staff. "I wouldn't say I got any special treatment at the company," he said, "but it was special to me. Mack was so fair, such a straight shooter. He didn't want me to feel any discrimination. Personally, it was almost too good to be true."

— Chapter Four —

Leaders in Their Fields

IT WAS JUST BOYD'S LUCK. NO SOONER HAD HE SET UP HIS office at the Pepsi-Cola Company than the entire soft-drink industry was hit hard with a drop in sales. The "worse-than-seasonal slump" began in October 1947, and at the start of the new year, consumption was still stalled. "We don't know what's behind the drop," one bottler told *The Wall Street Journal* in an alarmed front-page story in February 1948. "Sure the weather has been bad but that can't be the whole story."

The problem, various reports suggested, began with a glut of bottlers, some seven thousand across the country. The end of sugar rationing made an already competitive field heat up further. Things got worse when the price of a bottle of cola—just about every brand except Coke—started to rise at certain locations throughout 1946 and 1947. Half of the Royal Crown Cola bottlers had increased their price to six cents, for example, only to see their sales plummet. Robert Woodruff of Coca-Cola was right about the psychological barrier of the nickel bottle, and so was the little girl at Mack's famous stockholders' meeting who demanded to know why some stores charged more than others. "That dirty-faced kid with a nickel clenched in his fist is one of our best customers. And he's a tough one to get more money from. When a soft drink goes to six or seven cents a bottle, it has been priced out of Junior's market," another unidentified bottler told the *Journal*.

Added to that problem were rising production costs, particularly labor. Equipment prices were up 30 percent since before the war, bottle caps up 20 percent, glass bottles up 12 percent, labor up 50 percent, and sugar, even after two price cuts, was up 50 percent at the start of 1948. Estimates were that a bottler had to sell to the small retailer at no less than 3.33 cents a bottle, pushing up prices at the retail level.

Mack put on a calm face. "What's all the fuss about?" he asked one reporter early in the crisis. Sugar will eventually come down in price, he reasoned, and "the nickel bottle will return."

That rollback was already happening by early 1948, after manufacturers had learned their hard lesson from Junior. Some 90 percent of the Royal Crown Cola bottlers who had raised their prices returned to the nickel bottle. Pepsi-Cola's Bryan Houston said that by February about half of Pepsi's five hundred bottlers also had returned, "and eventually all of them will be back at a nickel." Subsequently, Mack was being pressured to cut the size of the twelve-ounce bottle. But he was far less willing to let go of the size than the price. "Never," Mack vowed, "will the size be changed, nor will there be any need." He did, however, allow eight-ounce bottles to be introduced at ballparks and other public places, and sold them for a nickel. In those days, the twelve-ounce bottle was considered too large a serving for an average person to drink in one sitting. (By the end of the century, it became the standard can size.)

The price rollback, however, didn't help every manufacturer. In less than two years, many soft-drink companies had journeyed through a meteoric rise and a subsequent freefall into bankruptcy. The smallest producers were the most vulnerable, including many returning vets who had enjoyed the special privilege of being exempt from the sugar rationing. The biggest companies knew their best chance to survive was by bringing down per-unit production costs and expanding sales. Thus, even in the middle of this terrible slump, companies started increasing and modernizing production. Coca-Cola barged right into Pepsi's turf, building a new plant in New York City with equipment that could turn out 300 bottles per minute, compared with the 144 of its old machines.

Soft-drink producers also prepared for aggressive sales campaigns. Pepsi took the lead. It sponsored contest giveaways totaling an almost unprecedented two hundred thousand dollars. For six months, the company handed out fifty-one cash awards and three big national prizes for completing the line: "Pepsi-Cola hits the spot because . . ." A $25,000 grand prize and forty-three other cash awards were handed out for the best statement on "how the sales of Pepsi-Cola can be increased." The contest was open to all, but advertised only in the white press. It signaled the beginning of the era of the amateur jingle-writing competition.

Finally, soft-drink manufacturers concluded that new markets had to be opened in some locations to ease the production glut in others. They turned their attention to the underserved populations in America. Canada Dry licensed nineteen bottlers in new territories from the end of 1947 to early 1948, up from five. Nehi added thirty-five new franchises in about the same time. In six months, the Charles E. Hires Company added more than one hundred bottling companies. They also jumped into selling soda pop in corner drugstores, offering more flavors.

Mack had no desire to add plants. Instead, he planned to chase new customers, particularly in the black population that had been so loyal to Pepsi-Cola. That was a big break for Boyd, of course, and Mack was ready to keep his word on the hiring of African-American sales representatives. But Boyd got nothing but bad news on budgets for the

Negro market. He was told that he had to be careful in spending. For a start, he got to hire just four men of the planned staff of twelve.

———————

What sort of candidates did Boyd have in mind? "I wanted clean-cut guys with an education, youngish, well turned out, a certain personality," he said. "That is, attractive in terms of meeting the public even if they hadn't been salesmen, because few black people had extensive experience."

There was no need to advertise in the newspapers. In fact, Boyd didn't dare. "I didn't want to be besieged," he said. Instead, he started making contacts, using the help of the National Urban League, as any corporate executive looking for African-American employees would have done in those days. The Urban League had established a well-run network—respected in U.S. business circles—that connected young, educated people with companies that could help them launch professional careers. For a generation of black professionals, the joke was that the Urban League had the most overqualified telephone receptionists in the country. "Everyone wanted a job answering the telephones at the National Urban League," said Julian Nicholas, later a Pepsi team member. "When someone called with a really good lead, you'd give them the usual line, 'I believe we have a fine candidate for that position I'd like you to meet. Let me make an appointment for an interview tomorrow.' The receptionist would then hang up, get his or her résumé ready, and show up at the meeting. No way that message was getting passed along!"

That's exactly how Boyd hired his secretary, Norma Bowler. He had worked with her boss at the Urban League on the thirteen-city community-relations project. He asked Bowler if she knew anyone who would be interested in being a secretary for the new Pepsi-Cola national sales team for the Negro markets.

"Why, I'd be interested!" she said.

Bowler was from a family of domestic servants who worked for the wealthy in the town of Darien, Connecticut. Such domestics were the backbone of the Negro market. They typically shopped for their affluent employers and thus influenced buying choices. And unlike in typical working-class households, they became accustomed to the higher-quality products their employers used and found ways to budget those same items into their own households, despite the cost.

After high school, Bowler went to secretarial school, and Boyd was impressed with her outgoing personality. "She met people well and developed many friends among the secretaries at Pepsi," Boyd said of Bowler, who was the first African-American secretary at headquarters.

Her people skills and ability to organize complex schedules proved to be invaluable. Keeping track of a traveling sales team in the days of paper-and-ledger transactions was hard enough, but executing complex travel and lodging changes at the last minute for tired, upset salesmen because of arbitrary acts of discrimination took a special talent. Norma Bowler was the sweet and calm voice at the other end of the phone. She took her seat in the center of the ring of offices, outside Boyd's door.

Shortly after Bowler was hired, she married Cliff White and changed her last name to his. Boyd immediately recalled the first name of her spouse nearly sixty years later. Indeed, he remembered the names and family histories of almost all his salesmen's wives, and was surprised that anyone should suggest that it was remarkable to do so. In the small circle of African-American professionals at that time, the wives' connections were often better than those of their husbands. Black women were seen as less threatening to white society, Boyd said, and thus could start a professional career more readily than their husbands. Perhaps more so than whites, he suggested, black men accepted the idea that their wives would work outside the home. Boyd was always proud that his wife worked as a Time, Inc., librarian on magazines such as *Time* and *Fortune,* and had her own interests in life.

Although he wasn't opposed to the idea, Boyd never hired a woman for his sales team. "Not a single woman approached me," he said.

Boyd began interviewing candidates, keeping in mind the regions they were from. His first hire was David Foster Watson, a sharp, likable thirty-six-year-old who had just completed a year of work in Atlanta, Georgia, "promoting the welfare of Negro citizens," according to an article in *New York Age,* one of the many black newspapers covering the new hires. "He impressed me the first time I saw him," Boyd said. "He was just a nice person, the kind of person I was looking for."

Watson came from a family that typically held government jobs in Atlanta, and he was a graduate of Morehouse, so the Watson name was familiar to many in the area. He married into a family that was known nationally. His new bride, Beulah Clark, was at ease in any social situation, and the Watson home in Queens was often the scene of a dinner with the boss or a party with the whole team.

Beulah was the sister of the famous psychologist Kenneth B. Clark, a longtime leader in the fight against segregation. In 1940, he became the first African-American to earn a PhD in psychology at Columbia University. When Boyd met Beulah, Dr. Clark and his esteemed wife, Mamie, had just founded a center in Harlem for emotionally disturbed children. Their most famous work, however, was a study showing how young African-American children showed a preference for white dolls over black, which the couple linked to the psychological damage of segregation. It was a pivotal finding used in the *Brown v. Board of Education* case in 1954, which outlawed segregated schools and debunked the notion of "separate but equal." Kenneth Clark went on to participate in President Lyndon Johnson's War on Poverty. He died in May 2005.

The second hire was H. Floyd Britton, thirty-four years old, a native of Pittsburgh. After high school, Britton went to work for the advertising department of *The Pittsburgh Courier,* and after three years rose to managing the paper's New York office. During the war, he did "work of a confidential nature," as he described it to the press. He then joined the Pabst Brewing Company's expanding black sales team.

Boyd admired Britton's sales skills. He was an energetic person and was especially good at working the local nighttime haunts, particularly in Harlem, when the team started to take orders from bars and clubs. "Britton was the kind of guy who knew all the bartenders and club owners who, like us on the staff, had aspirations," Boyd said. "Those men belonged to powerful organizations and could introduce us to other groups."

Britton was serious about his job but determined to have a good time while on the road. And that would ultimately create friction with Boyd, who knew his group was under constant scrutiny and pressure to be good examples—a "credit to their race," in the parlance of the day.

Boyd's third choice was Harold W. Woodruff, from Houston, Texas, whose late father had been a professor of agriculture at Prairie View A&M College. Woodruff attended Kansas A&M College, specializing in electrical engineering. During the 1930s, he was in the radio and refrigeration businesses, and during the war he worked for the Sun Shipbuilding and Drydock Company in Chester, Pennsylvania.

In addition to being older than the other hires and the only representative from the Southwest, Woodruff was very light-skinned, a deliberate move by Boyd. Having his team reflect the wider community they served not only helped sales, it was practical when the team hit the road. "There came times when we could use Harold," Boyd recalled.

Selecting the final member of his sales team turned out to be a trying experience for Boyd—one in which he got his first introduction to the pressures of the old-boy network. Mack told Boyd about a call he got from his political crony, Jacob K. Javits, who had won his first election to Congress. The liberal Republican from Manhattan had an African-American aide who had helped him in his campaign, and he wondered if Mack could find room for the man on the new special-markets team.

It was a good tip. But, from the moment he laid eyes on the aide, Boyd knew it wasn't going to work. He could see why Javits had hired him: He was mature, of imposing stature, could talk "on the street level," was persuasive, and looked like he could take care of himself in a tight spot. But what worked selling a politician just wasn't going to work selling a soft drink—and vice versa, as Mack himself had learned working with Willkie. "He didn't have *it*," said Boyd. "He didn't have the appearance and approach I wanted."

When Boyd met with Javits, he thanked him for the referral, but said the man didn't fit the bill. Javits was furious. "He got real uppity, and stood up and started yelling," Boyd said.

"Mr. Boyd!" Javits started. "Walter Mack is a good friend of mine and I'm going to report this. I'm sure this is a good job for you, and I'm going to tell him about this."

"I hope you will," Boyd replied.

Boyd remained calm and tried to exude confidence, but he was worried. Mack had promised to give him final say on hiring, but he knew that Mack was serious about his standing in the Republican Party, and that Mack and Javits were cut from the same political cloth. As soon as Boyd left the congressman's office, he headed for a pay phone and made an appointment to meet with his boss the minute he arrived at work the next day.

Boyd's next stop on his way home was *Time* magazine headquarters at Forty-ninth and Rockefeller Plaza, where his wife, Edith, worked. This was the first of several times over the next few years that Boyd would make a trip to her office. Whenever he needed a sounding board, he'd ask Edith to take a break from her research work and go down to a lounge just off the main lobby. Boyd told her his problem. "I wanted to prepare her for the fact that I might not have a job the next day," he said.

"Ed, you have to stand up for your principles," she told him, as he knew she would. "Do what you have to do."

The next day, at their meeting, Mack was surprisingly reassuring. "Hell, Ed, Javits is just a political friend, that's all. I'll back you up. You know what you want."

Boyd went back to his office. A few minutes later, he heard Mack's end of a loud argument with Javits on the telephone. "Mack put him in his place," Boyd said. About three years later, Boyd moved into the Upper West Side neighborhood where Javits lived. He sometimes encountered the congressman in the nearby park along the Hudson River. "But he'd never say hello to me," Boyd said.

The incident cemented Boyd's admiration for his boss. Mack must have felt a certain satisfaction about Boyd's stand as well. In his book, Mack never referred to the hiring incident, but he did say that the Javits brothers were the lawyers who had settled the shareholders' case against Phoenix Securities almost ten years earlier, which had so infuriated Mack.

Boyd's fourth hire was already working inside the company. Again, Mack told Boyd the final decision was his. This time, it was clear from the start that Alexander L. Jackson was the type Boyd wanted. Jackson came from a Chicago family. He was refined and sensitive and was accustomed to the privileges and respect that came with his family's achievements. He was a Harvard graduate, the son of a Harvard graduate, and the brother of a Harvard graduate. His father was the college classmate of Pepsi-Cola vice president Toby Freeman, and Freeman had gladly hired him. Jackson had been working at Pepsi since 1943, spending the war years managing Pepsi's voice-recording unit, which allowed servicemen to send messages home. When the canteens were converted to information centers after the war, Jackson was assigned to work on sales development for the company-owned bottler in New York. Joining Boyd's team promoted him to the national level.

The black press hailed the formation of the team—and the caliber of its professionals. Mack was widely quoted: "People the country over know of the wholesome and worthwhile community projects which Pepsi-Cola Company has sponsored through the years. Now, with the employment of Negroes in its national marketing staff, Pepsi-Cola Company has taken the initiative in still another direction. It is with a great deal of satisfaction that we are able to announce a program of this character and magnitude and we are confident that it will fulfill our every expectation."

———————

Pepsi-Cola's new, all-black sales department raised the hopes of black entrepreneurs in more ways than one. Joe Louis had teamed with sales pioneer William Graham to develop and market Joe Louis Punch. ("It's a Knockout!") It was a unique black product that was instantly appealing to whites as well. When Louis was winning in the ring, sales would soar. But it also had a peculiar problem: Fans would take home the bottles, and even the advertisements that outlets displayed, as souvenirs. "We have no trouble selling the drink, but we do have trouble keeping enough bottles to supply our distributors," Graham complained. The signs were replaced daily. It was a costly predicament. The company tried to diversify by selling other flavors, including orange and ginger ale, but it never got wide distribution. Its greatest hope was that a big soft-drink concern would acquire it. Graham's star salesman,

Harvey Russell, did due diligence on Pepsi-Cola to see if it might be a potential buyer.

Mack never showed an interest in the company, but Russell was impressed by the Pepsi-Cola Company. Boyd wasn't making any more hires that year, but Russell waited for an opportunity to join the sales team.

———————

Harvey C. Russell was born on April 14, 1918, in Louisville, Kentucky. He came "from a long line of eggheads," he liked to say. His grandparents were among the first African-Americans to graduate from college, his father was president of West Kentucky State College, his mother was a high-school teacher, and his three sisters counted fourteen degrees among them. He graduated from his father's school, where the six-foot-two-inch athlete played football. He had started attending Indiana University to pursue a doctorate in sociology when World War II broke out. President Franklin D. Roosevelt's promise to black leaders to include black workers in the war industries landed Russell a factory job. He was given a 4A deferment as an essential war-plant worker. But after working there a year, he grew bored with the monotonous work and decided to volunteer in the service.

He decided to join the more integrated coast guard, as an apprentice seaman. One year later, after he went to Manhattan Beach, California, for boot camp, he passed the exam to go into officer training. He was happy to report to New York City, fleeing the kind of racial strife he had experienced in Indianapolis, a center of KKK activity. In 1942, Russell became one of the first three African-Americans to graduate from the reserve officers' course. He was a lieutenant junior grade, commissioned as an ensign. He served two years.

After the war, he returned to New York City but had no illusions about opportunities there. "When I came to New York, you couldn't even eat on 125th Street, in the heart of Harlem, if you could imagine that," he said. "The only hotel you could really stay in without any problem was the Theresa, the black hotel on 125th Street. You couldn't go to theaters; you couldn't go to the restaurants, so all the entertaining was done primarily in or around the home. But New York was considered very liberal compared with most other places."

Russell's ideas about a career changed when he was introduced to Bill Graham. Family members thought he was "off his rocker" when he chose a business career over academia, but they didn't discourage him. Graham, the president of Joe Louis Punch, was another pioneering African-American adman; he had built his reputation selling Pabst beer to the Elks. He opened the first black professional advertising office in Times Square—55 West Forty-second Street—in 1946. W. B. Graham & Associates, despite its problems with Joe Louis Punch, was doing brisk business that year buying space in the new *Ebony* magazine and in the black newspapers for black-owned businesses such as Rose Meta Cosmetics, Murray's Pomade, and other products. It was also trying to get *Ebony* placed in more stores.

Russell stayed for two years with Graham, agreeing to work for a modest salary to learn the advertising, public-relations, and soft-drink industries. He called upon all his professional connections and his fraternity brothers for contacts. Russell was a member of the oldest black Greek-letter organization in the country, the Sigma Pi Phi, "a close-knit society—close-knit not by choice," he said. "Blacks were 10 percent of the population, and only 10 percent of that were college educated or professional, so these professionals knew each other all over the country."

When Graham's top accounts hit shaky times, Russell started looking for other work. He did a stint with Rose Meta Cosmetics and even tried his hand at his own cosmetics-distribution company, but nothing worked out. In the meantime, he took a job with the board of trans-portation in New York City as a claims examiner, which paid twenty-four hundred dollars a year—double his best salary. For extra money, he worked as a navigator on boats that affluent African-Americans had bought during the war. The owners were mostly doctors, and mostly heading for Oak Bluffs, an affluent black enclave on Martha's Vineyard. These contacts would prove invaluable, and Russell waited for an opportunity to put his skills to better use.

Meanwhile, the new Pepsi-Cola hires were getting enthusiastic press coverage beyond local interests. The trade magazine *Modern Industry* hailed the move as one of the most ambitious campaigns to reach the black consumer. "This hand picking of superior men to pioneer Negro employment is stressed by most Negro leaders," the magazine stated. One of those leaders was Julius Thomas, of the National Urban League, who pointed out the sterling educational credentials of the new hires. "Employers should select exceptionally well-qualified personnel for their first try," Thomas advised about attempting to integrate the workplace.

Boyd cultivated a relationship with Thomas, head of the league's pivotal industrial-relations division, to help with recruitment and training. Thomas was eager to have the team succeed and so open the door to similar ventures. The two men put the new hires though an intensive program—from sales techniques to how to set up store displays. Just how far ahead of the game the Pepsi-Cola effort was can be seen in what *Modern Industry,* in that same article, was offering as advice for selling to black Americans. "Negro market-research man" David J. Sullivan was still getting mileage out of the sales tips he wrote for white pitchmen at least as early as 1943. Some of his tips are shocking for what they suggest was the norm of the day; others stand out for how long it took advertisers to implement them. Some of his "do's and don'ts":

- Don't exaggerate Negro characters with flat noses, thick lips, etc.
- Don't portray them as dull-witted domestics. Negroes resent radio characters presented this way, and boycott products advertised by them. They do approve of "Rochester" [opposite Jack Benny] and "Eddie" from *Duffy's Tavern* [the popular radio and television show] as intelligent individuals.
- Avoid incorrect English usage and grammar and dialect.
- Don't belittle clergymen.
- Don't lampoon Negro children or call them pickaninnies.

"These common-sense admonitions for good taste are rarely violated today," *Modern Industry* assured its readers, "though some conspicuous exceptions have meant years of explaining for some companies." The magazine added that the list should be followed when selling to white audiences as well as black.

Modern Industry predicted success for Pepsi-Cola and any other company venturing to hire for the Negro market, because of the black population's "don't spend where you're not employed" attitude, spearheaded by the powerful black press. The article contrasted Pepsi-Cola's scholarship program for blacks with the dubious record of an unnamed soft-drink manufacturer that had held a carnival in a park that banned blacks. Other companies had been no less subtle, it suggested, offering as contest prizes vacations at resorts that didn't welcome African-Americans.

The magazine also equated the spending power of America's fourteen million blacks to that of the entire population of Canada—a comparison that was quoted endlessly from that point forward.

Boyd's group began its efforts in metropolitan New York and northern New Jersey. While the budget was tight, the team did public-relations work, much like the original special-markets agents. The men would make appearances in communities, hand out samples of Pepsi to garner new customers, and encourage outlets to do more promotions. But Boyd wanted the force to cut a wider and deeper swath through communities. He wanted them to establish relationships with the bottlers, and add more clubs, bars, and colleges to the effort. He himself sometimes worked alongside the team, especially if a salesman wanted to lavish a bottler or a store owner with special attention from the boss. "I'm not a club man, but I'd go with our salesmen to talk to the owner if I had to," Boyd said. "Floyd Britton was good at knowing when to do that."

There were still a lot of clubs in Harlem, although not as many as during the war years. Choices, of course, were limited for African-Americans. Frank's, next to the Apollo, was off limits then, as was the Cotton Club, Boyd remembered. Sometimes people who wanted to see their friends entertain would sit in the balconies or even wait in the kitchen, then go backstage afterward.

Just as important for sales as any club, however, were the local churches. Boyd insisted that his men approach all the houses of worship in a black community—not to push the product, of course, but to introduce themselves to the parishioners, the softest of sells. It was expected that the company representatives would contribute to the parish funds.

It was all part of Boyd's effort to have a big enough team presence in any location to result in a significant spike in sales. They were gradually to go further than their predecessors and learn to seek out and expand orders from establishments. Beyond writing up a detailed expense report, the men had to write a narrative of what they did, where they went, to whom they spoke, and what aspect of their pitch worked best. The job was grueling. The salesmen had to work long days and there weren't many days off, especially if you included the church work.

Two months after their hires were announced, the five men began their first campaign on the road. "If the Southern girls get a look at this glamour crew, Pepsi's sales should soar . . ." wrote Lillian Scott, of the *Defender,* in her Along Celebrity Row column. From then on, she followed the comings and goings of the team. Not three months later, in mid-July, Scott wrote of "a rumor to the effect that the Pepsi-Cola sales force did such a good job down South that they may go out again. That's the group headed by suave Ed Boyd." It also made her column when most of the crew returned from Texas in September feeling ill—from "virus T," she joked.

———

Whenever the men were in the Greater New York region, they reported to desks at the Queens plant. They didn't have to make the trek for long, however. Mack had secured office space at 3 West Fifty-seventh Street, where Pepsi-Cola rented all but the ground floor. "The move was a big deal to Mack," Boyd recalled of his status-conscious boss. "The building was next to the fashionable stores, like Bergdorf Goodman."

Boyd had fond recollections of the reception of his team by some at the new office. Pepsi's fountain-equipment unit, headed by Henry McGovern, would invite Boyd and his team to go out to dinner, and delighted in going to the Dodgers games with them to cheer on Jackie Robinson.

In some parts of the country, it was still a privilege for a black man to watch a Robinson game up close. In April 1948, when Robinson and Roy Campanella became the first blacks to play professional ball in

Texas in a Fort Worth game, several thousand African-American fans had to stand behind a rope behind the foul line, or on a levee outside the left-field wall that separated the park from the river, to watch the game—and were charged bleacher prices. Still, they broke the attendance record for the field. Other ballparks relented under pressure from fans. In Dallas, reserved seats in back of the grandstand were opened up for the first time, and black fans quickly accounted for more than half the crowd—which was yet another record attendance.

The friendship Boyd forged with McGovern lasted long after they stopped being Pepsi colleagues. George O'Neil, vice president in charge of purchasing, was another matter. He kept his distance, watching as the new black sales team was put to the test. He didn't have to wait long. Things were going to be different with the Negro team around.

The special-markets team never went into any territory except at the invitation of the bottler. Some were more open to the idea than others. The franchise owner in Delaware was one who was eager to have the special-sales team visit his area. The young man, Boyd knew, was a good friend of Walter Mack, and the team came highly recommended. The new salesmen thought of a program whereby the Wilmington bottling plant would open its doors to local schoolchildren for a tour. To Boyd's horror, the plant was filthy.

Boyd had to report on the visit at the regular weekly managers' meeting at headquarters. "Watch out," Bryan Houston warned him, "he's a friend of Mack's." But Boyd's review was scathing. He told how dirty the plant was and what the team had to do before admitting the schoolchildren. The other managers held their breath, expecting Mack to take offense at this criticism of his friend. Instead, he thanked Boyd for his candor. He had suspected trouble there but no one else had had the nerve to identify the problem.

"O'Neil was friendly after that," Boyd recalled. "He came into my office the very next day to tell me how pleased he was that I made the report, because they had been afraid to because of the bottler's friendship with Walter Mack."

Mack was growing fond of Boyd as a colleague and as a casual friend. He and his wife, Ruth, occasionally invited Boyd and his wife to dinner at their favorite French restaurant, and they included Boyd at their table for special arts benefits or book-signing parties. Boyd recalled that the Macks had a diverse circle of friends that frequently included a gay couple.

Boyd's strategy to boost sales in 1948 was four-pronged. The first line of action was to have the sales staff do public relations in an area and increase orders. Next, Boyd planned a large newspaper and magazine ad campaign, featuring advertisements geared toward the black consumer. Then, he planned a letter-writing campaign to bottlers and African-American organizations, preparing for the various campaigns across the country. Finally, he wanted point-of-purchase advertising pieces and packaging displays for stores.

Mack's community charities were incorporated into the broader goals of the Negro-market department. In 1948, Pepsi-Cola's scholarship board selected 17 Negro high school seniors among the 232 students awarded full-tuition scholarships, at a cost of $330,000. Scholarship board member Dr. Mordecai W. Johnson, an eminent scholar and president of Howard University, made the announcement. The awards were designed to discover outstanding young students who could be trained for "leadership within their own fields," as Pepsi-Cola described it to the press.

That phrase became the core slogan of the Negro-market campaign. Boyd and his colleagues conceived of Pepsi ads that would be informative, featuring top-performing black professionals in a series titled "Leaders in Their Fields." Pepsi would be contrasted as a "Leader in Its Field." The campaign would add to Pepsi advertising the kind of educational element that was becoming popular in classrooms as the observance of Black History Week spread in the black population. The Urban League, in fact, had just published what the black press was calling "the first Negro comic book," an illustrated book of Negro figures in history.

Boyd wasn't interested in historical figures but in living professionals who were making a difference in their fields of endeavor. He brought the idea to Herb Fox, on Newell-Emmett's creative team, and to Pepsi-Cola's advertising boss, Al Goetz. They liked it. They began working on a layout that would include a photograph and a short, snappy profile of the subject. As the ad campaign took shape, the search began for impressive profiles.

It was a fad in the 1940s to have real people—famous or not—represent the "real face" of a product, like Mack's campaign that portrayed the "average American family" or his salute to professionals in his "Good Taste–Better Taste" series. Compared with those, Boyd's version was more imaginative in style. In concept, it was revolutionary. He was applying highbrow, noncelebrity testimonials to the Negro market. Manufacturers trying to reach black consumers at that time typically didn't see the need for unique ads. But "after pulling a few boners," *Modern Industry* said, "manufacturers decided it's best to gear ads to the Negro market." Ultimately, most settled for using entertainers and sports figures. This is not to say that those two groups weren't deserving of admiration. Sports heroes were breaking color barriers daily, and jazz was entering a golden age that redefined American popular culture and gained a worldwide following. In addition, many stars in both fields became outspoken activists for equal rights. Still, most white Americans knew about blacks or related to them only as sports figures and entertainers. "I kept saying, I wanted to make something impressive," Boyd remembered.

Impress he did. "Pepsi-Cola, planning a series of ads for the Negro press, is breaking away from this pattern of theatrical celebrities and getting endorsements from successful but little-known Negroes in fields like chemistry, medicine, business, banking, etc.," *Modern Industry* reported.

Boyd found all the profile subjects and wrote the copy himself. There was no blatant sales pitch for Pepsi and no price appeared in the ad, thereby avoiding equating the lowest price to the black population. No one was paid for his or her appearance in the ad, except for a symbolic one-dollar fee.

Boyd's first choice for a notable African-American was easy. The man who had aspired to be the greatest diplomat in the world chose to honor the man who actually was the greatest diplomat of his time: Ralph Bunche. Bunche was also a brilliant academician, bringing serious scholarship and an internationalist's perspective to race issues. He had just been named by the United Nations to direct aid toward emerging nations and the disenfranchised, after winning praise for his work for the U.N. on the confrontation between Arabs and Jews in Palestine. "There was nobody greater than Ralph Bunche then," Boyd said. "It was quite a coup to get him. He was reluctant at first, but he did it mainly because of our family ties."

Boyd picked five other notables:

- Cornelius E. Ford, former president of the Buffalo, New York, livestock exchange, who bought and sold livestock for meatpacking companies in North America.
- Walter Franklin Anderson, director of the music department at Antioch College in Ohio, whose compositions were performed by

the Cleveland Symphony Orchestra. He had "distinguished himself through experiments with applications of music to problems in social work."

- P. Bernard Young, Jr., editor-in-chief of the Norfolk (Virginia) *Journal and Guide,* who had won a journalism award for his coverage of the 1946 United Nations conference.
- Dr. Paul B. Cornely, the medical director at Washington's Freedman's Hospital, a consultant to national health organizations and foundations, and the author of sixty-five scientific and popular articles.
- Rachel Ratcliffe Wilson, executive director of a division of the Association for the Blind in Harris County, Texas, who performed years of effective volunteer work among juvenile delinquents.

The ads made their debut on April 24, 1948, in about fifty of the nation's leading black weeklies. One newspaper was so excited by the Bunche ad that it enlarged it with its own headline: "CONGRATULATIONS, DR. BUNCHE. HIS RECENT APPOINTMENT AS PROFESSOR OF GOVERNMENT AT HARVARD UNIVERSITY HELPS ESTABLISH HIM AS A . . . LEADER IN HIS FIELD."

The black media began to get a taste of the advertising largesse enjoyed by their white counterparts. Adrian Hirschhorn reported in his thesis on *Ebony*'s share from June 1947 through June 1948: 485 national advertisers placed orders in the magazine. *Ebony* reported that total billings in 1947 for the two hundred black newspapers topped the $5 million mark, with *The Pittsburgh Courier* alone taking in $2.5 million. "Today's ad linage is double that of the prosperity years of the 1920s when advertisers included Chevrolet, Lifebuoy soap and White Owl Cigars," the magazine stated.

Black publications persisted in trying to coax white companies to send more ad dollars their way, growing increasingly impatient. *Ebony* did a profile in May 1948 of the new black salesmen—dubbing them "brown hucksters"—and some of the big companies they worked for. It took the opportunity to chide the American Tobacco Company for not keeping up with its rivals in creating ads for the black consumer. The article also complained that "the biggest soft drink maker Coca-Cola has no Negro sales representatives," and pointed out Pepsi-Cola's success. In response, Coca-Cola made a classic dodge, claiming it was "studying the employment of one" national sales representative. But after the article ran, American Tobacco got busy. By August 1948, it was running a series in the black weeklies that paired its Lucky Strike brand with African-American luminaries, from the late Booker T. Washington to jazz sensation Duke Ellington, the first African-American to play a full concert at Carnegie Hall. Echoing Pepsi-Cola's Leaders series, it took as its slogan: "First in Negro History . . . First in Cigarettes."

By then, Mack had switched ad agencies. He chose Biow & Associates. Biow also created the famed Philip Morris ads featuring the bellhop. It, too, took a cue from Pepsi-Cola's Negro-market campaign. The diminutive Johnny, which *Modern Industry* had predicted would never be sacrificed to conform to the Negro market, was suddenly relegated to a small corner of the new Philip Morris ads. In his place was a salute to black professionals who claimed "No Cigarette Hangover!" when smoking the brand. Pepsi-Cola had once again taken the creative lead in its industry for promotional work—this time with the help of Edward Boyd.

———

Pepsi-Cola prepared a second batch of five notables for the campaign that ran in the fall of 1948. For one, Boyd had to look no further than his family. Biow gave these ads a slicker look, "cleaning away the spinach" as Mack might have put it, and further softening the pitch for the product. Five new names finished the series:

- Jesse H. Mitchell, head of Industrial Bank of Washington, D.C., a former teacher and former real-estate investor who had graduated from Howard University Law School.
- Dr. Theodore R. M. Howard, a Mississippi surgeon and Boyd's brother-in-law, who performed more than five thousand major operations since 1942, as well as founding and managing a recreation center for Mississippi Delta youth.
- Dr. Percy L. Julian, director of research at the Glidden Company, Chicago, held a doctor of philosophy degree from the University of Vienna, had ten U.S. patents, and wrote many scientific articles and books. Dr. Julian was a fixture in the black press.
- Joseph S. Dunning, MIT graduate and aeronautical engineer at Douglas Aircraft Company, Santa Monica, California.
- Mildred Blount, a hat designer, who had worked on numerous Hollywood films, was the former chief designer for John-Frederic, Inc., of Beverly Hills, and had begun working under her own label for exclusive West Coast shops.

Boyd might have scored another one but one potential profile declined, a chemist who said he "didn't need the exposure" and wanted to be paid for his service. Otherwise, the professionals Boyd approached were happy to appear in the popular press. Boyd aimed for dignified treatment. All were photographed in a suit and tie—even Cornelius Ford, the livestock trader, who was shown in a cow pasture with a trench coat over his suit.

The series stood out amid the flurry of advertising activity in the black press that had begun in mid-1947. The "Leaders in Their Fields" ads were such a hit that individuals and black schools, even universities, across the country began asking for copies of the series. But as highly praised as the ad series was, at that time it was unthinkable that it would ever appear in any white-owned publication. National brands that portrayed blacks at all were still using one-dimensional stereo-types. African-Americans had to be "funny or faithful," like the Aunt Jemima "I'se in town, Honey" ads, as a *Fortune* magazine survey of ad styles described them. Smaller, regional companies often had extremely offensive caricatures, such as the jet-black silhouette of a running boy for Inky Eraser, and others showing exaggerated facial features or bare bottoms. Still, when American Airlines made a blun-der by using a cartoonish illustration of a black butler in a press release in 1946, one African-American editor noted, "It has been a while since anyone did something this stupid."

To understand how foreign a concept the "Leaders in Their Fields" ads would have been to the mainstream media in 1948, con-sider the career of Norman Rockwell. Rockwell was born on Febru-ary 3, 1894, a few months and several blocks apart from Walter Mack on Manhattan's Upper West Side. He was *The Saturday Evening Post*'s most popular illustrator from 1917 to 1962, with a mandate to depict "the American way of life." (Rockwell was an avid Coke drinker. His famous 1960 *Triple Self-Portrait* at the Rockwell Museum in Stock-bridge, Massachusetts, shows his ubiquitous glass of the cola at his side.)

Rockwell's name became synonymous with the culture of simple, small-town life, notable for its homogeneity. He also painted many covers for the magazine of the American worker as the rugged white man. At the start of his career, one recurring theme of his work was the lampooning of the so-called feminization of American culture as men abandoned hard labor to work for corporations. This fear of losing a masculine culture stemmed from anxieties over the close of the fron-tier, female suffrage, and expanding urban lifestyles, according to information at the Rockwell Museum in Stockbridge, Massachusetts.

Rockwell, however, came to resent being cast as champion of a one-dimensional view of American culture. He considered himself a liberal and a "citizen of the world" and rebelled against his narrow-minded editors. He told an interviewer later in life that he was once asked to "paint out" an African-American he had featured in a group portrait because *Saturday Evening Post* policy dictated that African-Americans could be shown only in service-industry jobs. (It wasn't until the 1960s that blacks were regularly depicted any other way.)

Rockwell did what he could to undermine the rule, he said. In 1946, he drew *Boy in Dining Car* for the two-million-circulation magazine, showing a young white boy struggling to figure out the bill for his meal while a smiling black dining-car waiter looked on. Rockwell said he took pains to draw the waiter as an individual with a personality, and not as a caricature. One of the reasons he jumped to *Look* magazine in 1962, the artist said, was for the freedom to draw political themes, particularly race issues. He made up for lost time with a series of illustrations with a civil rights theme. One illustration of the 1964 murder of three civil rights workers in Philadelphia, Mississippi, raised the hackles of timid editors. The illustration ran showing only the victims, not the white police and Klansmen he had shown holding weapons. He also once drew two wounded soldiers—one black and one white—on a battlefield in Vietnam, with their spilled blood mixing in the dirt. But that "made the publishers nervous," he said, and was censored.

What was the image of the African-American that most advertisers sought in those days? *Ebony* did a feature story on the man it dubbed "the world's most photographed Negro," a dark-skinned South African immigrant to America with a soft, friendly face. If you saw a black man in a cigarette or whiskey ad, the magazine stated in 1947 (before the wave of new ads using models from the handful of new African-American agencies), it was likely Maurice Hunter. He was a model for Calvert and Four Roses whiskeys, among others, and had amassed a collection of about two thousand costumes for the "thousands of billboards, posters, magazines, and store windows all over the country" in which he appeared. "Look at a Coca-Cola ad and you'll see Hunter as [one of] several bemused natives watching GIs sipping Cokes," *Ebony* said.

Most recently, he had appeared as a bass fiddle player in a gasoline ad. "Most of his poses, however, are in the run-of-the-mill butlers, chauffeurs and Pullman porters," *Ebony* reported. Despite his monopoly on the male Negro model business, Hunter made very little money. "Twenty-five dollars was the most money I ever got for one job," he groused. "That was for a whiskey ad and I had to pose all day." At the New York World's Fair, an eight-foot poster of Hunter in a white jacket and an attendant's cap was featured in front of the Railroads on Parade exhibit. He was paid only five dollars for that job. By 1947, Hunter had made plans to leave modeling for an acting career.

Ebony itself was fighting the servile image of the black man. Since its inception, *Ebony* had been criticized for its lack of a strong political voice and its tendency to portray the softer side of African-American life. If the magazine steered away from some of the gritty details of the civil rights movement, its ability to break down stereotypes was an important front in that battle. In fact, Boyd got several of his "Leaders" profiles from features that had appeared in *Ebony*.

The battle over the image of black Americans came to a head just as the Pepsi team was getting started. As Hollywood's influence on popular culture worldwide grew, the NAACP moved to set up a bureau to consult on films and help abolish the stereotype of the "gin drinking, bowing and scraping" black by meeting with producers to discuss their scripts before they began shooting. But all efforts were brought to a swift end in September 1947, when the House Un-American Activities Committee began investigating the motion-picture industry for communist influence, questioning forty-one employees in Hollywood. All testified, naming nineteen more colleagues considered left-wing activists. Ten of those nineteen refused to answer questions before the committee, invoking their constitutional rights to free speech and not to incriminate themselves. When their case went to court, the ruling went against them, and they were sentenced to up to a year in prison for contempt of Congress.

The plight of the so-called Hollywood Ten, though all white, sent a chill through the black leadership. They saw racism behind the anti-red campaign, and thought it was no coincidence that the assault was heating up just as African-American actors were gaining recognition. *The Pittsburgh Courier* wrote a story in late 1947—RED PROBE BLOCKS SEPIA FILM ROLES—covering a "free the movies" rally led by Thurgood Marshall, counsel for the NAACP and later the first black U.S. Supreme Court justice. He spoke out against HUAC for harassing movie producers and spreading fear in Hollywood. "Every movie script has been reexamined and every instance in which Negroes have appeared in a decent light or [been] called Mr. or Mrs. have been struck out," he told the crowd. The Screen Actors Guild, the weekly reported, confirmed that unemployment among its black members had reached a point "more alarming than at any time in Guild history" and that "Negro parts were cut out of plays and books for screens or rewritten for whites."

Canada Lee was a case in point. Boyd broke his rule against using celebrity promoters for Pepsi only once—to have a publicity photo of himself taken with the superstar, one of the most popular African-American leading men on stage and screen. In 1946, the multitalented Lee had become Broadway's first black producer when he staged *On Whitman Avenue.* He followed that achievement with another landmark stage performance: He put on whiteface to play two roles—one black and one white—in *The Duchess of Malfi.*

The following year, Lee had snagged his biggest role to date, starring as Kid Chocolate opposite John Garfield in *Body and Soul*. He boasted that it was the most respectable, substantial role ever played by a black man in a Hollywood film, and many agreed. Lee also praised Garfield for his support and respectful treatment of him personally on the United Artists film set. In the movie, Garfield plays a Jewish middleweight who has to beat Canada Lee to win the championship title. He defeats the Kid with the help of the corrupt businessmen who control the ring. Both men are seen as fighting for the honor of their people, critics noted.

HUAC screened the film and identified it as an example of "the manner in which Commies and pinks, in the field of communication and ideas, gave employment to each other." Lee was thereafter labeled "a fellow traveler."

Lee, born Lionel Canegata, of Puerto Rican heritage, also had made a bid to become a New York state senator for the American Labor Party, although he quit the race by the end of the summer of 1948. Lee consistently denounced communism and its American supporters, but the hounding never stopped. By 1952, Canada Lee was dropped by the American Tobacco Company as a promoter and was thus banned from some forty TV shows it sponsored, although he did find some work in film overseas. That year, he wrote to Walter White of the NAACP: "I can't take it anymore. I'm going to get a shoeshine box and sit outside the Astor Theater. My picture [*Cry the Beloved Country*] is playing to capacity audiences and, my God, I can't get one day's work." Shortly after that, he died of a heart attack, distraught and financially ruined, at the age of forty-five. His wife blamed his demise on his persecution by HUAC.

In all, more than 320 artists were blacklisted, or barred from working in Hollywood, including John Garfield, Larry Parks, Pete Seeger, Lillian Hellman, and Dashiell Hammett. Actor/singer Paul Robeson's career was also destroyed, and his $300,000-a-year income dwindled away. He had tried to sound an alarm in the black community back in April 1947. He, W. E. B. DuBois, and eighty other activists signed an ad in the black press asking the president and Congress to block the move to make the Communist Party illegal. "We call upon the President and Congress promptly to enact legislation to guarantee fair employment practices, to abolish poll tax and other barriers to free elections, to out-law lynching, and to establish a national code of civil rights. This pro-gram, we submit, is far more consistent with the democratic ideals and aspirations of the American people than the fascist-like proposal to illegalize the Communist Party."

HUAC grew into an ominous weapon in the black population—bent on reversing job gains, particularly in unionized industries and federal government agencies. The committee had been around under other names since 1937. It had a mandate to investigate terrorism and rout out communists. Many citizens were waiting for it to go after the Ku Klux Klan for its murder of thousands of U.S. citizens. But the founding chairman, Representative Martin Dies, a Texas Democrat, was active in the Klan, as were other members. Lem Graves, Jr., of *The Pittsburgh Courier,* wrote about HUAC: "Watching a hearing, this reporter was constantly aware that one of the guiding spirits of the House committee was the arch Negrophobe of the U.S. Congress, Rep. John Rankin of Mississippi." Committee member John S. Wood of Georgia, openly a member of the KKK, defended the committee's refusal to investigate the group by arguing that its actions represented "an old American custom." Counsel successfully argued that there wasn't enough information on the Klan to warrant a probe.

Even the name *Un-American* was a hijacking of the term typically used until then to characterize the undemocratic treatment of minori-ties. "What the committee was doing sickened me," Boyd said. "Although at that time I was a terrible anti-Communist." That didn't matter. Boyd didn't know it at the time, but he, too, was guilty by association. Following a Freedom of Information Act query in 2004, the Justice Department confirmed that a file had been opened on "Edward Boyd of New York," but later had been destroyed. Boyd guessed it was due to his affiliation with the Screen Actors Guild. HUAC, which changed its name to the Internal Security Committee in 1969, was abolished in 1975.

African-American cartoonist Jay Jackson won an award from the Chicago Newspaper Guild for his skewering of HUAC's attack on Hollywood. Jackson, forty-two years old, a native of Oberlin, Ohio, was known for his biting satire of racists and red-baiters. With an oeuvre that would likely have had him banned from work in many places, Pepsi-Cola's special-markets department hired him to draw a series of advertisements for Pepsi in *Ebony* for the second half of 1948.

Al Goetz made the announcement in the black press. Calling the ads a departure for national advertisers, he explained: "Embodying light cartoon treatment, the preparation of these advertisements draws upon the best kind of talent available. It is only natural, therefore, that in adapting this advertising technique for Negro publications, we have tried to secure the most capable talent available in that field." Jay Jackson, it noted, attended Ohio Wesleyan University and the Art Institute of Chicago and was widely published in both the black and the mainstream presses.

The first of the Jackson series ran in *Ebony* in June 1948. It shows a scrubbed schoolgirl visiting a museum with her father, dressed in a suit. They are standing in front of a painting of a giant Pepsi bottle. "Mmmm, Daddy! Now that's art!" the caption read. Another shows well-built youths in swimsuits, and in another, an attractive secretary is fleeing from her boss, who is really heading for a Pepsi vending machine. The five ads were light and humorous. Jackson had a sassy, slightly bawdy style. His women were shapely, the men handsome, the kids hip and happy. Although the subject matter may seem outdated by today's standards, at the time, the drawings—like those of his colleagues in the black press—made a mockery of the simplistic, offensive cartoons of blacks that appeared in the mass media. Pepsi-Cola itself during the war had created a cartoon ad of two black, big-lipped, grass-skirt-wearing natives celebrating a victory of the Allies with Pepsi.

One Ohio minister, who had been using *Ebony* to teach his Bible-school students the reality of African-American culture, objected to the sexual content of the Jackson ads and of *Ebony* magazine in general. "Do you have to accept that kind of ad?" he asked.

Ebony's advertising hit home with its core readership. Another letter, sent by a group of female university students, stated: "We have noticed increased patronage by national products, many with Negro models (which is quite a refreshing innovation).... [W]e are keeping a list of the companies that recognize us as a segment of the American public, and using their products wherever possible."

In the fall of 1948, Boyd started to send out letters to bottlers and outlets to get them working together, while his salesmen got ready to take to the road across the country. The men had just rested and recovered from the Texas trip when they had to pack their bags again. "The Pepsi boys—that personable sales gang led by Ed Boyd—may hit the road again, much to the general consternation of their wives," Lillian Scott wrote in her column. They were to encourage sales on college campuses and other institutions and venues selling Pepsi. The letters were sent on Pepsi stationery, looking slightly gaudy with a big red-white-and-blue Pepsi bottle cap at the top of the page with its 3 West

Fifty-seventh Street address and Murray Hill (MU) phone exchange number, flanked by color cutouts of a Pepsi bottle and a logo-emblazoned glass filled to the rim with the caramel-colored liquid.

In one of his earliest letters, dated September 21, 1948, Boyd attempted to get black colleges to promote Pepsi at their home games. If white consumers were being sold "the sizzle and not the steak," the black consumers also were being sold something entirely outside the product itself: the high principle behind the venture. There was nothing subtle about the appeal as he tied racial pride to Pepsi's offer of a handsome football program the school could sell at its games. The language used by Boyd reflects the formality considered proper business style in those days:

Dear Sir,

I am sure you are aware of the interest this Company has shown in worthwhile activities among the Negro race. I am certain that you, as we, are highly conscious of the ideal and ambitions of the racial group of which you and I are both members. You are, no doubt, doubly conscious of these factors because of your intimate contact with youth and your ability thereby to observe the frustrations which beset them. This awareness will certainly impel you to support, by very concrete means, those companies, individuals and organizations who indicate respect for the group by affording Negroes some of the benefit of their support. . . . I am enclosing a sample of the football program cover design which, you will observe, utilizes Negro football players as subjects. I think you will agree with me that the approach represented herein is most acceptable."

Boyd took the onus off the white, Southern bottler to contact the school administrators. The letter continued:

May I suggest that you immediately contact your Pepsi-Cola bottler by a personal visit, telephone call or special delivery letter and when doing so, be prepared to tell him the number of home games, and the expected attendance.

———————

In the fourth prong of his four-prong strategy, Boyd focused on the main front of his campaign: the grocery stores where most Pepsi was sold. From his earliest meetings with Biow, he had insisted that point-of-purchase promotions were important. Negro stores, *Modern Industry* magazine concurred, had been neglected by display experts. "This extra touch makes a big difference," the magazine said of Boyd's efforts, which would be fully realized the following year.

The store displays were big cutouts, some life-size, situated near the shelves of Pepsi. Boyd kept his ban on celebrities. Instead, he wanted to show a black family in the same kind of idealized setting as those used in mainstream ads. Boyd thought a friend's son would make a perfect model for the boy of the family. The seven-year-old was handsome, bright, and full of energy.

"I knew Ronnie and how he looked, and asked for him specifically," Boyd said. Ronnie's father, William Brown, was a former federal housing expert selected to be the manager of the Hotel Theresa in Harlem. "Ronnie used to run around the Hotel Theresa, in and out of the bar, greeting people," Boyd said. "He was very precocious. We were concerned he'd come to no good."

Ed Boyd was introduced to the Brown family in early 1949 when his wife, Edith, joined a new women's group called the Smart Set, a club started by sisters who regularly had gone to Atwater summer camp in Massachusetts as children. The club was intended to preserve their friendships and to encourage achievement among professional black women. When Boyd asked Ronnie's mother, Gloria, to allow her son to appear in the ads, she agreed immediately.

All the models met at a photographer's studio for the shoot. First, the background was shot, showing a father pouring his daughter a glass of Pepsi. The three models used in addition to the young boy were from Barbara Watson's Brandford agency, which was barely two years old. Boyd liked Watson and gave her plenty of business.

To everyone's surprise, when it was the young boy's turn to pose, he was poised, cooperative, and professional. He did his shoot, smiling and reaching up for a six-pack of Pepsi held by his "mother." The result was a handsome tableau of a black family enjoying their middle-class life.

The boy, Ronald H. Brown, grew up to become secretary of commerce in the Clinton administration. When he was killed in a plane crash during an official assignment in Croatia in 1997, Boyd was given the original Pepsi ad, which Brown had kept as a cherished memento in his Washington office.

— Chapter Five —

The Brown Hucksters

WHEN THE VICTORIOUS HARRY TRUMAN HELD UP THE *Chicago Tribune* in November 1948 with the banner headline "DEWEY BEATS TRUMAN," a thousand hearts sank in the marketing world. The pollsters—so revered for bringing precision to the seat-of-the-pants business of selling everything from paint to politicians—had gotten it dead wrong. The election debacle prompted a full quarter of subscribers to drop Gallup, the only one of the top four "quiz masters," as *The Wall Street Journal* called them, that made money on political polling. In a single stroke, the nascent polling industry had lost its reputation as a foolproof science. For some time, armies of survey takers had been marching across the country to record families' buying habits, data that were then sliced and diced according to gender, class, and whether the household was urban or rural. The average person was so thrilled to be chosen to participate in these opinion surveys that the pollsters were often invited to stay for dinner. The promise was that these polls were the first step in matching product supply to consumer demand in a perfect way that would benefit everyone. And because those products needed salesmen to introduce them to eager buyers, advertisements for—and from—pitchmen choked the want ads of daily newspapers. In 1945, the *Journal* marveled at how marketing companies knew "an amazing lot about the American consumer's mind," while lamenting that "the general public, however, knows next to nothing about these commercial poll takers."

Four years later, consumers felt that they knew more than they ever wanted to about pollsters, products—and especially salesmen. Selling, *Fortune* magazine declared, was to the twentieth century what production had been to the nineteenth: the one defining activity. And because much of the rest of the postwar world was in an austere mood as it recovered from deep wounds, America became "the one great glittering Bazaar left." Everyone seemed to be selling something. "The American citizen lives in a state of siege from dawn till bedtime," the article complained. And, as if product surveys weren't enough, a professor from Indiana University named Alfred Kinsey was knocking on doors across the country, recording Americans' preferences regarding the most intimate details of their sex lives.

Many were skeptical about consumerism and questioned the nation's postwar values. Some of the best-sellers Americans were reading were books like *Point of No Return,* by John P. Marquand, about a banker who, while awaiting a promotion, returns to his hometown to review his life, and *The Hucksters,* by Frederic Wakeman, about a veteran coming to terms with his new career in advertising. *The Hucksters,* an enduring favorite, was made into a popular movie starring Clark Gable as the conflicted protagonist and Sydney Greenstreet as his new boss, a doughy man so repugnant that in their first meeting he emphasizes a point by spitting loudly on a table and rubbing his palm in it. "Irritate! Irritate! Irritate!" the tycoon orders the man he hires to sell his soap. Like many boastful executives at the time, this boss gloats that his product is no different from any of his rivals'; he is simply smarter at selling it. Pride of product took a back seat to clever commercials.

Amid all the public bashing of the seller and the sellout, nothing was as symptomatic as the new play *Death of a Salesman*. Directed by Elia Kazan, the play opened to rave reviews in early 1949 and earned its thirty-three-year-old playwright, Arthur Miller, a Pulitzer Prize. In the drama, hailed as one of the most significant in American theater, Willy Loman, a salesman "riding on a smile and a shoeshine," ends up selling more than he planned—the trust of his family and eventually his life and identity—in a failed attempt to achieve the American Dream.

Ed Boyd went to see the play on Broadway with a visiting friend and was devastated by Lee J. Cobb's powerful performance as the shattered salesman. "I went out into the street crying, I mean sobbing, it was embarrassing," said Boyd. "I related to it so, the life of a traveling salesman. I had seen so many pretend one thing at home with their families and do another. Here was a guy who was a success, but in the end, it all came back down on him."

The public reaction to the play was so strong that *Fortune* magazine felt it necessary to publish a lengthy defense of salesmen, salesmanship, and business in general. Arthur Miller was asked to explain how the fact that Willy Loman is a salesman "is important, but secondary." "[He] has lost his essential—his real—nature, which is contradictory to his assumed one, until he is no longer able to know what *he* truly wants, what *he* truly stands for," Miller said. "In that sense he has sold himself." But an accompanying article admitted that the public's reaction had wider implications, and pointed to a *Harvard Business Review* survey showing that "a majority of the people believe that very few businessmen have the good of the nation in mind when they make their important decisions."

At least two members of Pepsi's special-markets team would see the play by year's end, and it would give them a more sober view of their jobs. But, unlike the mainstream media, the African-American press didn't join the chorus of criticism of business. Some writers did complain about the new push to consume, but they were paid little heed by a black press looking for ad dollars, by veterans and other young people seeking sales jobs as entrée into business careers, and by civic organizations demanding deeper participation by blacks at every level of the economy. And, far from being inundated with surveys, black Americans were still all but ignored by pollsters, whose clients wanted their business but didn't want to publicize their patronage. So when Professor Kinsey debunked racial stereotypes about male sexuality in his report, the black media gratefully took notice. The report concluded that attitudes toward sex were determined mostly by class and education, not ethnic or racial identity. (None of the Kinsey researchers was black.)

Ebony magazine wrote its own passionate defense of salesmanship and business in an editorial in late 1949, decrying the "modern-day puritans" who criticized black consumerism. It called the popularity of Cadillacs among blacks, for example, a "weapon in the war for racial equality." General Motors, it insisted, was trying "to curb sales to colored customers lest their prize species of the automobile trade be labeled 'a Negro car.'" Corporate ambivalence toward black consumers—welcoming them but only to a point—still hindered Negro-market campaigns.

Ebony had been following the careers of black salesmen since it started running Pepsi ads. It counted a mere forty black salesmen across America in mid-1948, and just six black-owned ad agencies. But their impact was greater than their numbers would suggest. In *Ebony*'s article, "The Brown Hucksters," the magazine recognized a decade of achievement by the "colored prototype of the bouncy, gregarious character popularized in the [Wakeman] book and movie. . . . In a little more than a decade, he has scored spectacular successes in changing the selling habits of many of the country's leading consumer-goods companies and the buying habits of the colored common man," the magazine said. "Working against trying handicaps of the past—prejudiced executives, lack of adequate marketing research, low standards of Negro newspaper advertising columns, Negro suspicion of high-pressure tactics—these business pioneers have nevertheless succeeded in transforming Negro Americans into the most brand-conscious buyers in the nation," it said. Among the best-recognized brands in the special market were Pepsi-Cola, Chesterfield, Seagram's, and Vaseline.

Most of the brown hucksters were employed by beverage distributors, *Ebony* noted, citing William B. Graham and Herman Smith for their pioneering work at Pabst and Pepsi-Cola, respectively. Smith had devised a "bang-up promotion campaign" at Pepsi before moving to Schenley, it added, and lauded Pepsi-Cola's "astute president" Mack for organizing a national force. The brown hucksters, *Ebony* wrote, were admittedly green, but could claim some stellar individual achievements: Graham was earning five hundred thousand dollars a year placing ads for the soft drink Joe Louis Punch. Louis took Chesterfield cigarettes to first place in Harlem and in Chicago's South Side by endorsing the brand; the legendary James "Billboard" Jackson was soon to retire, but he was training Wendell P. Alston to replace him at Esso; Abbott Laboratories had Richard B. Alphran selling to black pharmacies; and James W. Adams was heading a staff at Pabst that had grown to eleven in his five years there. Others included T. G. Laster at IBM and Etta Curry and Robert K. Barr at Old Gold cigarettes in Chicago. Clarence Holte had become a national salesman for Lever Bros. And not to be outdone by Philip Morris and its use of "the world's smallest bellboy," Cresta Blanca hired the very short African-American Frankie Dee to sell its wines.

Ebony optimistically declared that the worst employment difficulties faced by African-American salesmen were fading by the late 1940s. Though economic pragmatism was surely spurring the change, it added, "perhaps their best ally has been a general trend towards more interracial good will in America. . . ." That trend seemed to be taking hold at the highest levels of government in 1949. President Truman, who won 69 percent of the black vote, promised that civil rights would take top priority in his administration, and many in the Republican leadership were determined to participate in any successes. For months, the black press reported details of preparations for the inauguration, and celebrated the modest blows to segregation. The architect for the outdoor ceremony, the first inauguration ever televised, removed the Jim Crow signs from the portable toilets put on the Capitol grounds for the workmen building the reviewing stands. Washington National Airport announced it would put an end to all forms of racial segregation of passengers using its ground facilities. And not only would the inaugural ball be integrated for the first time, but the main entertainment would be provided by vibraphonist Lionel Hampton, one of the more vocal artists advocating equal rights.

Opponents to bigotry were getting bolder. In the streets, whites, or at least white students, began to take on racist organizations with new fervor. That spring, University of South Carolina students confronted Klansmen as they paraded through Camden on their way to hear Grand Dragon Sam Green speak on white supremacy. The students pelted them with gravel and stench bombs and ridiculed their garb: "Hey, honey, your slip is showing!" they taunted. A few months later, Green was named Imperial Wizard of the Klan, and the black press couldn't help noting that, like fellow racists Theodore Bilbo and Eugene Talmadge, he died before he could take office.

———

Mack kept himself in high profile with his civil work, collecting yet another award—the Thomas Jefferson Prize for the Advancement of Democracy—for his scholarships to Southern blacks and his interracial youth clubs in New York City. But Coca-Cola remained disinclined to go mano a mano with its rival in pursuing black consumers. Instead, it utilized vending machines, the ultimate color-blind sales force that was a huge success in diverse neighborhoods and businesses around the country, from Harlem hair salons to factories everywhere. *Fortune* reported that Coca-Cola had installed a million new vending machines in the first year after sugar rations fell. In no time, the machines were accounting for 20 percent of Coke sales. Pepsi lagged behind, burdened by a bottle too large for the machines. It waited until 1948 before installing machines that dispensed eight-ounce bottles.

Playing also-ran in the vending-machine race was just one of Mack's blunders, as he suddenly seemed short of a strategy to boost sales. The mainstream press was remarking about the comedown of this former darling of the business beat. Pepsi sales had become stuck in a long slump and the company's stock price was falling. Bottlers continued to agitate for an end to the bargain bottle. Earnings in 1948 were dismal: net profit plunged 53.5 percent to $3.15 million, from $6.77 million in 1947. And the first months of 1949 showed nothing to suggest that the slump was reversing.

"Only the giant Coca-Cola Co. was riding the storm unperturbed," *Newsweek* reported, although the company did drop plans for opening three plants in New York and New Jersey. Woodruff, with his genius for positioning his drink in popular culture, picked up sponsorship of ventriloquist Edgar Bergen and his sidekick, Charlie McCarthy, on CBS radio.

Mack, no longer able to play the daring upstart, began raiding his rival for talent. He lured away Alfred N. Steele, Coca-Cola's vice president in charge of domestic sales and the future Mr. Joan Crawford, and made him director and first vice president for sales and operations. Steele joined Coca-Cola in 1945, and during his four years with the company, the affable executive handled relations between the main office and the bottlers.

Steele was a native of Nashville, but his father was an international secretary of the YMCA, "so Steele saw the world from London to Manila before [he was] out of knee pants," according to a *Business Week* profile. He had extensive advertising experience. Before joining Coca-Cola, he had spent seven years as vice president in charge of the New York office of the D'Arcy Advertising Company, which handled the Coca-Cola account; and before that, he was advertising director of the Standard Oil Company of Indiana. He also had once been ad manager at the *Chicago Tribune*. News of the hire sent Pepsi shares up a point to $10.25; they had been as low as $7.50 in November 1948.

Meanwhile, the Biow ad agency appointed Samuel A. Alter, another former Coca-Cola executive, as vice president and head of its Pepsi account. Mack also announced the promotion of Herbert L. Barnet to assistant vice president of the company and vice president of the Pepsi-Cola Metropolitan Bottling Company. Steele and Barnet would work closely together in the years to come. The more ambitious of the Pepsi team members felt confident they could compete with the new talent for promotions.

Pepsi's big bottle exaggerated the central problem in the industry at the time, and that was the stubborn refusal of consumers to pay even one penny more for a soft drink. It was the main gripe at the state bottlers' convention that convened in New York City in April 1949. The preceding year, industry executives were in the mood to forgive Little Johnny for not wanting to part with more than a nickel for his soft drink. But by early 1949, members of the New York State Bottlers of Carbonated Beverages, Inc., had changed their tune: Johnny needed to be reeducated. Mack argued that drink manufacturers were failing to point out that they had offered the same product at about the same price for the past ten years, while food prices had more than doubled. This notion—that a bottle of cola was worth more than people had been paying—was the message Mack was trying to convey when he told bottlers that year that Pepsi planned to move away from the "nigger bottle." He suggested more advertising to solve the problem.

As soon as the bottlers' convention was over, Mack hired out Town Hall in Manhattan to face his shareholders. That gathering bore no resemblance to the lovefest of 1947, or to the charmingly discursive meeting of 1948, when kids asked the tough questions. Stockholders, who had gone a year without seeing a dividend payout, were angry. The annual reports weren't even ready ("Printing problems," Mack said). When one shareholder suggested that the company's "deadwood" be thrown overboard, he was greeted with enthusiastic applause from the crowd of 250. All Mack could do was promise that by year's end he would raise the price on the twelve-ounce bottle and sell more eight-ounce drinks for a nickel. The following month, Mack was barely able to put down an opposition slate of directors. He found himself increasingly on the defensive about Steele's three-year contract, which gave the executive an annual salary of eighty-five thousand dollars and options for sixteen thousand shares. You can't get good people to work for nothing, was Mack's rejoinder.

Not long after he was hired, Steele dropped by Boyd's office to discuss the Negro-market campaign. "He told me he had been aware of what we were doing when he was at Coca-Cola," Boyd said, and suggested some at Coca-Cola regretted the sales they had forfeited by ignoring the Negro market. "He gave the impression that he was on our side," Boyd said, but he didn't feel at ease with the new executive or the move to hire Coca-Cola executives, which he thought was changing Pepsi-Cola's corporate culture.

It wasn't easy to maintain the department's success, for the team was shrinking. Tumbling profits had forced Boyd to lay off half the sales staff. He found two ready volunteers to depart: Harold Woodruff and Alexander Jackson. "Woodruff was a wonderful person, but not cut out for sales," said Boyd. "He wanted to be a builder." Boyd regretted losing Jackson as well, but traveling across America was traumatic for the second-generation Harvard graduate from Chicago. "The first time he saw a white bus driver order a black man to sit at the back of the bus, he nearly had a stroke," Boyd said. "He just couldn't take it—or any of the separate-but-equal laws of the South, with the water fountains and restrooms and such."

It was still difficult even to buy bus or train tickets and to wait for departures in the segregated stations of the South. Once on board buses and trains, it wasn't just that seating was separate; the bars and curtains that separated the races in buses and dining cars were movable. Black passengers had to accommodate whites in every instance, even if it meant not getting a seat at all. And there was always the danger of confrontation. It took a tremendous amount of courage to stand against a crowd of harried, often hostile passengers, but many African-Americans refused to acquiesce to segregation. Often, the dissenters were women, who depended on public transportation more because of their jobs as domestics. They also were somewhat less likely to be beaten or killed for taking a stand.

Incidents of dissent had been on the rise since the 1946 Supreme Court decision stemming from a case involving Irene Morgan, who had refused to give up her seat on a Greyhound bus in Virginia. The ruling stated that interstate transportation couldn't be segregated. Greyhound immediately complied, but many companies, and many local authorities, refused. Even on those complying lines, and in states that didn't have segregation laws, transportation companies tended to bow to the various rules and regulations along their routes—rather than the other way around—and sold only certain seats to blacks. The companies claimed they were simply sparing black passengers any insult, injury, or aggravation. But more and more, black passengers were choosing to face the consequences.

As the Pepsi team began traveling the country, reports of protests by blacks and some white activists were in the news. In New York, black passengers were getting whites to buy tickets for them to allow them regular seating. Five whites were reported injured in December 1948 in a shootout on a Tennessee bus when a black rider, James Philips, refused to give up his seat. Weeks later, Martha Thibodeaux fought with a passenger and then with police after she attempted to move the Jim Crow screen on a New Orleans bus to accommodate an overflowing black section. In June 1949, Mrs. Smithey Reynolds refused to take a back seat on an interstate bus and the driver in North Carolina delayed the departure two hours rather than let the fifty-seven-year-old sit where she wanted. Two white and two black members of CORE, the Congress of Racial Equality, were sentenced to 30 days on a state road gang for violating Jim Crow travel laws, despite the fact that they were legally integrating the seating on an interstate bus. More than a dozen activists traveled through the upper South to test compliance with the Supreme Court's interstate-desegregation ruling. Bayard Rustin led these protests on buses, trains, and in hotels. These were the forerunners to the more famous Freedom Rides of 1961.

Boyd went one better than Mack in trying to avoid conflicts on the road. Rather than use Pullman cars on trains, he encouraged the men to drive their own cars or take planes, which catered to a select group of passengers. With only Watson and Britton available for travel, Boyd often accompanied them. Pictures from the time show him mingling with ordinary students and churchgoers as well as the mighty: New York City Congressman Adam Clayton Powell and black insurance magnate C. C. Spaulding of Durham, North Carolina.

But it was advertising that Mack wanted to focus on, and Boyd got busy on two new campaigns. Pepsi-Cola stuck to newspaper and radio ads. Television wasn't enticing business the way radio had in its infancy, though ad spending overall hit a record $4.8 billion in 1948. Nearly 52 percent of all ad revenues were in periodicals, 12 percent in radio. Companies were fighting over limited billboard space, wishing to put their brands in front of the growing number of drivers venturing onto the nation's roadways. Coca-Cola was still the biggest buyer of billboards. Ironically, it was the oil concern Texaco that diverted $1.25 million of its ad budget from roadside billboards to sponsor comedian Milton Berle on the "video medium."

Advertising in the black press took a leap forward in 1949, growing in quantity, quality, and variety. Bulova watches, Chevrolet cars, and Underwood electric typewriters were some of the national brands that ran at least one ad in black newspapers. Colgate was a frequent advertiser, with elaborate vignettes showing smartly dressed young blacks. Noxzema regularly featured a black nurse. Philip Morris even featured Ron Brown's father, "William H. Brown, manager of America's largest colored hotel, Hotel Theresa," in its "No Cigarette Hangover" series. Pet Milk started a charming and popular series of ads profiling African-American families in their homes. Some budget-conscious companies, such as Beech-Nut gum, ran stock ads that merely depicted the product. Lucky Strike continued to buy space in the black media, but also appeared to be cutting costs. Rather than create new ads featuring black subjects, or even rerun its "First in Negro History" series, the company ran generic ads featuring several white tobacco buyers or warehouse operators in the industry. By year's end, even a niche product like Manischewitz kosher wine was using black entertainers for endorsements in the black press. ("My Favorite Too!" said trumpeter Erskine Hawkins.)

As expected, the new proliferation of big national ads lifted the overall quality of advertising in the black press—and often the news coverage as well. The effectiveness of the campaigns in terms of dollar sales was not in doubt; but big advertisers also received goodwill and the tacit agreement that they wouldn't be boycotted by the increasing commitment to "buy black." And that term came more and more to mean not just black-owned businesses but those that hired black professionals and recognized black consumers. The success of major corporations selling to black consumers was such that *The Pittsburgh Courier* worried it might ultimately drive out Negro-owned businesses, just as the integration of baseball was killing the Negro League. Would integration of the marketplace be a two-way street, with money flowing *into* the black community from big business as well as *from* the community, keeping black neighborhoods vibrant?

Few of the ads in the black press could match the popularity of Pepsi's "Leaders in Their Fields" campaign. Boyd decided to update and relaunch it in 1949. He reran the two most popular profiles, of Ralph Bunche and chemist Percy Julian. For its debut on April 16, 1949, however, he chose another famous name that had unexpectedly returned to the news: polar explorer Matthew A. Henson. The first explorer to set foot on the North Pole, on April 6, 1909, Henson was finally being awarded medals and honors in belated recognition of his achievement at the side of his colleague, Admiral Robert E. Peary. News stories told the sad tale of how, after his last expedition, Henson had been reduced to jobs parking cars and serving as a messenger in the Customs House in New York City. He had retired from the latter job on a meager pension, despite the repeated attempts of three lawmakers to get Congress to grant him more money. When Boyd visited the eighty-two-year-old former explorer in his 150th Street apartment in Manhattan, he found him going blind and suffering from lumbago. Henson had hoped Pepsi-Cola would pay him for his endorsement. "He needed the money, and I felt bad, but I couldn't give him any more than the dollar that we gave for legal reasons," Boyd said.

The eleven new ads also featured:

- Dr. Harold D. West, biochemist and professor at Meharry Medical College.
- Dean Dixon, successful conductor of the American Youth Orchestra.
- James J. Johnson, collector for the IRS for the Third District of New York and member of the New York Bar.
- Dr. John W. Davis, distinguished educator.
- Walter A. Gordon, chairman of the California Parole Board, lawyer, and former football star for the University of California.
- J. Finley Wilson, Grand Exalted Ruler of the Elks and founder of the Norfolk *Journal and Guide* weekly.
- Fred Jones, chief engineer for U.S. Thermal Control Company.
- A. A. Alexander, contractor and engineer, lately of the newly completed "$4,000,000 Whitehurst Freeway" in Washington, D.C.

Get "More Bounce to the Ounce" was the new slogan introduced in the special-markets campaign, in the profiles of Gordon and Wilson. It was a slogan associated with Steele and his wish to emphasize Pepsi's higher calorie count and its large size. "Yes, ounce for ounce, Pepsi gives more quick food energy.... Why Take Less ... When Pepsi's Best!"

For a second ad campaign, to run in magazines from July through December, Pepsi-Cola wanted to make a bigger impact in the youth market. Boyd suggested a six-ad series centered on the black colleges in the South. The first was prominently placed in *Ebony*'s July issue. It featured a group of actual campus leaders at Howard University—popular and attractive sorority girls and lettermen—enjoying Pepsi. The "More Bounce to the Ounce" slogan was used in some of those ads and was emblazoned on a lighted scoreboard that Pepsi-Cola donated to Hampton Institute's football field. The gift was unveiled during a game by Boyd and Hampton's newly installed president, Alonzo Morón— the first black and the first Hampton graduate to head the school.

As usual, Boyd personally selected the student models with input from campus officials and wrote their profiles. He went along on every shoot, just as the school year was ending in the spring of 1949. While Boyd was scouting standout students for the ads, he also kept his eyes open for talent to recruit for his sales team, slated for expansion by midyear. That mission made him a doubly welcome guest. On the Hampton campus in Virginia, he asked the dean of placement to recommend promising seniors for possible employment. The dean immediately suggested a bright, easygoing, and well-liked student—Chuck Wilson—and contacted him. Wilson dropped everything and went to meet Boyd, who was in the middle of a photo shoot. The two men agreed to meet over breakfast the next morning.

Wilson was honest about not having noticed Pepsi's advertising campaign. He had been focused on his studies. "Pepsi was foreign to me," he recalled later. "I liked Nehi's flavored drinks, and the only cola I knew was RC."

Boyd described the Pepsi-Cola Company to Wilson, stressing the employment opportunities. It seemed to Wilson that he had managed to meet the right man at the right time. Hampton, for the most part, lived up to its promise that every graduate would get a job. But in reality the prospects were limited, especially after the war. "You could almost forget Corporate America," Wilson said of the choices open to graduates, a bleak situation that had changed little over the past decade. Those who didn't want to be self-employed still gravitated to teaching; a select group headed for large, black-owned companies, such as insurance. Those looking for an integrated workplace tended to choose government jobs, especially in the growing fields of social work and employment. After all, even at Hampton, most of the instructors were white, including the dean who had recommended Wilson to Boyd. The newest additions to the staff were European academics who had fled the Nazis during the war, Wilson said. He had two offers: one in Georgia working in rodent-and-pest control and another teaching high-school chemistry. "I wasn't too happy about the Georgia job," he joked. To be offered work with a company like Pepsi-Cola "was unheard of," Wilson said.

The interview went well, but no offer was made, and no other meeting was scheduled. Boyd had a lot more territory to cover. Wilson put the job out of his mind and turned his attention to school, finishing his work just in time to graduate in June 1949. He had made it through school with barely a nickel to spare for a train ticket home to Atlantic City, New Jersey. He couldn't wait to get back to his favorite fishing spot along the seawall. One night, not long after he arrived, he was happily casting and enjoying the sunset when his Uncle Cheatham drove up and handed him a telegram. Wilson held it in the car's headlights to read the message: "In the event you are still interested in employment at Pepsi-Cola, report for work on Monday." It gave an address, an hour, and a contact.

It was Sunday! Wilson raced home. He wasn't sure what he should wear or where he should stay once he got there. But, within a couple of hours, he was dressed in a suit and tie and sitting on the night's last direct train to New York City. He arrived before sunrise and waited patiently in the station for the workday to begin before making his way to Pepsi-Cola headquarters on Fifty-seventh Street. He found his way to personnel and, after filling out papers, went to see Boyd.

"When Mr. Boyd said national sales, the word *national* struck me," Wilson said. "When he said we'd be taking the lead in special marketing, that hit me, too."

Within an hour, he was formally offered the job. "I was a little suspicious of the whole thing," Wilson recalled. He had his heart set on medical school, and nothing would change that. Finally, he asked, "How much money are we talking about?"

It was about thirty-six hundred dollars a year, plus expenses, with a thousand-dollar contingency fund to start with, Boyd replied.

Wilson was thrilled to have it. It was enough to allow him to save for medical school and to marry. Before Wilson knew it, he was on his way to Long Island City to tour the plant. It seemed like a massive operation, and he was pleased with his new colleagues. "Pepsi gave me the chance to be exposed to blacks who wanted to go somewhere, who were involved in the hard work. I met people with force, with energy, with desire."

Wilson felt proud and knew his grandmother Carrie would be, too. "My family was broadcasting, 'Eloie is with Pepsi-Cola Company!'" he said. (He was known by his middle name until arriving at Hampton.) It was the kind of achievement she had hoped for him. She told him he would be successful if he worked hard, saved, got an education, and kept true to himself and his beliefs. To an outside observer, however, a corporate job in New York City might have seemed an unlikely way station in the journey Wilson had begun in life.

———————

Charles Eloie Wilson was born on April 24, 1926, in Crisfield, Maryland, the eldest of three children of a single mother, Aretta. By the time he was eight, his mother had died, as had one of his sisters. He knew his sister had succumbed to scarlet fever but not why his mother had lived only to her twenties. He didn't know his father and didn't care to, but years after his mother's death, Wilson was told that his father had probably been a white man, not the African-American he had met a couple of times. He promised himself then, as a young man, that he would worry not about what he was made of, but what he made of himself—and that he would never judge his mother's choices in life, only his own.

He couldn't complain, he reasoned, because nothing had been missing from his childhood. That he felt this way amid such sorrow is a credit to his grandmother Carrie. She brought Wilson and his sister, Julie, to live with her and her eight children, even though she had split from her husband. Wilson and Julie were raised as her own, and they came to call her Mother. "If there is anything in this world that I had a surplus of, it was love," Wilson said.

Grandmother Carrie was the daughter of former slaves, and she and her family made sure that they worked harder for themselves than they ever had for any master. Crisfield was a major center of the seafood industry, and most of the family, children included, found jobs in local food-processing plants. One sister worked as a domestic for the same family for seventy years, from age thirteen until her death. The only memory Wilson keeps of the seafood plants is the sight of carloads of people pulling up alongside a building to hear the workers inside singing.

None of Carrie's children had much formal education, a source of deep regret in a family led by wise and formidable women. Throughout his life, Wilson heard the same drumbeat from his grandmother: education, education, education. And she was equally committed to instructing her children at home in the ways of the world. In a society that often sought to strip African-American males of their manhood, she taught her three sons and grandson how to behave as men. "Son, get your hands out of your pockets," Grandmother Carrie used to scold Wilson. "Don't stare down at the ground, or it'll come up and hit you in the face. Look at the peacock. He thinks he's the greatest thing in the world, strutting around with that great tail. Then he looks down at his feet and his tail drops. Walk with your head up."

As a child, Carrie had witnessed a white mob bludgeon a black man to death with a sea buoy and drag him through the streets of Crisfield. She and her mother, Lucy Brown, nicknamed Noon, lived in terror of someone in the family being killed, and they did everything they could to protect their children from racists. When Wilson was twelve, he confessed to Noon that he had been in a fight. He had been swimming at a local beach with friends when a white boy yelled to them: "You *niggers* shouldn't be swimmin' off this pier." Wilson punched him. He remembered thinking that of all the boys who would say such a thing, how odd that it was the son of a "honey-dipper," slang for a man paid to shovel out outhouses. Certainly he had no business putting on airs. Wilson was furious and vowed to get even.

"Never throw dirt, son, you only lose ground," his great-grandmother told him.

"That stuck with me my whole life," Wilson said at age seventy-eight. "Noon would always give me words of wisdom."

Lucy Brown, who described herself as part Indian, part black, and part white, spent some sixty years as a chef in a hotel in Ocean City, Maryland. She never lived in the hotel basement with the rest of the help; instead, she walked across the bridge to her own quarters on the segregated beaches of the mainland. She made good money between her regular job and all her extra work, from filling picnic baskets and party platters for the well-to-do to being a wet nurse.

The Wilson home was filled with three generations of enterprising women: Carrie, her five daughters, a granddaughter, and several of her sisters. Noon lived next door with her husband, Toby Miles. Some of Wilson's aunts went to live in Atlantic City, so his summers were divided between trips to visit them on the New Jersey shore and to the former Makepeace plantation, where his great-grandfather Toby had been a slave. In Atlantic City, one uncle by marriage was active in a powerful local Republican club. Wilson's family was part of a minority of blacks who didn't defect en masse to Franklin D. Roosevelt's Democratic Party in 1938. They remain mostly in the "party of Lincoln" to this day. "I'm a Catholic and a Republican, and I get hell for both," Wilson said, seeming to relish going against the grain.

The family story is that Toby Miles was willed a parcel of land by his master, and the Miles family settled there and became carpenters. His wife's parents, too, had been owned by a lawyer who contracted tuberculosis. He promised them that when he died they would be freed, as long as they helped his wife and children work the land. They stayed on, more or less voluntarily, as "friendlies." Noon's mother, known as Ma Brown, was likely the owner's daughter.

Carrie's husband, Algie Wilson, came from a family that ran barbershops. Another branch, based in Baltimore, became affluent by opening pharmacies in Langley, Virginia. It was that branch that started a tradition of attending Hampton Institute, and even though Wilson didn't know those relatives well, he became infatuated with the idea of attending Hampton.

Grandfather Algie, the only father Wilson knew, set up a home with a second wife three blocks away after his split from Carrie, but he continued to support the ten children with money and attention. He enjoyed a good reputation in his community. He had a good job with the railroads, calling freight to alert the workers that a shipment was on its way. Many in the town knew him through his membership in the large and powerful Elks organization of black workers, and he played tuba in the Elks band.

In Crisfield, the group's members congregated at the shop of a local barber who was also an Elk. The barber donated his upstairs space for a makeshift classroom, and Wilson started school there. Schools were completely segregated at the time, and there was no "colored" high school. So, after grammar school, the children in his family were sent to live with relatives in towns with black high schools. Wilson went to Atlantic City.

Wilson loved school. His teachers were exceptional, he said, many of them overqualified graduates of the black colleges who could find no other jobs. One teacher in particular had a profound impact on his life—Miss Sherill in the fifth grade. She had Wilson enter an intercounty reading contest and coached him herself: hold the book with one hand, stand erect, avoid licking your fingers to turn the page, look straight and then to the sides to address an audience. Wilson took first place and won a dictionary. "Every day you will come to me with a good word," she told him. "One like *parsimonious*. What could be prettier than that word?"

Wilson studied hard, knowing early in life that he wanted to be a doctor like the one black doctor in town, who delivered most of the African-American babies. As far back as he could remember, Wilson was preoccupied with finding work, perhaps because he was adopted. "I think the main thing was I didn't want to be in the way, a burden, with no mother and no father," Wilson said. "I believed in hard work as a little boy. Still, to this day, I believe in hard work."

He got his first job at age six, for fifty cents a week, helping his uncle Miles deliver candy and syrup for two Jewish brothers who owned a diner and a wholesale candy business. Wilson worked every day after school until dinnertime, and all day on weekends. When he was fifteen years old, he worked at the diner's soda fountain, where he learned how to handle money. Meanwhile, he picked up odd jobs: separating grades of oysters from a captain's boat, baiting crab pots with eels, digging up terrapin eggs for a processing plant, gutting fish on a party boat. If he made a dollar, Grandmother Carrie took out eighty-five cents and pushed it into his bank. He took the rest and immediately went for a movie and a root beer.

Of all his jobs, his favorite was as a driver and errand boy for a Catholic couple who owned seafood and dry-cleaning businesses. She was a teacher from a wealthy farming family. They were childless, so they lavished attention and modest gifts on Wilson. They helped him get his driver's license when he was still under sixteen. Wilson worked for the couple for two years, until he had saved enough to realize his dream of entering Hampton Institute in the fall of 1943. He became the third of five generations of Wilson men to attend the school by the end of the twentieth century. While he was attending, he read the teachings of Hampton's most famous graduate, Booker T. Washington. Wilson has read his *Up From Slavery* countless times and owns a recording of one of the famous debates between Washington and his philosophical rival, W. E. B. DuBois. He paraphrases Washington's writings to sum up the philosophy of his family: "Never let a woman or man pull you down so low as to make you hate yourself. When you look into that mirror you're looking at a human being with potential. Take that potential and make it work. Stay good, stay honest, and you'll stay fearless. And always believe in God."

Wilson loved Hampton, but he was able to complete only one year before his precious education was interrupted by the war. He was drafted into the army in July 1944. He remembers the day he was on an army bus outside a post office in Atlantic City in a light rain. His grandmother, who had moved to New Jersey a couple of years before to be with her daughters, was there to see him off. "Son, listen to me," she said. "You promise me that you'll come back to me just the way I'm sending you."

Those words turned over in his head the myriad times he almost came to blows with other soldiers and officers. At eighteen years old, he was facing the consequences of racism for the first time on his own, and at times he feared for his life. It started in boot camp at Fort Leonard Wood, Missouri. The base had a majority of white American soldiers, and it also housed thousands of foreign prisoners of war. At one end were Italian prisoners, who did quartermaster work such as shoe repair, laundry, and hauling food and supplies from the railroad depots. At the other end were prisoners from Rommel's desert campaign, mostly Germans. When the black soldiers returned from their training in the valley, they had to pass the prisoners' barracks on their way back to headquarters. As the soldiers passed, one prisoner stuck his head out the window and shouted to Wilson in German: *"Hey, Schwarzer! Soldat! Schwarzer! Sing! Sing!"* ("Hey, black man! Soldier! Black man! Sing! Sing!")

Wilson thought it outrageous to be taunted by a Nazi on an American base and asked permission to break rank and speak to his captain. The captain, white, gave him a withering look, ending the complaint, and Wilson fell back in line. The two despised each other. Wilson was relieved when he was assigned to engineering school at Fort Belvoir, Virginia, then to pilot and navigation training at Keesler Field, Mississippi. But the same troubles followed him. On his way to the latter assignment, Wilson traveled with a group of black soldiers. A porter had told them there were Pullman cars available for their overnight trip. But when they approached a white conductor, he told them, "No vacancies." They were sent to the segregated cabin to sleep sitting up all night. Walking along the station platform to their cabin, they looked up and saw a Nazi officer, a prisoner, being transported by military police. He was chatting with an American MP in a Pullman car. "This Nazi was in the same line of cars we were in, but in a Pullman with dining, showers, pull-down bunks—and we were in uniform! We were American soldiers . . ." Wilson said, his voice breaking, still stung by the humiliation and anger.

"It was actually more acceptable to fraternize with the German troops than it was to be friendly with a fellow Black American soldier!" confirmed singer Tony Bennett in a remarkable story about army segregation in his autobiography, *The Good Life*. He said that when he was stationed in Mannheim, Germany, during the war, he was elated to have run into a high-school friend on Thanksgiving Day, 1945, and invited him to the mess hall for a proper dinner. As he entered the lobby of the building with his African-American friend, both in uniform, he was stopped by an officer who flew into a rage at the sight of them. The officer took a razor blade out of his pocket, sawed off

Bennett's corporal's stripes, spit on them, threw them to the floor, and yelled that he was "a private again." As part of his punishment, Bennett said, he was reassigned to Graves Registration, where he dug up soldiers from mass graves for reburial. "We all suffered" from the segregation rule, said Bennett, who went on to become a lifelong supporter of the civil rights movement.

Wilson never actually attended the training classes. The school was suddenly closed when training for single-engine planes ended. "When we were leaving the base to go to town and board the train, they played 'Bye-Bye Blackbird,' " Wilson remembered. He laughed.

Wilson then went to Camp Lee, Virginia, where he was invited to attend Officer Candidates School, and became a platoon sergeant training recruits there. Not long before being discharged in 1946, he contracted rheumatic fever and was hospitalized for ten days on the base. A white American nurse who was caring for him gave him a book to read while he was recuperating. It was the 1944 historical novel *Freedom Road*, by then-Communist writer Howard Fast, about how efforts to bring racial equality to the South during Reconstruction were crushed. The book had a profound impact on Wilson's thinking about race and politics. "It was like someone turned a light on things," he said. The illness, unfortunately, also had a lifelong impact, forcing him to live with heart disease.

Wilson returned to Hampton in the autumn of 1946, physically and emotionally changed. Racists like Senator Theodore Bilbo, who said the black man would become dangerous if he was given a gun during the war, were right in a way, Wilson thought. He felt empowered: a bigger, stronger man physically, despite his illness, and emotionally. He was ready to go after success and reward, and capable of fighting for his rights. The nonwhite troops in World War II had proven themselves in battle as exemplary soldiers.

Back at college, Wilson began to explore his spiritual side and converted to Catholicism. Other African-Americans were taking a similar path. *Ebony* did a feature story in 1949 about the growing population of Catholic blacks, noting that blacks accounted for about 10 percent of all converts. Around that time, it became known that the Catholic Church would elevate the first black to sainthood: Martin de Porres, a sixteenth-century Peruvian.

Religion unexpectedly became a touchy subject during Wilson's tenure at Pepsi-Cola. While on the road, he balked at having to visit non-Catholic churches on Sundays as part of the Pepsi promotional campaign.

———

The very afternoon Pepsi-Cola hired Wilson, the company put him on a plane with Floyd Britton to the West Coast to work territories there. It was Wilson's first commercial flight but he would take many more. He especially appreciated the opportunity—and the flair—of flying back to the Hampton area to work those markets and see his girlfriend, Mary Shelton, who had two more years at Hampton Institute before graduation.

"When he got that job, I thought it was phenomenal because he was a biology major," said Mary, who later became Wilson's wife. "He certainly didn't have it in mind to go into business. It was a tremendous opportunity, a big plus."

During his first three months on the job, Wilson stuck close to Britton and Watson—the two remaining members of the original sales team, who trained him. Wilson learned the drill: how to check the local papers for events, how to arrange for a tent for the big occasions, and to set up drinks and snacks for the smaller gatherings. Their mornings were spent with bottlers, which included riding with driver-salesmen to seek more sales opportunities along their routes. Their afternoons were spent with merchants, helping them set up in-store displays and promotions. Nights were spent at social functions; Saturdays at conventions or other special functions; Sundays in churches.

Late at night, Wilson would study the department's instruction booklets on sales techniques. He belonged to the easygoing, "make a friend" school of salesmanship, and he quickly became a popular figure at the local gatherings the team would infiltrate. "I never did anything slick," Wilson said. "Pepsi-Cola and I were partners; we were buddies. I never wanted to do anything that I felt would hurt Pepsi," Wilson said.

The technique worked just as well on the bottlers' employees. The morning sessions at the plants included addressing the driver-salesmen. In those earliest attempts at diversity-training seminars, the team members described how they would win them more sales by making contacts with the black store managers. Not all the truck drivers appreciated the advice, and many were uncomfortable working in uniforms alongside an African-American in a suit, with a clipboard in his hand. But Wilson found the drivers, on the whole, to be welcoming. One of the first he met took Wilson home to have breakfast with his family after learning he was a veteran, and Wilson spent the morning reading comics to the man's son. Another time, Wilson was riding with a driver-salesman when they stopped for lunch. Wilson declined to go into the segregated restaurant and asked the man to bring him a sandwich when he finished his meal. The driver went inside and emerged a short time later with two lunches, choosing to eat with Wilson in the truck.

At the end of his training period, Wilson was able to travel and handle the outlets on his own, except for those times when Boyd orchestrated a market siege and all hands reported to the same area. Wilson preferred working with the others. Whenever he could, Wilson would get his colleagues to take time off for a fishing trip when they were in the countryside, or go to see a play in the city.

Watson and Britton had very different approaches to their clients and to the myriad situations they encountered on the road. "Watty was a Southern boy who knew the Southern way," Wilson said. "He didn't rock the boat one bit."

Wilson was also cautious, but controversy followed the Pepsi team, anyway. Wilson remembered once going to check in at the Biltmore Hotel in Omaha. He never made it to his room. First, the taxi driver brought him to the service entrance; then the clerk lied about having lost his reservation, and offered him the name of a boardinghouse. When an African-American bellhop heard the argument he joined in the fight with the clerk. "Can't you see this gentleman doesn't want to stay in a place like that?" said the older man. When Wilson politely told him not to interfere lest he jeopardize his job, the man left the area quietly, but made a call to the local NAACP. Members of the group appeared in the lobby to help Wilson find another hotel, then took legal action against the Biltmore.

Britton had the opposite temperament. Wilson described him as shrewd, "a poker player; but he had savoir faire. It was, 'look at me,' and it was effective," he said. Britton would get indignant about the disparities between the relatively fine dining and lodging enjoyed by Pepsi-Cola's white salesmen and what the team had to endure. "We're doing the same thing they're doing, except here we are in Maggie Whittington's backyard paying two dollars a night," he'd complain.

And it wasn't easy to find even those backyard lodgings. Rather than take their chances after rolling into town, all the brown hucksters carried a travel guide called *The Negro Travelers Green Book,* published out of Harlem by Victor B. Green. It covered the United States, Alaska, Canada, Mexico, and Bermuda, offering tips on lodgings, hotels, and gas stations that would welcome African-Americans. The book—less than one hundred pages—started as a local guide in 1936 but with the help of the U.S. Travel Bureau expanded to cover sites across the nation in the 1940s, and continued annually until 1963. "This copy presented with the compliments of James A. Jackson, 'The Esso Man,'" read one customized 1947 cover. The cover of the 1949 edition had an illustration of an improbably long line of bumper-to-bumper traffic on a three-lane highway. "Travel Is Fatal to Prejudice," read one quote under the drawing. The author was quick to point out that he couldn't vouch for the quality of many of the suggested retreats—some of them simply a room in a private home. Many accommodations were unpleasant, to say the least. Wilson learned to supplement the book with lists put together by local organizations and churches in a town.

Such accommodations sometimes were offered informally by whites who were against segregation. For example, Albert Einstein famously opened his home to Marian Anderson when she couldn't find accommodations in white-only hotels in the Princeton, New Jersey, area. It was one reason that Congressman John Rankin of Mississippi took aim at Einstein on the House floor that year, calling for his deportation for "communistic activities." But Einstein remained a vocal opponent of segregation. "Racism is a disease of white people, and I don't want to be quiet about it," he once said.

The green book came in handy, as 1949 was shaping up to be a very busy year for Boyd's shrunken sales team. Wilson started at Pepsi during a fortuitously long and hot summer across the United States. Breweries and soft-drink makers with disappointing first-quarter sales suddenly were overwhelmed by demand. Coca-Cola boasted that it doubled its sales in the second quarter, compared with the first. At the same time, production costs were falling from previous year's highs.

With demand high and the Pepsi team shorthanded, it made sense to push vending machines. "They're the silent merchants; when you're sleeping, they're making money," Wilson said, reciting his sales pitch. Suddenly, with the help of the special-markets team, the round-topped Pepsi vending machines started appearing everywhere: in the subways of New York City and across the South in the furniture factories and textile plants that were moving down from the North.

Wilson especially liked working the college campuses. Not only were the college officials happy to offer their students soft drinks, but they liked having the men on campus as role models and usually gave them lodging. "This is what you can do after you graduate, this is what you could become," was the message Wilson conveyed. He went to his alma mater first, peppering the Hampton campus with vending machines. The Norfolk-area bottler was thrilled with the results, so much so that he wanted Wilson to be the plant's exclusive salesman. He declined.

In the home office, Boyd handled consents from bottlers for marketing assistance. But it was up to each team member to find new outlets in the small towns and communities located in-between the bottlers' territories. "We might spot a popular youth hangout that might accept a vending machine, or a small Catholic school, or a meeting of hairdressers, or a string of black merchants in a section of town," Wilson said. Or he might gain entrée into a group or store through a fraternity brother from Alpha Phi Alpha.

For the smaller, noncommercial outlets, Boyd armed his team with copies of a thank-you letter to his customers. In a letter dated August 8, 1949, Boyd alluded to the company's history of service to the black community—while making a rare pitch about the value of the product:

Dear Customer:

We, of the Pepsi-Cola Company, are desirous of having a little chat with you, our customer, because we want you to know that we appreciate your patronage. . . . This Company has striven to contribute its part toward the elevation of standards of living among people generally. In whatever activities this Company has engaged, it has consistently endeavored to make sure that the benefits of those activities were extended to each and every segment of our society regardless of race, creed or color.

I am sure that in this period of high living costs you find it necessary to spend your food money extremely wisely. It is in this connection that Pepsi-Cola makes its greatest contribution, for it affords you more for your money. May I suggest, therefore, that you consider these advantages as you undertake to provide for your family's food needs in the most economical way.

Again, may I thank you for the support you have given us in the purchase of our product. I should like to think that we may continue to count you among our group of "Pepsi" boosters. With very best wishes, I am,

> Very sincerely yours,
> Edward F. Boyd,
> Assistant Sales Manager

Wilson loved to meet these individual customers and they loved him back. He called on shoeshiners, field workers, and the fishermen and crabbers along the Southeastern coast. "Hi! I'm Chuck Wilson. And I'm here from New York to talk to you about Pepsi." He drove rented cars at first, then bought a car with a veteran's loan to take advantage of the company's generous mileage reimbursement. Every month he filled out an expense report, chalking up an average of 250 miles. The reimbursement checks were sent to the bottlers, according to schedule. If one was late, the bottlers would sometimes give the salesmen an advance. The team moved quickly, and Wilson ended up crisscrossing the country twice. "We were moving so fast, we'd leave a suit behind and have to buy another one in the next town."

On occasion, he would fly into an area and use a bottler's two-door coupe, emblazoned with the Pepsi insignia, to get around. But not all bottlers were comfortable with this arrangement. "Some preferred we weren't seen in Pepsi cars," Wilson said.

The men almost never used trains and buses by 1949. Chuck Wilson took exactly one train ride for Pepsi-Cola, and that was to represent the company on a cross-country Elks Club junket that carried black lodge members to the organization's convention via reserved Pullman trains. Wilson took the Great Northern from New Jersey to Chicago and through Montana to the San Francisco convention site. At night, the team organized games with prizes for the passengers. They had cases of scotch, beer, and other liquor brought aboard, along with cases of lemons and limes—all of which the men stored in their own compartments.

Wilson and his colleagues were affable hosts, serving beers or mixing cocktails. They also collected the Elks' postcards and letters each morning and mailed them at the next stop. One morning, Wilson was stopped by one of the Elks, who admonished him for not taking the time to speak to him.

"He looked like a little turtle," Wilson recalled. "He had the horned-rimmed glasses and he's sitting there with his feet up on the seat." Wilson apologized and, when the man lowered his feet, sat down opposite him to chat.

The man, from Kentucky, told him: "I worked in this bank all my life, cleaning, mopping, running errands, opening doors. They'd get out of their cars and give me their deposits and I'd bring it in and bring back the deposit slip. They'd give me tips and at the end of the day, I'd put them in my savings account." With those savings he bought land cheaply, he said, and ended up selling it at a tidy profit to the local A&P for a new store site. It was enough to send all six of his children to college. "I had to out-dumb The Man," he told Wilson, "but my children and you, you're going to outsmart him."

Wilson was a quick study and was doing very well in sales. In no time, he was ready to be a mentor himself. He got the chance when Boyd hired a fourth man in late 1949. Richard L. Hurt was also a Hampton graduate, one year ahead of Wilson. The Rhode Island native had studied journalism. After graduation, Hurt worked at a liberal Harlem newspaper called the *People's Voice* and did extensive reporting on the integration of professional baseball. He had a clear and easy writing style that made him invaluable when it was time to write up the narrative field reports, a task his colleagues were only too happy to delegate to him. He missed writing, and so put journalistic flair into the reports. Wilson and Hurt, two handsome, single men, liked working together—and double dating—and became close friends.

The golden age of advertising had coincided with a golden age in jazz, and that made it fun for the sales team. The *Chicago Defender* had an events column: "What the Cats Are Doing While Squares Sleep." The Pepsi cats were hitting the biggest clubs for business. Wilson and Hurt got along well with other brown hucksters, and when they met up with the Schenley liquor or Pabst Blue Ribbon beer salesmen, Wilson remembered, they liked to invent new mixed drinks they imagined could rival the popular rum and Coke that was killing sales of Pepsi to bars. Boyd, however, kept the team on a short leash even after hours. They resented it, but acquiesced.

Wilson and Hurt also took advantage of Mack's offer of free Broadway theater tickets for employees. Wilson went to see *Death of a Salesman*. If he'd had any doubt about whether he would stay in sales, that clinched the No vote. But that didn't mean he wasn't enjoying his work. He grew to like road travel. In those days, long drives were a pastime—and offered vistas of the far corners of the country that relatively few had seen. New places and situations gave Wilson perspective on his work. "I learned that this country had its problems, and I wanted to be part of the solution," he said. "I felt I could make doors open."

However many obstacles he faced, Wilson said, "I never let anything linger with me so long that I became bent out of shape." Once, when he was crossing South Dakota, he treated himself to a trip to Mount Rushmore. "Something like that wiped out all that adverse, negative crap you were dealing with a day ago."

The negative incidents were frequent in those days "before the revolution," as he called the pre-civil-rights era. One hot morning in Mississippi, he was driving down a highway when he saw about fifteen women and children working in a cotton field. He decided to offer them a cold drink, and pulled to the side of the road.

"Hi, I'm Chuck Wilson. I'm out of New York. I came here to say hello to you."

"You're from New York! And you came all the way down here to be with us?"

"That's just what I did," he said, and went to the trunk of his car to dig into the cooler he was carrying. He started popping open some bottles of Pepsi and handed them out still dripping with ice.

Suddenly, he saw a pickup truck headed down the road. A man slammed on the brakes and jumped out.

"What in the hell is going on here?" he shouted.

"I'm Chuck Wilson with the Pepsi-Cola Company. I saw the children working here and thought I'd stop."

"You're trespassing, boy!" he said. "You're on my goddamn land."

"No offense, sir," Wilson said. "I really didn't come here to offend you. May I offer you a bottle of cold Pepsi-Cola?"

He stopped and growled. "No, I had enough belly wash for one day."

"Excuse me," Wilson said, and took off.

That was how he dealt with the bigots, Wilson said. "You don't worry about race relations. You don't worry about 'separate but equal.' You work out a system."

Another part of that system was using humor. Wilson, fond of puns and storytelling, spent his driving time thinking of new jokes, or putting his own touch on an old one, to tell his colleagues when they met up. Most were Stupid White Man jokes. "The jokes were a treat, and a treatment, like human laughter always is," Wilson said.

Take the one about when he stopped along the road at a small mom-and-pop stand to get some home-cooked chicken. Some white guys were loitering outside, and he says hello and goes inside. He comes out and heads for a table, holding his chicken in a box. One of the white guys says, "Boy, whatever you do to that chicken, we're going to do to you next."

"So I pick up the chicken and kiss its back end," Wilson deadpanned.

He even had a few jokes about lynching, which was still a threat. One Southern sheriff pulled a body out of a creek with forty-eight bullet holes in it. The sheriff takes one look at the body and declares, "This is the goddamnedest case of suicide I've ever seen."

The hucksters never shied away from political humor. One of Wilson's favorite jokes, which he took credit for, was about driving his new Chevy into town.

"It had started to rain and this cop steps out in the middle of the street and holds up his hand and stops me.

" 'Boy, what you doin' down here?' he asks.

" 'I'm with Pepsi. What's the matter, officer?'

" 'Your windshield wipers are going left to right stedda right to left! Follow me to the courthouse.'

"[I go] before the judge. The judge says, 'Boy, you familiar with our Constitution?'

" 'Yes, sir.'

" 'Read it!' he says, and hands [me] a copy of the Constitution. [I look] at it . . . it's in Russian. . . .

"I read it. They put me in jail for being a Communist!"

This joke was inspired by headlines he saw during his first summer on the job. The House Un-American Activities Committee was continuing to destroy lives and reputations and spreading fear. The list of subversives—some watched by authorities and others accused by grandstanding politicians—grew to include such well knowns as Helen Keller, Dorothy Parker, Danny Kaye, Fredric March, Edward G. Robinson, Frank Sinatra, and Lena Horne, plus many women's rights advocates.

In the African-American population, it was no secret that some activists were Communists, but over time even the most hard-core became disillusioned by how the party used race relations as a propaganda tool. Moreover, communist sympathizers made trouble for everyone by giving HUAC the ammunition to force blacks out of their newfound jobs in government. Many African-Americans were called to speak before the committee, although not all were suspect. By the end of the 1940s, one newspaper estimated black membership in the Communist Party at no more than fourteen hundred. It created quite a stir, then, when Paul Robeson said in a public speech that no black man would take up arms against the Russians.

When Jackie Robinson appeared before the committee in July 1949, he spoke against the black Communists in general and Paul Robeson's latest actions in particular. But he went on to deliver a harsh and unexpected rebuke of the committee's efforts. He told HUAC: "The fact [that] it is a Communist who denounces injustice in the courts, police brutality, and lynching when it happens doesn't change the truth of his charges. Just because Communists kick up a big fuss over racial discrimination when it suits their purpose, a lot of people try to pretend that the whole issue is a creation of Communist imagination. . . . Negroes were stirred up long before there was a Communist Party and they will stay stirred up long after the party has disappeared—unless Jim Crow has disappeared by then as well."

The ballplayer's calm defiance filled many fans with as much pride as anything he had done on the field. "EXTRA! JACKIE HITS HOMER AT RED PROBE" was the *Defender's* headline. Some four years before Edward R. Murrow's famous assault on Senate red-baiter Joseph McCarthy started to turn the tide on such investigations, African-American leadership had united to form a coherent response to accusations of disloyalty.

On the same front page as the story on Robinson's appearance before HUAC, the *Defender* reported that the committee was told "in cold, blunt language by leading Negro spokesmen that whatever inroads made by the Communist Party in the Negro population of America are due to the stupid failure of this country to live up to her professions of democratic ideals." Those leaders included Lester Granger, executive director of the National Urban League; Dr. Charles R. Johnson, president of Fisk University, and Thomas W. Young, president and general director of the Guide Publishing Company, Inc., publisher of the Norfolk *Journal and Guide* newspaper.

The following month, the National Alliance of Postal Employees, representing twenty-five thousand black postal employees, fought to reverse the purges of nearly one hundred of its workers accused of being subversives. The alliance blasted the federal Loyalty Oath because it denied those accused the basic rights to defend themselves and face their accusers. (Did you protest the segregation of blood in blood banks? was one question asked of prospective federal-job candidates.)

The poisonous political atmosphere hardly motivated the private sector to accelerate efforts to target black consumers. The trade magazine *Printers' Ink* ran an updated feature on the Pepsi team by Adrian Hirschhorn, based on his earlier graduate work at New York University. The September 1949 article, titled "Pepsi-Cola's Campaign to the Negro Market," recorded painfully few strides forward in the three intervening years, underscoring the glacial pace of progress in moving

African-Americans into sales and management positions. "America's
Negro population today is our largest and most important underde-
veloped market," the article began. Hirschhorn saw Pepsi's "Leaders in
Their Fields" ads as "designed to compensate for the Negro's feeling of
suppression and to tie the product in with the idea of leadership." He
declared the series a success and worth "the specialized planning and
preparation costs involved."

Coca-Cola, for one, wasn't convinced. The *Defender* decided it
would court Coca-Cola with one of its big, favorable company profiles—a piece that took up the better part of a page and was accompanied by photos of seemingly contented black employees in Chicago. At
Coca-Cola, the writer stated almost apologetically, "There is no question about the fact that the Negro market is respected. It is." The feature spelled out the history of the company from its founding to the
1,050 bottling plants and some 100,000 fountains operating by October
1949. If Bob Woodruff's mandate was that "every customer must be
a friend," it said, using the boss's informal name, the cola plant at
Seventy-third and State in Chicago was making some friends in the
local community of five hundred thousand blacks. "It's a precision
plant where there are no flunky jobs and where men regardless of their
color are placed in positions where they can function best," the article
said. It offered proof: blacks employed as local special-sales representatives, as a wholesale driver assigned to sporting events, as the supervisor
of the syrup room; and as the bottle tester. Without providing specifics,
the paper said that the plant was "quietly carrying on a long-range welfare program in this market" and the people in charge hoped "to
develop more good will among Negro buyers."

The ploy to win over Coca-Cola didn't work. Coca-Cola's main
office still didn't advertise in the *Defender* or any other black periodi-
cal, and didn't hire African-American national sales representatives.

That left Pepsi's Walter Mack virtually by himself in the Negro soft-drink market at the decade's close.

———————

The team usually found itself back in the New York office at Christmastime. Wilson recalled how they'd gather around their desks waiting for word on year-end bonuses. "We'd sit and wait with bated breath, then all of a sudden the intercoms would come on and announce that the board had approved bonuses and we'd cheer."

Christmas parties were fun, with lots of alcohol, but Mack demanded a certain decorum. One young accountant made the mistake of getting tipsy at a gathering and calling Mack by his first name. He was fired the next week, Boyd remembered. The formality of office culture in those days didn't encourage bosses to be friendly with their employees. But around the same time, Chuck Wilson finally got to meet Mack after several months with the company and caught the boss in a different mood. He ran into Mack as the two were getting into the elevator at headquarters, and they introduced themselves. Wilson remembered Mack pulling out of his pocket a bawdy postcard that he seemed to keep at the ready for an encounter with his traveling salesmen. Mack seemed attentive and sincere, genuinely concerned about his employees. "Is there anything I should know?" he asked Wilson. And he continued to ask the question at other chance encounters.

Mack had mixed news for bottlers at the Southwest convention in Dallas at the end of the year. Sales had made a remarkable rebound, from 30 percent below 1948 levels for the first five months of the year, to a gain of 4 percent for all of 1949. But annual net profit was again spiraling downward, to $2.14 million from $3.15 million in 1948. Looking back at the close of Mack's decade of corporate leadership some years later, *Business Week* noted the contrasts. In 1949, it stated, the average person could still turn on a radio and hear the famous Pepsi jingle, "one of the oldest and best of its kind," and still look up and see the Pepsi name in the sky. But it was also the year the company was on "the brink of bankruptcy."

What good fortune the company had—summer heat wave aside— Mack attributed to the continuing transition to a standard eight-ounce bottle for "on-the-spot consumption." It made him optimistic about future sales.

The greatest glimmer of hope, however, was news that got only second billing from Mack and the reporters covering the convention: Pepsi-Cola's plant in Cairo, open just six months, had passed a milestone of one million cases sold. The venture into Africa was much more exciting for the special-markets team—and was watched carefully by the black press. The salesmen were more adaptable than their white colleagues to the changing scenario, and quickly grasped the significance of the move. They found a way to introduce the highly successful Egyptian plant into their sales pitch, and eventually incorporated the Pepsi logo written in Arabic script into Negro-market displays. Pepsi-Cola, like the rest of the soft-drinks industry, was beginning to think globally; and Boyd's salesmen were going to prepare themselves for the advance.

— Chapter Six —

The Cola Color Wars

THE SALES TEAM OFTEN FOUND THEMSELVES ON THE WEST Coast in 1950, working to promote Pepsi in the large, modern supermarkets cropping up around California. Mack, Wilson remembered, got war-surplus searchlights to place at the stores' entrances to comb the sky, as if at a Hollywood opening. Inside, the team set up an "electronic eye" trip wire at the door to set off a recorded voice as customers entered: "Hello! How are you? I'd like you to come over here to see me. If you buy a carton of Pepsi, I'll give you one free!" The men would sell case after case of Pepsi, stacked high in a central display. They repeated their success up and down the coast.

The trip wire was a great sales tool. Most Americans at the half-century mark were fascinated with gadgets and thrilled at the prospect of technology changing their lives. They already were able to fly, watch television (some twenty hours a week of color programming was in the works by CBS), cook (at least commercially) in microwave ovens, and even, for the first time, play Duke Ellington on an LP record. The *Chicago Defender* ran a feature suggesting that a man contemplating marriage might consider asking of his future bride, "Is she a good mechanic?" The article explained: "The hand that rocks the cradle now runs washing machine, dishwasher, vacuum cleaner, sewing machine, and an increasing number of other mechanical servants."

New Year's predictions, with an eye toward 2000, contemplated bored housewives sitting in their kitchens killing time while electrical pots and pans, or some incredible machine, cooked dinner. Some twenty-five years before the height of the feminist movement, it was easier to imagine a robotic housemaid than it was to imagine a woman working outside the home. It was the same for African-Americans. While many white Americans could see exceptional African-American individuals succeeding in business, the arts, and sports, the idea that average blacks might be fully integrated into society and reach the highest positions in a corporate structure was almost too foreign a notion. Society had yet to learn one of the lessons of the women's movement: that discrimination has many sources, and is not necessarily a product of hate or unfamiliarity.

Nevertheless, the more enlightened saw that social progress was lagging behind technological innovation, and they wanted change. The *Defender* did a series asking prominent citizens to predict what race relations might look like by the year 2000. The first to write was Alabama Governor James E. Folsom, forty-one years old, who predicted that the U.S. Constitution would end discrimination. "This will be true because I think man will become more Christ-like. . . . Racial issues will break down and in their place will arise class issues. I believe that the professional Negro will pursue activity of a nature similar to other professional groups. . . . I believe that fifty years from now, people will have taken off their cloaks of prejudice as they would a pair of dirty overalls, and cast them aside as a thing unwanted, a thing unclean."

Folsom backed up his views shortly thereafter by declaring a week in February Brotherhood Week in his state. Many schools and districts embraced the concept and paired it with an observance of Negro History Week, founded in 1926 by African-American historian Dr. Carter G. Woodson, who would die before the end of 1950.

The black community was less optimistic. Dr. Benjamin E. Mays, head of Morehouse College, wrote the week after Folsom: "There will be no Utopia for the Negro in the year 2000. . . . Even if discrimination became illegal, as with the Jews, discrimination would survive," he argued. "So, as paradoxical as it may seem, the second half of the twentieth century holds for the Negro at least three things: larger opportunities, greater competition, and continued discrimination. And I predict that he will meet all three with dignity, pride, and success."

Ebony magazine continued to cajole its readership into integrating major companies. Despite the success of many professionals, and of many large, black-owned businesses, critics thought the battle of the next generation was to break into mainstream jobs that would win them a share of the real wealth and power of the nation. Instead, many sought safer, less lucrative careers in jobs that served only their communities. "Smug in their towers of ideology and theory, these men to whom the black masses look for guidance are content with the pittance of a teacher or preacher while billions flow into the white man's coffers."

Manufacturers in postwar America were turning out a dazzling array of new consumer products for a beguiled public. The spread of products was changing the buying habits and social life of typical Americans. Consumers were becoming increasingly more sophisticated, and African-Americans were no exception. Trumpeter and composer Erskine Hawkins, for example, said dance halls in black communities were in an unprecedented slump as jazz musicians began to play "for listeners" rather than "for dancers." These audiences wanted the sort of improvisational music that musicians once reserved for after-hours jams among themselves. This kind of jazz, Hawkins said, would have been "too rich a diet" for the dance fans that used to fill the clubs.

To sell these new products, the advertisers had to make some adjustments. For one, the emphasis shifted to spotlighting the gadgets themselves. It was a far cry from the days when Mack and his counterparts perfected sales techniques in order to stand out in a pack of products acknowledged to be fairly interchangeable. Black periodicals won ads for such new toys as Motorola, Admiral, and Victrola 45 television sets; Zenith radios; and Spartus, "the only camera with a built-in flash attachment and built-in bulb tester." The companies selling the latest technology were not inclined to use black models. Companies that did, targeted the same demographics as they would for their white consumer counterparts. More and more, the so-called questionable products—charms and the like—were replaced by brand-name products and fashion novelties like the popular be-bop eyeglasses in the style of Dizzy Gillespie.

Also, advertisers adopted a new look: a cleaner, lighter, less self-conscious tone—the thin line drawings, polka-dots, and text bubbles that came to represent fifties style. In the black press, Pabst hired boxer Ezzard Charles and Cleveland Indian Larry Doby to pose for ads; but rather than show them in their sports uniforms, they were photographed wearing suits, sitting in luxurious lounges, and drinking beer from elegant glasses. Jackie Robinson remained the ubiquitous spokesman for companies big and small, selling everything from Wheaties to underwear. Other regular advertisers included Hellmann's mayonnaise, Pet Milk, Manischewitz, Noxzema, Carnation evaporated milk, Carolina rice, Lysol, Quaker, Seagram's, Chesterfield, Blatz beer, Vaseline, Lifebuoy, Kool-Aid, Rinso, Lucky Strike, and Philip Morris.

Beech-Nut gum may have been the biggest employer of black models, as ad after ad showed a new female face—attractive, affluent, and hip. Even Aunt Jemima was changing. The *Defender* introduced its readers in early 1950 to Edith Wilson, a mature, attractive woman who would be "the modern Aunt Jemima of radio and television." Colgate was another big spender, consistently running large ads that featured a variety of black families; and for every white dentist shown in an ad, there was also a black dentist. Popular hair and skin products, such as Perma-Strate, Royal Crown Pomade, Pluko hair treatment, and Black and White Bleaching Cream, got lots of ad space. Perma-Strate could afford top-notch talent for endorsements, including musician Dizzy Gillespie and actress Isabelle Cooley.

In the fall of 1950, the American Tobacco Company launched one of the smartest new campaigns. Its "Be Happy, Go Lucky" series presented an array of positive black images of both genders. It wasn't a celebration of actual achievers but an imagining of the possibilities: lifeguard, policeman, secretary, beauty-contest winner, archer, and writer. *Negro marketing* had become so common a term in the ad industry that in January 1950, a new graduate of New York University advertised a specialized study in the field in a *New York Times* want ad.

Everyone was chasing the black consumer. Boyd remembered the moment when he realized just how far the Negro market had come in gaining recognition—and just how well the leadership of Pepsi-Cola understood it. "I remember Bryan Houston using the example of Florsheim shoes and how blacks were the ones who set the style for many fashions," Boyd said. Houston, the executive vice president under Mack, used Florsheim's rising shoe sales as an example of how a product could become popular in the general market only after winning favor among African-American shoppers. For a time, Boyd added, he felt his team "might have been treated better than anyone else in the ad department."

The need for strong new markets was critical. Pepsi-Cola reported a first-quarter loss of $100,000, forcing it to sell its Cuban sugar plantation. Coca-Cola announced that it would shut down its Pittsburgh plant and lay off two hundred people amid declining earnings in a saturated domestic market. Yet, Pepsi-Cola was conspicuous in its absence from the pages of the black press early in the year. Beverage companies, instead, were beginning to direct their special-market funds to the country's robust foreign-language newspapers, seeing them as influential links to overseas markets. Carstairs Whiskey, for example, announced its latest ad campaign of 244 newspapers would include many immigrant newspapers.

The Wall Street Journal wrote in a May 1950 article about the success of the industry's global push. It also suggested the limited experience of businesses, and business journalists, with foreign markets, writing that "turbaned Arabs, sombreroed Argentineans and derbied Britishers are learning to gulp U.S.-type cola beverages, ginger ale, and fruit drinks as never before. The biggest current offensive is directed at countries not far from the Equator where throats get dry faster." Pepsi-Cola counted 66 plants in thirty-seven countries outside the United States and Canada. Of course, Coca-Cola still dominated the foreign markets with its 275 plants in seventy countries. Like Pepsi-Cola, Coca-Cola did extremely well in Cairo, selling one million cases in ten months of operation. It took twenty-four years for a U.S. bottler to manage a million cases in one year, the story said. The companies didn't report separate foreign and domestic sales to the public, but Coca-Cola credited one-third of its 1949 net profit of $37.79 million to sales abroad.

Pepsi-Cola announced that the capacity of its first Egyptian plant would be increased fivefold and that a second plant was in the works. It sent specialists in management, production, accounting, and distribution to help new foreign bottlers. Coca-Cola was more of a believer in formal training. Key Coca-Cola managers were "groomed for eighteen weeks" in the United States or in a foreign center about sanitation, merchandising, advertising, and making glassware and bottle caps. Most of those managers were officials of the host country's government who could overcome obstacles, such as limits on conversion of profits into U.S. dollars, strict controls, and a ban on bottle imports and sugar rations. The success of the American colas worried local industries. Soft drinks cut into sales of German beer, Italian wine, and Japanese sake. In France, wine merchants backed an unsuccessful effort by the Communist Party to block the sale of Coke because it was a symbol of American business expansion in Europe. The battles of the litigious Coca-Cola Company were beginning to take on a deeper political dimension—abroad and at home.

At Pepsi-Cola, it wouldn't be Mack who led the charge into global markets. Pepsi-Cola directors wanted change. On March 1, 1950, Walter Mack was named chairman of the board and Alfred Steele took over as president, almost one year to the day after Mack hired him away from Coca-Cola. Herbert Barnet was appointed vice president in charge of domestic operations.

Steele announced in the annual report his plan to undertake a massive effort to pump up the most lucrative markets and to invest in infrastructure. He resolved to advance region by region, working more closely with bottlers than in the past to increase sales, and made no apologies for the cost of his plans. He said he'd continue to expand overseas amid strong sales, with plans to add twenty-two new bottling plants and three concentrate-making plants.

Steele liked being the underdog but had the advantage of his successful tenure at the undisputed market leader, where Mack had not. Mack was once the turnaround king, yet there was no doubt that Steele embodied the modern business strategist that was replacing the paternalistic corporate chief of the first half of the century. "Steele works more on strategy than inspiration," *Fortune* said by way of comparison.

Steele had a hard task ahead. Restive bottlers were starting to sell "flavors" such as orange and grape alongside their colas to help profits. Steele was adamant that the bottlers could do much better in their markets selling Pepsi alone but selling it better. The high-energy executive seemed the one to lead the charge. He vowed that before his three-year contract was up he would double sales, making Pepsi about half as big as Coke.

———————

Boyd was wary about the reorganization, but the team benefited immediately from the change of guard. Steele wanted to spend money where individual bottlers could see quick results, and nothing could push sales figures higher faster than a blitz by the Negro-market team. The month after Steele became president, Boyd sent a letter to bottlers that confidently hailed an end to the company's doldrums. Finally, headquarters could repeat a partnership program that had done well in 1948, tying local bottlers to school sports teams. "For 1950–51, you, the Pepsi-Cola Bottler, now have ready a new and better sales weapon," the letter began, using a Cold War–era metaphor. And because it was still the era of Jackie Robinson, the letter continued:

> While this essentially is a school plan, you should know that the entire Negro population is intensely excited about Negro athletes, perhaps more intensely than the general United States white population is about white athletes. The attention you pay to Negro school promotion will fan out to almost the entire Negro population in your franchise.

The so-called weapon promised for the coming football season was a double-page program handed out to fans at games that would promote the local bottler, splitting costs with the home office. Steele emphasized a break with the troubled past, and Boyd followed suit:

> I call your attention to the fact that we have had success in Negro school promotion although we had practically no tools with which to

work. This year, we have the support of a special Negro football ad, Negro-type cover designs, and, of course, the great advantage of the 50-50 cooperative fund.

The Negro high school principals and athletic directors will be intrigued by your special program and should give you thorough attention and cooperation. . . .

The bottlers had final say on selecting which of six cover designs to use on their programs. The various covers, Boyd noted, used color drawings that only partially showed players' features, and so could "be interpreted as Negro or white" and used for any school.

Boyd concluded: "So far as I know we are the only soft-drink company to offer a special program for the Negro market. Take advantage of it this year while we have the exclusive.'"

If, judging by that last sentence, Boyd was truly concerned about other brands muscling into Pepsi territory, he needn't have worried. When the Pepsi marketing team blanketed an area for merchandising, the men still had the field to themselves. And with Steele's enthusiasm for spending one dollar to make two, Boyd was permitted to hire more men. Candidates' résumés were beginning to show more sales experience and more study at major universities than earlier ones. The profiles of the current team also took on a more professional tone in the newest press releases. Gone was Britton's mysterious "war work of a confidential nature," he was now "H. Floyd Britton of Birmingham, a graduate of the University of Pittsburgh School of Business, former sales employee of Pabst Breweries and U.S. Steel." Watson's public-sector service was no longer mentioned. He was "David F. Watson of East Elmhurst, N.Y., a graduate of South Carolina State College and Atlanta School of Social Work, formerly an insurance sales manager."

The new hires for 1950 included the former sales manager of Joe Louis Punch. Harvey C. Russell finally sealed his future with the team when he and Boyd met on the boat of a mutual friend. It was still unusual to meet an African-American who knew the soft-drink industry and by the end of the trip Boyd knew that he had found a team member. Russell was made staff field coordinator and paid more than the others—a meager four thousand dollars.

Boyd also took on Baltimore native Frank L. Smith, a graduate of Fisk University and the University of Iowa, who was a counselor for the Veterans Administration. The third hire was another Harvard graduate, Paul D. Davis of Columbus, Georgia, who had sales experience in real estate and insurance.

With a newly expanded department of eight, Boyd finally was closer to the manpower and visibility that he had originally envisioned. As the salesmen started a Baltimore campaign, the *Afro American* newspaper touted their role at the Pepsi-Cola Company: "INTEGRATION AT WORK: PEPSI-COLA PERSONNEL HERE TO EXTOL DRINK." The team planned to blanket the area in "an intensive merchandising and sales campaign" for three weeks. They were still pushing the "More Bounce to the Ounce" slogan, but it was becoming less appealing to a public learning that extra calories add pounds. Two years into the Negro-market campaign, Pepsi-Cola had no new charities to trot out.

The men worked hard in Baltimore: three weeks of the usual drill of visiting churches, schools, fraternal meetings, social agencies, and community events. Then, suddenly, their main rival handed them a sales weapon more powerful than anything they could have planned. The June 26, 1950, issue of *Time* carried a brief article on a Georgian kingmaker running the reelection campaign of Governor Herman Talmadge, son of Gene Talmadge, the notorious white supremacist who had died immediately after his own reelection in 1946. At a campaign dinner, Coca-Cola president Robert Woodruff stood up and gave a toast to the younger Talmadge, in anticipation of what was clearly going to be a victory: "To the second-greatest governor, sired by the first greatest governor."

The second-greatest governor? This was the segregationist who tried to take over the governorship after his father died; the man who promised to pass educational requirements for voting at a time when only 20 percent of black Georgians had completed the sixth grade. This was the governor who was reported to have KKK leader Dr. Sam Green on his personal staff; who called civil rights legislation a communist conspiracy; who vowed never to integrate schools, over the protest of three hundred Southern university educators and students. This was the leader who infuriated African-American businessmen when he ordered the state real-estate commission to revoke the license of anyone who sold white-owned property to blacks, causing one African-American agent to lose his livelihood.

If Woodruff was merely trying to be gracious to his host while gaining a little political collateral, he ended up being unnecessarily provocative. Woodruff and Mack shared an industry and a political party; but while Mack was pragmatic in business and altruistic in his politics, Woodruff was the opposite—and it didn't always sit well with the public. The fact that Coke was so much a symbol of American culture only exaggerated the company's missteps.

The campaign manager, Roy Harris, told *Time* that with such big money behind his candidate, he wasn't worried about the black vote. The article printed his vulgar goading of activists: "The *niggers* are a little disgusted. They thought they were going to get equality and now they have found out they are not. Now you have to pay the preachers to get 'em out." And Harris didn't think it was worth the expense, the article continued.

Black business leaders gave an angry, highly charged response to Woodruff and his segregationist cronies the following month. They had the perfect forum: the convention of the National Negro Insurance Association, or NNIA, held in Los Angeles that year. The NNIA was a powerful business group. Under C. C. Spaulding its leadership had come to stand for promoting equal rights and fair employment, in the same vein as the NAACP or the Urban League. The business leaders didn't pull any punches.

The Pepsi team was ready to join forces for an all-out attack on the race front. It had plenty of time to get the conventioneers fired up and to help forge the response to Woodruff. The convention train from Chicago took five days to reach the West Coast, and two Pepsi-Cola representatives rode with participants, providing the refreshments. After they arrived at the convention, the team set up new life-size cardboard cutouts that Boyd had ordered up of two women—one black and one white, in starched-collared waitress uniforms—serving Pepsi. It made a good photo opportunity for the press. The face of the black model, pencil tucked into her cropped hair, was used frequently in future ads, smiling behind a large Pepsi bottle.

The salesmen took every opportunity to slam Coca-Cola's hiring policy as they saw it: Coca-Cola had vowed never to hire a black man above the job of janitor. There is no evidence that anyone at Coca-Cola headquarters ever actually stated such a policy, and, in fact, many Coca-Cola bottlers had given jobs to minorities. But no one could deny that headquarters did little to accommodate demands for fair hiring practices.

During the convention, keynote speaker Eugene M. Martin, secretary and first vice president of the Atlanta Life Insurance Company, urged the fifteen hundred delegates to join the economic fight for equality against "ruthless manufacturers who do not think of the race issue except in terms of economic benefit to themselves. They are not interested in democracy in America or abroad, but only in the new cheap raw materials they can obtain."

He ripped into the Southern power structure and the ethics of white businessmen, saying Herman Talmadge represented "the worst" in race relations. "How tragic," Martin continued, "that the president of a great firm like Coca-Cola should cast its lot with the worst enemy of Negroes when Negroes drink Coca-Cola all over the world. I dare say if all the Negroes in America knew that the Coca-Cola Company, through its chief officer, was helping to perpetuate in office one of their worst enemies, that the dividends of [the company] would feel the effect. . . . Herein lies the great tragedy of the race problem. Men like [Herman] Talmadge, [Strom] Thurmond, are maintained in office by firms who garner millions from Negroes and not only give them no jobs save those of menials, but often use these funds to promote and perpetuate in office men who would kill the forward march of practical democracy and keep Negroes as a people in a state of serfdom—or at most, second-class citizens."

Martin then asked business leaders, fraternities, and churches to band together and "withdraw support from firms who deny jobs save in servile capacities and whose officers are never seen in the councils of freedom and democracy, but who are well known in the councils of the Dixiecrats and other rapers of American and World Democracy."

His attack was called courageous by the black press, and fitting for a leader who was used to facing down racists in Georgia. African-American business leaders like Martin were at the center of the equal-rights movement and made no attempts to separate race and politics from their work.

The following week, attorney Ray W. Guild, former head of the Boston branch of the NAACP, entered the battle with a speech in which he described the Talmadge political machine as one supported in the North by some of Wall Street's leading businesses. "With one of Talmadge's chief money supporters being Coca-Cola tycoon Robert Woodruff, there must be a new and more vigorous organized effort to counteract such moves on the part of any big business," he said. "It's hard to believe that Coca-Cola, which followed our troops at a great profit to World [War] II . . . in their fight for freedom and equality for all peoples, can express itself as being opposed to equality for colored citizens in Georgia."

Guild urged consumers to use their economic power and align themselves "with those businesses which respect our purchasing power and give us equal employment opportunities throughout the nation."

If the language was harsh, the frustration of African-American civic leaders was deep. In 1950, it was still news when a black got a single corporate job. "CHASE BANK HIRES NEGRO" was a page-one story in the *Chicago Defender* in February, when a woman named Inez Smith was hired as assistant librarian in the bank's New York City headquarters. Even then, the event was announced by an official of the local Urban League, suggesting that outside pressure had played a part in her hiring.

Even Branch Rickey, the model of the progressive boss, couldn't seem to commit fully to the integration movement. At an awards dinner early in the year, the Brooklyn Dodgers general manager, responding to a question, affirmed that he'd be open to running for Congress in a Negro district. But he wanted it known that he would vote against the Fair Employment Practices Act, which black leaders were then trying to push through Congress. Instead, race problems should be solved "on a social level," he said. Black sports writers, meanwhile, had stopped writing effusive stories about the integration of sports. They noted that while black fans had flocked to the games, filling the coffers of sports franchises and bringing the Negro League to its knees, only a handful of black ballplayers had made it to the Major Leagues in the three years since Robinson and Doby broke the color line.

But another, more important, reason prompted the tough call to action by Eugene Martin that went far beyond the Talmadge-Woodruff fiasco or the usual frustrations of a businessman. The NNIA audience, like the African-American community at large, demanded strong leadership at that moment. There had been stunning news the preceding month. On June 5, 1950, the U.S. Supreme Court struck what was called the mightiest blow for freedom and full citizenship for African-Americans since the Civil War. In three separate decisions hours apart, the high court ruled:

• Segregation or discrimination against Negroes in railroad dining cars was illegal. The ruling in the case of Elmer W. Henderson reinforced "the stubbornly ignored Interstate Commerce Act that made it unlawful for railroads in interstate commerce to subject any person to undue or unreasonable prejudices or disadvantages whatsoever."
• Racial segregation in higher education was unconstitutional under the equal-protection clause of the Fourteenth Amendment. Herman M. Sweatt was ordered admitted to the law school of the University of Texas.
• G. W. McLaurin must be allowed to enter graduate school at the University of Oklahoma under the same constitutional protection.

The rulings, seen as a victory for the Truman administration, stopped short of the plaintiffs' demands to reexamine the whole doctrine of separate but equal. But it dealt a significant blow to Jim Crow. "The complete destruction of all enforced segregation is now in sight," declared Thurgood Marshall, special counsel for the NAACP.

As the beginning of the school year neared, the *Defender* published photos of smiling white classmates welcoming McLaurin into the University of Oklahoma under the headline "WE'RE GLAD YOU WON." Well-wishers were not in short supply, as white civic, business, and religious leaders lent their support. RCA president Frank M. Folsom announced that he backed a fair-employment law. More than a dozen restaurants in Washington, D.C., took down their segregation signs, and some segregated universities promised to open their doors to all. Tennis officials ruled that the talented Althea Gibson could play in the U.S. Open tournament. Monsignor Fulton J. Sheen, the popular radio cleric, preached that the purpose of the Catholic Church is "to lift people up from class hatred, from enmity, from bigotry, up to eternal life with God." Even the Metropolitan Life Insurance Company in New York City finally agreed to remove race barriers at its Stuyvesant Town apartment development after a long fight.

The Actors Equity Association came up with an idea to offer monetary incentives to hotels across the country that rejected segregation. It gave the designation "Equity hotel" to all operators who welcomed black actors, guaranteeing a show's entire cast, including its biggest stars, would stay there, giving these establishments free publicity.

As always, the backlash was immediate. This time, it came from lower-court judges who declared that segregation was still permitted in restaurants. So when Woodruff made his effusive toast to Talmadge after all that had just passed, the gesture had wider implications of supporting Jim Crow laws.

————

Riding high after the insurance convention, the team stayed on in Los Angeles for a six-week sales blitz. Boyd threw a lavish party, complete with a mariachi band, in a style that was much more welcome under Steele's tenure than under Mack's. The elegant party was held in his mother-in-law's home, where Edith Boyd's family had finally landed after being forced to move, after several lawsuits, from their newly purchased house in an affluent white area of Los Angeles. The party's purpose was to make contacts among local fraternity leaders who were prominent in the business community. It was a success.

Boyd, always delighted to be working on his home turf, took the team to the Bay Area for another four weeks. His ties to the state were played up in the papers. The media seemed to have renewed interest in the team's work and gave the campaigns big play, even if the articles consisted mainly of corporate press releases and photos produced at Pepsi-Cola headquarters. One widely circulated photo gave a rare look at the team sitting around a conference table in the New York offices. Dressed in white summer suits were Paul Davis, Harvey Russell, Charles Wilson, David Watson, Ed Boyd, secretary Norma White, Floyd Britton, Richard Hurt, and Frank L. Smith. The text described their sales efforts as a vital lesson in doing business in the "color market," one providing interested parties "an opportunity to witness a national firm, Pepsi-Cola, carry on an intensive merchandising and sales program using eight sepia national sales representatives."

While the Pepsi-Cola team was still touting the company-sponsored canteens for World War II soldiers, the men got the dubious assignment of helping to send off a new generation of fighters. Boyd and his men were part of the talent brought in to bid farewell on behalf of Pepsi-Cola to two thousand soldiers and more than five thousand of their guests from around Southern California. The Sixth Engineer Combat Group, an all-black unit comprised of the 1401st and 1402nd Engineer Combat battalions, was headed to Korea, where the "tan soldiers" were already distinguishing themselves in combat. "NEGRO GIS FIRST HEROES" read the early headlines from the front lines, as papers claimed that the first major U.S. victory of the war was won by black soldiers taking the city of Yechon. The euphoria was muted by the lingering insults of segregation stateside, particularly reports that minority trainees had to eat in the backyards of Southern restaurants while white soldiers ate in the dining rooms.

With more money available to develop markets, and the special impetus given the Negro-market team by Coca-Cola's blunder, Steele had allowed Boyd three more hires that summer. Boyd was looking for people with strong contacts in the upper Midwest, and another with experience in Texas and the Southwestern region. As usual, he put the word out through the National Urban League that he would be interviewing for one day only at Chicago's Sherman Hotel.

Boyd got one surprise in his new search. One of the first in line for an interview was Allen McKellar, who had been one of the two African-American Pepsi-Cola interns in 1940. Since leaving the company in 1943, he had done a stint in the army and then moved to his wife's hometown of Chicago. She worked as a teacher while McKellar continued his career in sales and public relations, becoming a salesman for the Pioneer Atlas Liquor Company, where he handled the most difficult accounts. A friend of McKellar's had called him from the local Urban League office to tell him about Boyd's interviews. He, in turn, called two friends, William E. Payne and Jean F. Emmons, both educated Chicago natives looking to jump-start their careers. Payne had attended North Carolina State College and the University of Iowa, and had worked with the USO, the National Youth Administration, and the City of Chicago Recreation Department. Emmons had graduated the year before from the University of Chicago, with a master's in business administration and a concentration in finance.

"Allen said, 'Hey, Jean, Pepsi-Cola is going to be in town, and they're interviewing for positions in marketing and merchandising,'" Emmons recalled. McKellar told them about his own history with Pepsi-Cola early in the decade, and Pepsi-Cola's longstanding commitment to the community.

"It seemed too good to be true; I couldn't believe I was finally getting a break," Emmons said.

Opportunities had been few for the six blacks in his class at the University of Chicago's business school. Neither the five men nor the lone woman had gotten a single job offer among them, despite the growing economy. "The white graduates from the department had multiple job offers," he recalled, "but no one even pretended they were considering us for employment. I came out and there were no offers. Nothing! Nothing! I didn't know what to do."

More frustrating, Emmons felt, was that even companies known to hire African-Americans, such as International Harvester, seemed mostly interested in recruiting at black colleges. "Very few African-ancestored Americans then had the credentials I had—very, very few," said Emmons, using his preferred term for black Americans. "If America had the proper conscience, I should have been recruited like they recruit pro ballplayers today, but America didn't consider black academic excellence, and that hasn't changed much today."

When the three men entered the large conference room at the Sherman Hotel, there were already about a dozen other candidates gathered. Boyd was sitting at a table with his secretary, Norma White.

One by one, the men were called forward for an interview. Emmons told Boyd about his work experience. After teaching finance for a year at Southern University in Louisiana, he had returned to Chicago, where he worked for the U.S. Employment Service, but he hated the depressing atmosphere. Emmons also recounted his sales experience, while an undergraduate, in the insurance industry. When Emmons explained that he had earned an MBA with honors, Boyd was impressed.

Boyd gave Emmons the usual brief description of the untapped ten-billion-dollar market, and how few companies were taking advantage of it. It wasn't a marketing issue taught at the University of Chicago or widely known in the community. But Emmons had begun reading about it in the black press, and he thought the recognition was long overdue.

After the morning interviews, Emmons, Payne, and McKellar had lunch together and, along with several others, were asked to return for second interviews. Boyd seemed to be moving quickly; he was preparing for the NNIA convention then and wasn't staying long in Chicago. By the end of the day, Boyd let the three know they were hired. In addition to having stellar résumés, they were already friends and so could work well together.

"My wife, everybody, was happy. It was a big deal," said Emmons. But before he even started at Pepsi-Cola, an unexpected conflict materialized. He was being considered for a management-training program at the Ford Motor Company in Chicago. Discussions with the company had just started. He was tempted—very tempted—to go with the giant car company because it seemed a more certain path to a career in management. Ford, like Pepsi-Cola, was committed to fairer hiring practices. But Pepsi-Cola was the first to make the offer, and that offer sounded excellent.

Pepsi-Cola would be the best of both worlds. It was a national brand, and he would be part of a whole group of African-American professionals, led by an African-American boss, and dealing directly with African-American consumers. Emmons spent his life moving easily between the sharply divided white and black worlds; but when it came to performance, he had found that the expectations and the challenges were greater when he worked for his own people. White professionals, he felt, sometimes expected, almost demanded, less of him because he was a black man.

———————

Jean Franklin Emmons was born July 11, 1924, in Chicago, the middle of three children. His father was a waiter from Knoxville, Tennessee, and his mother was a teacher from Alabama. Together, they represented the long span of migration from the South to Northern cities.

His father, John E. Emmons, had been a sergeant in World War I, where his duties were washing, cleaning, and moving supplies. While stationed in France, he taught himself French. His facility with that language enabled him to get jobs in top restaurants in New York City when he returned to the United States. Eventually, he made his way to the Chicago area, where his parents and siblings had migrated. John's father was a waiter as well, in the dining cars of railroad lines. The pay was poor but the tips afforded a relatively decent living.

In Chicago, John E. Emmons joined the Appomattox Club of middle-class black men, where everyone got to know everyone else. He was known for being always well dressed, in suits, ties, and shined shoes. If his French was less than perfect, his English was impeccable. He was a master of his craft in elegant dining rooms.

John Emmons taught his two sons and daughter that America was the land of opportunity and that a person could find a way to success, despite an unfair system. "You must take what you deserve," he told them. "If you do, you can be born a slave but die a prince." For the senior Emmons, part of that achievement was finding a cultured wife. He already knew he wanted to marry a teacher when he met Annarette Dudley, who taught school in Birmingham, Alabama. They were introduced by a friend in Chicago during one of her summers in the North. She attended classes at Columbia University in Manhattan to earn a teaching certificate.

Annarette was raised by a family focused on education. Her mother, Carrie, was the youngest of thirteen children, and the only one to be born in freedom. When Carrie and her husband split up, she became a nanny and sent Annarette to live with friends. The father of that household was the principal of the black high school in Birmingham. When Carrie retired, she moved in with Emmons's family. She lived to be over one hundred years old.

Emmons remembered his parents providing a comfortable life for the extended family. His mother gave up her career as a teacher to be a homemaker. Then the Depression came. "We went from prosperity to poverty overnight," Emmons said. The family started moving—six times in six years—and ended up on relief. "Once, we went to get a charity basket," Emmons said. "That was hard on my mother, who found it extremely difficult to adjust to the situation."

His mother started making money by taking in sewing. His father worked two or three jobs to keep the household together. He waited tables, washed dishes, swept floors—anything to stay afloat and anything to make life livable. He never seemed to despair. He had a favorite saying, "If corn goes to five dollars a grain, I'll still buy a bushel."

"In the worst of times, a man who thought like that found a way to make it," said Emmons. "My role models were my father and mother, no others."

But times were hard. Emmons remembered the children resorting to putting paper in their shoes when the soles gave out. Finally, the moving and the hard life came to an abrupt halt when World War I veterans were granted bonuses—something they had fought hard for over the previous years. In 1936, John Emmons took the money and bought a home on Chicago's South Side, so his family would never have to move again. They bought in a modest neighborhood so they could afford to make a showcase home: wall-to-wall carpeting, sunken tub, stainless-steel kitchen cabinets, washing machine, and an oil furnace with controls. Mrs. Emmons kept the house immaculate and made sure all her children knew how to take care of themselves.

Emmons attended a predominantly white elementary school where there were no black teachers. He liked the duality of living with blacks and going to school with whites. If he was teased in school, it was because his name was Jean, French for John but pronounced like the girl's name. "That name caused me a lot of trouble," said Emmons. "I fought all through elementary school."

His happiest time was when the school instituted a leadership program and he was elected mayor of the school by his classmates. "I won by a landslide—a black leader in a white school." His family was proud.

When it was time to go to high school, Emmons decided against the technical school and the white high school; he went to DuSable, named after Jean Baptiste DuSable, a Haitian who was the pioneer settler of Chicago. The student body was predominantly black, although the teaching and administrative staffs were about 70 percent white. Emmons took advantage of the extracurricular departments: Reserve Officers Training Corps, music, industrial arts, home economics, and theater.

He was thankful for his most demanding teachers. In the 1930s, even in the black schools, students were taught little about black history. Nevertheless, Emmons was introduced to W. E. B. DuBois, Langston Hughes, Frederick Douglass, and Booker T. Washington. He also read Cicero, Plato, and Virgil, and learned Latin, Spanish, and French. He did so well, he skipped a grade for the second time. He was bookish, intelligent, and somewhat aloof. "I was called arrogant, but I felt I was at ease with people; they just weren't at ease with me," Emmons said. "I didn't have a typical social life."

Emmons wanted desperately to participate in sports, but his teachers wouldn't permit it. He was a scholar, they said. At DuSable, students who showed promise were put on academic tracks. Looking back, Emmons was grateful he didn't attend a predominantly white school, where he might have been pegged as an athlete and, at six-foot-two and 170 pounds, pushed to excel in sports. When he couldn't join a team, he enrolled in ROTC, advancing to captain.

As disciplined as his school and the ROTC officers were, his home was more so. Emmons's mother insisted that all her children do chores in the morning and on weekends before they could play. She demanded good manners, too. Once, when she was watching Emmons play baseball in a vacant lot, she heard him swear at the pitcher. "I look over and there's Mother," Emmons said with a grimace. "She went out there onto the field, grabbed me, and beat me all the way home."

Emmons graduated in 1941, at the age of sixteen, but his family couldn't afford college, so he took a job washing dishes, working long hours for little pay. When the war escalated in Europe, Emmons got a lucky break. He got a job in a steel mill in Gary, Indiana. They were hiring relatives of workers and Emmons had an uncle there. The pay was good, forty hours for twenty-eight dollars; the Congress of Industrial Organizations had begun organizing the large plants, and blacks began to receive better treatment. He used his drive and tenacity to get promoted to head of a crew of black and white workers, and eventually earned close to two hundred dollars a week, he recalled. For three years, he got up at 5:00 AM, ate a big breakfast cooked by his mother, caught a train that took him into Gary at 6:30, and hopped on a bus that arrived at the mill at 7:15. Work started at 8:00, and "there was no such thing as late." Whenever he got laid off during the slow times, Emmons went to work in the city stockyards stacking boxes for the Campbell Soup Company or hauling beef for the Armour Food Company. The black workers, he said, would gather to carry four-hundred-pound loads of beef on their shoulders from the conveyor belt to the boxcar, while the white workers stood by taunting them: "Drop that and you'll lose your job."

Then it would be back to the mills.

Working in the steel mills was a mixed blessing. The pay was good, but the environment wore on his psyche. Some of the jobs were life-threatening, like those in the foul-smelling acid pits where steel was "cured." Others required working with red-hot sheets that occasionally went out of control, striking the worker and causing a loss of life or limb. Emmons couldn't get over how quickly the workers aged.

Then, in 1943, Emmons enlisted in the army. With his high-school

ROTC training, he expected to enter officer's training. He did well on his exams, one of which was for the signal corps, so he requested a naval officer's training assignment. But that was not to be. Nothing was easy for African-Americans in the segregated system. Emmons resisted the recruiter's assignments again and again. He was eventually drafted, but tested positive on a tuberculosis test and was designated 4F.

On his return to the mills, he had an epiphany. He had to go back to school. Emmons enrolled at Wilson Junior College, a community college near his South Side home. He did well, and two years later he started taking summer classes at Northwestern, later transferring to the University of Chicago, a better school that was closer to home. The tuition was difficult for the family to raise, so he worked three jobs: He mopped floors at night in a campus building, operated the elevator in the school library, and sold life and health insurance for a small, private company. "I always thought all work is honorable," he said.

Between work and school he had little time to socialize, or even to rest. Sometimes he'd take a blanket to work so he could catch a few hours of sleep in a corner before classes began. His grades started to slip. The dean of the school gave Emmons an ultimatum: quit the jobs or quit school. Emmons chose school, and his father promised to find a way to pay the bill.

Freed from the workload, Emmons was soon on the honors list and won a scholarship. In the summers, he worked as a dining-car waiter, like his father and grandfather before him. But the family tradition stopped with Emmons. He had none of his father's finesse, and was fired when he accidentally dumped a dish of spaghetti over a woman's fine dress. He became a "basket man," selling sandwiches to the passengers in coach. He learned how to supplement his pay by selling his own half-pints of liquor, shoelaces, toothbrushes, and sundries.

After three years at the university, he graduated with an MBA in June 1948. He felt he had done it on his own. He'd had no mentor, no one to take him under his wing, no guidance program. And he was too busy to cultivate many friends. As he prepared for graduation, he recalled some of his white classmates talking about their interviews:

"That corporation was great! Jean, tell us about your interviews."

"I didn't have one."

"What? What did you turn down?"

"I didn't even know you were interviewing, I was never called."

They couldn't believe it, and neither could Emmons. He went to see the head of placement, who told him that corporations didn't want to interview him. Feeling dejected, Emmons then went straight to the chancellor of the university, Robert Maynard Hutchins, who promised him that he would be interviewed. Emmons was called to the placement office, where he entered a private room and spoke with a company recruiter. But it was clear that everyone was just going through the motions. One company representative told him as much.

The one job he could get was, as usual, teaching. The dean of the school of business at Southern University in Baton Rouge, Louisiana, offered him a position, and he went to live and teach in the South for one academic year. The job gave him the financial means to marry his girlfriend, Ruth Elizabeth Yarber, the daughter of a Chicago dentist, who had graduated from the University of Illinois.

After one year he was ready to return to Chicago, where he hoped one of the many corporations that had their headquarters there would offer him a job. When they didn't, he took the job at the government employment office.

He had just quit that job to look for something better when McKellar suggested that he interview with Pepsi. Emmons credits Mack for the opportunity. "Walter Mack was a man of tremendous vision," he said. "Somehow, there occasionally emerges a person who challenges the status quo, even to his or her detriment, by insisting on the inclusion of others. Thank God for those people."

———————

It wasn't big news when, on September 17, 1950, Walter Mack resigned from the Pepsi-Cola Company. He had been fading into the background of Steele's leadership. After six months, Mack had found that the chairmanship "did not provide him with enough activity and he is therefore looking into new fields," the brief *Wall Street Journal* story stated. Mack said he would continue to advise the company. He made a point of adding that he would stay in business, but it was clear he had other things in mind. Just a week earlier, the Republican Party had put his name on the short list of candidates to run for mayor of New York City. *The New York Times* suggested that internal squabbles at Pepsi-Cola over policy may have hastened his departure from the company. Mack said only, "I stayed longer with Pepsi-Cola than I usually do in reorganizing companies."

It had been three years, almost to the day, since Mack had hired Boyd, and Boyd was uneasy about his mentor's departure. "I felt I was losing a friend," he said. Steele gave Boyd financial backing, but Boyd could see the new boss didn't share Mack's personal commitment to the team and wasn't likely to match his predecessor's involvement in black causes. Boyd also felt vulnerable because he knew some bottlers resented his lofty title of assistant manager and, as powerful members of the trade association with close ties to Steele, were a threat to his authority. And, as any of the team members could testify, Boyd had a way of escalating a conflict when he sensed he wasn't getting the respect he deserved. "Boyd stood his ground against bottlers, against the hierarchy, against whomever, and he had problems in that respect," Julian Nicholas said.

————————

Not long after Mack left, Boyd had to dismiss two team members. Britton and Smith were fired for letting their private lives intrude on their work. According to Boyd, he had a daytime meeting with Britton in a hotel during one of their sales campaigns and found that Britton was with a guest. Boyd never asked for an explanation, and Britton offered none. He left by mutual agreement, and there were no hard feelings. The two remained friends and Britton went on to other successes, keeping in close touch with Boyd long into his career. Smith was let go after he had an accident in a company car belonging to a bottler while driving a friend home after a late night.

In their place, Boyd hired a Minnesotan, William R. Simms, a 1949 graduate of the master's program in public relations at Boston University. He had an undergraduate degree from the University of Minnesota and had already launched a career in public relations, having worked for the American Council on Race Relations in Chicago.

————————

By the time Simms joined the team, the five-cent soft drink, *The Wall Street Journal* declared, was about to become "as rare as the whooping crane." The death of the nickel bottle had been prematurely announced before, but there was no going back at this point. By midyear, 55 percent of Pepsi bottlers sold the twelve-ounce bottle for more than a nickel, compared with 25 percent of all bottlers. Only Coca-Cola was demanding loyalty to the nickel price, aiming to demolish every remnant of Pepsi-Cola's "twice as much" claim.

This time, the public was more accepting of the increase. But complicating the pricing issue was the proliferation of vending machines. The machines required one-coin purchasing, and as much as bottlers wanted to leave the old price behind, they were hesitant to jump to a dime. One bottler taped two pennies to every bottle in his machines to make change for a dime, according to Frederick Allen in *Secret Formula*. Bottlers, in a remarkable show of their economic and cultural clout, began to insist the U.S. Treasury mint a new 7 1/2-cent coin. (The more pragmatic bottlers suggested a 6 1/4-cent coin to make it four to a quarter.) Even Woodruff began warming to the idea, and the movement gained steam. When *Fortune* wrote about Steele's new leadership at Pepsi, it concluded: "The biggest break he could get would be a 7 1/2-cent coin, minted by the U.S. Treasury. He can pray for it while he works."

The Treasury, of course, didn't budge, and the cola industry soon had a bigger headache than price to deal with when a Cornell University professor testified before Congress that the sugar in Coke caused cavities and the phosphoric acid was unhealthy. Clive M. McCay described how a tooth left in a glass of Coke would begin to dissolve in two days, an image that persisted for generations. Coke was portrayed as the culprit, but soft drinks in general got a black eye from health advocates. Edgar J. Forio, a top Coke lobbyist, railed against the "food faddists, Communists, crackpots, and the like." Coca-Cola got Harvard's School of Public Health to write an article, based on research funded by Coke for *McCall's* magazine, asserting that teenagers could improve their diets by drinking a Coke in the afternoon.

By the end of 1950, television had become the next big medium, and corporations scrambled to sponsor new shows while networks fought over talent. It was especially attractive to buy airtime because a sponsor's products were unabashedly promoted throughout a show— variety shows in particular. Steele, who shared many sensibilities with Mack where sales were concerned, decided to sponsor *The Faye Emerson Show,* renamed *Wonderful Town* after the actress jumped to ABC from CBS in December 1950. If Pepsi needed to bolster its image as a "class" drink for the sophisticated consumer, this shapely blonde pouring the drink into crystal goblets was the one to do it. Much was made of Emerson's sex appeal, with mainstream critics dismissing her as a pretty lightweight. But for the Negro market, her allure had another dimension. Emerson was the wife of Elliott Roosevelt, son of Eleanor and the late FDR and a Pepsi bottler. Readers of the *Chicago Defender* remembered her as being politically astute. In an interview with critic Lillian Scott for a series on "influential white Americans" and how they saw race issues, Emerson declared, "The greatest cancer in America is the race situation. It's un-American."

The glamorous star chosen to elevate Pepsi's image from the "bargain bottle" for blacks was embraced by Boyd and his advertising team. Emerson was chosen as the face on the TV screen in future Negro-market ads showing Pepsi drinkers relaxing at home.

Woodruff at Coca-Cola, always slow on the uptake but dead-on when he got there, saw the radio audience slipping and got Walt Disney to make his very first television appearance on Coca-Cola's Christmas Day special at the end of the year. But the effort stopped there. According to *Secret Formula,* Coca-Cola turned down sponsorship of a TV western. Television, Woodruff said, "wasn't a national medium."

The biggest help Steele ever gave to the team had nothing to do with race per se, but rather was something that he had brought with him from Coca-Cola: a belief in the value of intensive and formalized professional training. Under Steele, Boyd was given the means, the cooperation of the corporate hierarchy, and access to the company's buildings and grounds to organize a sophisticated training course for the team—part of a companywide training campaign that involved ten thousand employees. It underlined Steele's shift in emphasis from outlets and public-relations work to aiding the driver-salesmen working at the bottling plants.

The ten members of the national Negro-market sales team were given their own twelve-day seminar that began November 21. They were: Edward F. Boyd, David F. Watson, Charles E. Wilson, Richard L. Hurt, Paul F. Davis, Harvey C. Russell, William E. Payne, Jean F. Emmons, Allen L. McKellar, and William R. Simms.

Taken together, the lessons provided a fully rounded view of the business—the kind of information a future bottler might use, except the team members could entertain such dreams only if they had a white business partner to deal with the banks. Included in the courses were lectures on bottle, fountain, and vending sales; export; market research; sales promotion; corporate finance; advertising; product control; and various display techniques. Training also included working in bottling plants with the driver-salesmen—on their terms.

Sessions were held at the West Fifty-seventh Street headquarters, at the "world's largest bottling plant" in Long Island City, and at a New Jersey bottling plant. The seminar was done in a style that passed for business-casual in the 1950s. The program showed a drawing of a white saxophone player and illustrations of drum majors beating on Pepsi-Cola caps, under a rhyme that was unself-consciously corny: *Now's the time to give your all/Show you're really on the ball/No whit less than the very best/Like your Pepsi, pass the test.*

A dinner-dance was scheduled for the weekend, midway through classes, at the Starlight Room in the Waldorf-Astoria Hotel. The RSVP card read: "Naturally you can expect me at the Waldorf on December 1. Where else would I be? I wouldn't miss it for anything. By the way, reserve me a portion of: Roast Prime Ribs of Beef au jus; Lobster Thermidor or Piscatorial Perfection Supreme . . . (Halibut, to you, bub) and all the fixings.

"I hereby solemnly promise to come to the Pepsi-Cola whoop-dee-do and have myself the best damn time I know how to have, because I know there's no time like the pleasant."

The workload was also in the style of the day, and moved at a leisurely pace until the hands-on experience speeded things up. Mr. Boyd spoke first, giving basic information on employee benefits, and Al Steele closed the first day's session. After that, various speakers accepted the invitation to address the Negro-market department. Friend of the team Henry McGovern, assistant vice president, identified operational problems; Biow advertising-agency representatives J. Fulghum and Robert Braun gave their view on ads. After the team screened sales-training films, the veteran members lectured the newcomers. Their topics were perfectly suited to their personalities: David Watson spoke on "The Case for Friendship," Charles Wilson called his talk "Doin' It Naturally," and Harvey Russell spoke on "Doorways to Dollars."

The team spent the better part of one day at the Long Island City plant, where chemist and flavor specialist Tommy Elmezzi, by then a vice president, explained everything but the formula. The following week, every man on the team donned overalls to spend three days with a route salesman on a truck at the New Brunswick, New Jersey, plant starting at 7:00 AM. On the final day, Watson and his wife invited the staff and their wives to a party at their home in Queens.

The move toward training came at the right time, when many big businesses were targeted by tenacious activists determined to do more to put money and opportunity into the hands of those it took money from. The NAACP and other like-minded organizations continued to attack employment discrimination. Their method was to file a complaint of unequal hiring practices against a company, then have area blacks line up to hand in their job applications. In June, for example, the *Defender* put out a call on behalf of the NAACP asking "Harlemites" to apply for jobs with four major radio and television companies denounced for their "intentional or unintentional discrimination" in hiring. In the Midwest, the National Urban League got brewers to hire twenty-five blacks on the production lines of three big companies: Pabst, Blatz, and Schlitz. The *Defender* reported that "Negro salesmen have been employed for years by the breweries, but the production line was traditionally considered the restricted domain of white workers." That victory paved the way for the Harlem Trade Union Council to pressure seven New York brewers to start hiring African-Americans. "There are ten thousand workers in NYC breweries and not one Negro except a few in the distributing field," said a council spokesperson, adding that the electrical industry would be the next target. Others were seeing to it that the National Association of Real Estate Boards would finally end its Jim Crow membership policy.

All these victories in fair-hiring policies allowed James A. "Billboard" Jackson to cap his unique career with an announcement that "a big gap between Negro and white business training" was being filled by the establishment at Howard University of a student unit of the American Marketing Association. Jackson had become one of the first two black members of the group years before, after he started working as a sales representative for Esso in the late 1930s. There were about fifty AMA units on U.S. campuses promoting research and the business of advertising and publicity, but Howard's was the first at a historically black college.

It came as something as a shock, then, when four months after Woodruff was so soundly attacked for toasting Governor Talmadge, another Coca-Cola official stepped into another minefield. In November, James A. Farley, head of Coca-Cola Export and a former postmaster general, called for President Truman to rein in his civil rights efforts. His criticism of the Truman administration was made in a Tampa speech to the Florida Chamber of Commerce during the president's visit to the South.

This time the reaction by black leadership was more direct and immediate, and a boycott was called with the aim "to so cripple Coca-Cola's sales in Negro areas that executives of the world's biggest soda corporation will gladly follow the principle of fair employment," according to the Harlem-based National Fair Play Committee, which led the effort. Judge Charles E. Toney, head of the committee, said he expected the growing boycott to win more white-collar jobs for blacks across the state, and that a major victory was expected by March 15, the start of the main selling season for soft drinks. The judge said he was stepping down from his post at the end of the year and seemed ready to make the boycott his retirement hobby.

Allen McKellar saved press releases from the committee's headquarters. Coca-Cola's "lily-white hiring policy" was unfair to New York State's nine hundred thousand Negro consumers, one said. The action was aimed at the New York Coca-Cola bottler, but the committee sought nationwide support. "We'll hit them where it hurts," added Herbert L. Bruce, committee executive "It's going to take time, money, and lots of hard work but we'll win eventually because the fight for fair play represents justice, truth, and honesty."

The first action was taken by cosmetics maven Rose Morgan, vice chairman of the committee, who said sarcastically that she appreciated the installation and maintenance of Coke vending machines in her four House of Beauty salons, but that "the public has demanded [their] removal."

In another press release, datelined Los Angeles, the committee said *Spotlight News* had drummed up support for the boycott on the West Coast through a month-long series of articles. One lawyer said the entire group of national Negro salesmen, calling themselves "the

Marketing Pioneers

Pepsi-Cola's Negro-market sales team at its peak in 1951. The men broke through corporate color barriers while helping to define niche marketing. From left: William R. Simms, Paul D. Davis, William E. Payne, Richard L. Hurt, department manager Edward F. Boyd, Allen L. McKellar, an unidentified bottler, Julian C. Nicholas, Harvey C. Russell, Winston C. Wright, Charles E. Wilson, Jean F. Emmons, and David F. Watson. (BOYD COLLECTION)

Opening Doors

Pepsi president Walter S. Mack (right), congratulating Allen McKellar, winner of an essay contest and a one-year job. (McKELLAR COLLECTION)

The internship program, called a business first, drew First Lady Eleanor Roosevelt and (right of her) New York mayor Fiorello LaGuardia to its inauguration in July 1940. Jeanette Maund, (right of the mayor) won the second seat open to a minority. (UNIDENTIFIED NEWSPAPER)

Creating a Team

Herman T. Smith (right), Pepsi-Cola's first African-American salesman, led a promotional campaign in black communities across America, with McKellar (left) and a growing number of regional representatives. (McKELLAR COLLECTION)

Winning Fans

Jazz musician Lionel Hampton, on vibraphones, plugs Pepsi for McKellar (far left) as fans make the Double V sign, symbolizing victory for democracy in the war abroad and for equal rights at home. Salesmen (right) often drove bottlers' cars emblazoned with the Pepsi logo. (McKELLAR COLLECTION)

Edward Boyd (second right) was hired in September 1947 to build a full-scale national special-markets department, after it had faltered during the war. Julius Thomas of the National Urban League (with papers) helped train new hires (from left) Alexander L. Jackson, Harold W. Woodruff, H. Floyd Britton, and David Watson. (*MODERN INDUSTRY*)

By the time the team met for a 1950 meeting at Manhattan headquarters (below), the department had expanded to ten polished professionals, including (from left) Chuck Wilson, Jean Emmons, Bill Payne, Bill Simms, David Watson, Ed Boyd, secretary Norma Bowler White, return salesman Allen McKellar, Richard Hurt, Harvey Russell, and Frank L. Smith. (BOYD COLLECTION)

On the Road

Ed Boyd spreading the word about Pepsi's new Negro-market strategy to the San Francisco Links club, a church, and one bottler's driver-salesmen force, on a grueling schedule that took the team to every corner of America. Segregation laws at the time made the men dependent on local groups for food and lodging. (BOYD COLLECTION)

Inside and outside the office, Pepsi employees generally embraced Boyd (second from left, standing) and his team, which by 1949 included former journalist Richard Hurt (center, with mustache). (BOYD COLLECTION)

Ed Boyd (standing) and David Watson (seated) touted double-digit increases in sales in regions targeted by the team, as Pepsi plant owners from Egypt to Virginia listened at the 1951 bottlers' convention in Chicago. (BOYD COLLECTION)

Say Pepsi, Please

Ed Boyd hosts a party in his in-law's Los Angeles home to introduce Pepsi and his team to national fraternal organizations. (BOYD COLLECTION)

The Good Life

The team rests at the home of entertainment entrepreneur Edward Atkinson (holding papers) in Los Angeles. (BOYD COLLECTION)

Hits the Spot

The success of the team in the Norfolk area made them welcome visitors at the local bottling plant. (PEPSICO)

COCA-COLA
Discriminates

Omaha Coca-Cola Bottling Co. Has Refused to Hire Negroes Regardless of Their Abilities.

This Is A Complete Denial of the American Ideal of Freedom of Opportunity.

Refuse to Support Discrimination
DON'T BUY COKE

Distributed by Omaha DePorres Club

Cola Color Wars

A flyer calls for a boycott (left) after Coca-Cola president Robert Woodruff publicly praised Georgia's segregationist governor. The action spurred the Pepsi team to make a strong showing at the July 1950 National Negro Insurance Association conference (right), where group leaders blasted big business for supporting racist institutions. (BOYD COLLECTION; *THE CALIFORNIA EAGLE*)

"That means mission successful—ice the Pepsi-Cola."

Selling Stereotypes

Pepsi-Cola, despite its diversity policy, was among companies using condescending images of blacks to sell products, as in this 1944 ad. (*TIME*)

A New Point of View

United Nations diplomat Ralph J. Bunche, the first of many prominent, living men and women profiled in Boyd's innovative advertising series, starting in April 1948 for black newspapers. (BOYD COLLECTION)

LEADER IN HIS FIELD

Dr. Ralph J. Bunche — Top-ranking Director, Department of Trusteeship, United Nations Organization; Acting Mediator for Palestine; former U. S. Commissioner, Caribbean Commission; and Associate Chief, Division of Dependent Area Affairs, U. S. State Department. Shortly to receive the Spingarn Award for Outstanding Achievement at the Annual Convention of the National Association for the Advancement of Colored People.

LEADER IN ITS FIELD

1. FOR QUALITY—Quality always has been Pepsi-Cola's keynote . . . unswerving standards of quality that govern the making of Pepsi, from the original ingredients through every step of blending and bottling.

2. FOR FLAVOR—There's just one way you can really judge a flavor, and that's to try it. Try Pepsi-Cola. We're sure you'll make it your favorite drink.

3. FOR SIZE—Naturally you want more for your money. That's just good sense. And every big bottle of Pepsi-Cola holds not 6, not 8 but 12 full ounces. Compare that with ordinary soft drinks. Pepsi is the best buy—the best value.

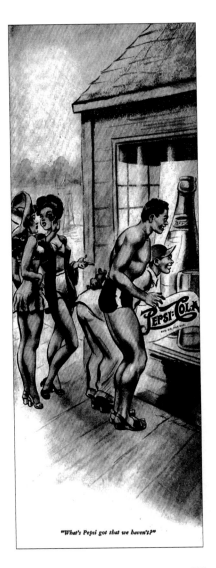

"What's Pepsi got that we haven't?"

"Now, I'm sure this is the right address!"

Hip and Sassy

Award-winning African-American political cartoonist Jay Jackson created a five-part Pepsi ad series for black magazines in late 1948. (*EBONY*)

In the Stores

Point-of-sale pieces punched up the special-markets campaign, and Pepsi-Cola hired some of the first professional black models, such as the popular Sylvia Fitt (above, left), who posed for this family tableau. To the crew, Boyd added a precocious young family friend, Ronald H. Brown, future U.S. secretary of commerce for the Clinton administration. (BOYD COLLECTION)

Salute to Students

A series of six magazine ads in 1949 introduced notable black students attending college. (*EBONY*)

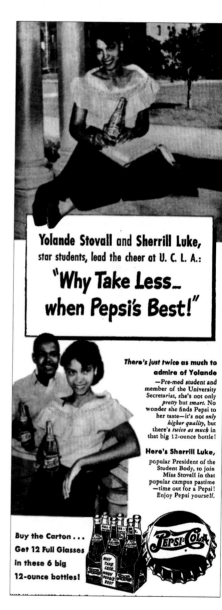

The often-used ad of a waitress (above) was falling out of favor in the early 1950s, as Pepsi's new president, Alfred N. Steele, focused on images (below) of young, affluent consumers. (BOYD COLLECTION)

More Bounce

This 1951 ad proof is one of a brief series, left partly unpublished as the team broke up, depicting the black middle class enjoying the American Dream. (BOYD COLLECTION)

A Fifties Update

Famous photographer Gordon Parks launched the final redesign of the "Leaders in Their Fields" campaign, which had become so popular that thousands of reprints were requested by schools and universities for use in classes. (BOYD COLLECTION)

Allen McKellar (above) hands out free Pepsi to Shriners, as the scattering of the team to regional offices, and subsequent dismissal of Ed Boyd, pushed the salesmen toward independent efforts. (McKELLAR COLLECTION)

Team veteran Julian Nicholas (below, left) works a promotion with Sam Hall (far right in bow tie), hired in 1955 as the first special-markets manager in the Philadelphia plant, ushering in the next generation of professionals. (SAM HALL COLLECTION)

MARKETING KNOW-HOW IS THE TRADEMARK OF NEW VICE PREXY

"NEGRO advancement in American business is an evolutionary thing," says Harvey Russell, Pepsi-Cola vice-president whose marketing know-how has become his trademark. "In 1945 you could count the companies with one or two Negro representatives on one hand; soon practically all companies had one or two. Now there's been a breakthrough toward the executive level. The next step is to appoint officers not in direct connection with the Negro market."

In the Negro market per se, business has also been laggard Russell states: "Very few companies have Negro marketing programs overall. Even in the soft drinks, tobacco and alcoholic beverages lines where there is more consciousness of the Negro, there is nowhere near an adequate program yet. In the past few years, however, the Negro has become a more sophisticated consumer and purchaser and this will be felt. It won't be long until no major market will be able to operate successfully without advertising and employment policies that include Negroes."

At the same time, however, he advises young Negroes that a marketing career will be open only to well trained young people willing to start at the bottom, and work up, learning as they go. Tartly, he declares: "You can no longer get a job on the basis of the 'twenty billion dollar Negro market' without knowing anything about marketing." At Pepsi, he has handled many company-wide, non-racial assignments including campaign for acceptance of firm's new 28 ounce bottle.

He believes full equality for Negroes will benefit American business as well as Negroes but sticks to marketing on his travels in the south, and does not discuss integration. "There are no moral issues here," he says. "This is a business entirely. We are devising ways and means of making as many potential Pepsi-Cola customers into actual customers as we can. This is what marketing consists of—a coordinated approach of advertising and promotion to build sales."

On corner before home office building, Russell commutes daily from Yonkers home. He has logged more than 25,000 miles a year visiting bottlers, coordinating participation in conventions. Ex-blitz star Jean Cleveland Steele is on Pepsi board.

Passing during national ad campaign talk with Ben Wright, Johnson Publishing Co., ad salesman, Russell accepts a light.

In research department, Russell secures material for speech from Frances Berkmeyer, field director of market research.

Discussing an advertising campaign, Russell (r.) makes point to advertising director Philip Hinerfeld, a vice-president (L.) and John J. Boughan, director of marketing services (also a vice-president and Russell's immediate boss) in company offices.

Planning special markets ad campaign, Russell meets with Batten, Barton, Durstine & Osborn, Inc., ad men: (L. to r.) Dick Pickens, Spanish language market specialist, Tom Sims, market specialist, Russell, and Bill Brown, account executive, at BBD&O.

34

A Corner Office

The Pepsi-Cola Company shook the business world in January 1962 when it named Harvey C. Russell as the first African-American vice-president of a major corporation. (*EBONY*)

Still Obstacles

Flyers (left) handed out by the Ku Klux Klan in the hundreds of thousands wrongly identify Russell's wife, Jacqueline, as white. Attacks got personal as Russell rose through the ranks. (HARVEY RUSSELL COLLECTION)

Below Picture of Negro Vice President Of Pepsi-Cola, At Left, And His White Wife, In Center

Pepsi Cola vice president negro Harvey Russell and wife Jackie give citation to one of company's salesmen, Bob Logan (right).

Let The Pepsi People Know What You Think Of Their Vice President And His White Wife

Leaving a Legacy

David Watson (far right) stayed with Pepsi-Cola for about thirty years, until his retirement in the late 1970s. The legacy of the Negro-market team was evident in the number of minority hires gathered on behalf of the company, by then known as PepsiCo. Inc., for an annual, national special-markets meeting. (SAM HALL COLLECTION)

Hucksters," would help put pressure on Coca-Cola to do more minority hiring.

The committee claimed to have investigated Coca-Cola's hiring policy and found that the Coca-Cola Company of New York "does not hire a single Negro salesman, distributor, clerk or stenographer. . . . When a Jim Farley tells a group of employers in Florida that fair play and the fight for justice should be abandoned because the South is threatened, he was simply reflecting the attitude of the company which employs him. That demonstrates how big business is frequently used to smother the political and economic aspirations of minority groups."

The committee warned that other jobs would be sought at other soft-drink companies after the drive against Coca-Cola. "What's the use of counseling Negro boys and girls to study salesmanship, marketing, stenography, and advertising if there's no opportunity for them to have and hold jobs in private industry?" the group complained. It was also frustrated, it said, that the city's big daily newspapers hadn't covered the boycott over the previous weeks.

Even without the coverage in the mainstream press, the word spread. Boyd kept a flyer from Nebraska, where Watson had just finished a month-long campaign. It was distributed by the Omaha DePorres Club, named for the first black saint, newly canonized. The flyer read: "COCA-COLA DISCRIMINATES. The Omaha Coca-Cola Bottling Co. has Refused to Hire Negroes Regardless of Their Abilities. This Is a Complete Denial of the American Ideal of Freedom of Opportunity. Refuse to Support Discrimination . . . *DON'T BUY COKE.*"

— Chapter Seven —

The View from the Threshold

GIANT COCA-COLA CERTAINLY COULD WEATHER A BOYCOTT by the African-American population, but individual bottlers were beginning to feel the impact. When some of the Pepsi team arrived in Wilmington, North Carolina, for a promotional campaign, they got wind of a counterboycott against Pepsi-Cola being spread in the region.

"What was the boycott about?" Harvey Russell asked rhetorically. "We were pretty sure the Other Bottler had dropped this bit of gossip that a Negro working in the plant had fallen into the syrup tank and died."

The fact that a black man was the subject of the rumor told the men that the lie was retaliation for their using race as a sales weapon. "To prove this wasn't true," Russell said with a smile, "we decided that I was going to walk around with a sign that said: 'I didn't die!'"

The sales team was enjoying the battle, but it didn't share the fun with company management. Boyd never talked to Steele about the boycott or his strategy for capitalizing on Woodruff's blunders. To Boyd, it was all part of his mission to build Pepsi sales, and he knew Steele had little patience for details.

Finally, Coca-Cola relented. On January 20, 1951, the company placed ads in the black weeklies for Coke—nearly three years after its rival. It didn't go so far as to put blacks in the ads, but it did make frequent placements. The first one, as it appeared in the *Chicago Defender,* showed a close-up drawing of a white woman's nose and mouth getting ready to take a sip from a bottle. "Ice-cold Coke is a part of any pause . . . the refreshing part." The price, five cents, appeared prominently in the ad. Ironically, despite its reputation for having given Pepsi a bargain-basement image, no ad from the Pepsi Negro-market team had ever mentioned price. But Coke was publicizing its ability to hold the price to a nickel.

When the Coke ads began running, former Woodruff publicist and adviser Ralph Hayes wrote a frank memo to his boss, stating that the company had been "too timid in integrating and upgrading Jewish people and colored ones in the Company's organization," according to *Secret Formula.* By May, the New York Coca-Cola plant had hired its first black salesman, Fred Graham. Internal letters suggest some Coca-Cola officers had been discussing race relations at least since after World War II. But the boycott seems to have helped push Woodruff to take action on behalf of blacks beyond his occasional charity work. Press reports show that Woodruff also joined the board of the Tuskegee Institute at the time of the race controversy in late 1950. That might have been where Coca-Cola officers finally got the word that the U.S. Negro market was the size of the population of Canada. The National Negro Business League held its fiftieth-anniversary conference at Tuskegee in September 1950, and a conference speaker made note of the comparative markets. If the Business League seemed a bit late to the table, it promised to take a more proactive role in 1951 with the opening of an office in Washington, D.C., to support much-needed research into black business and marketing.

The boycott had put the team back in the headlines and had given the salesmen a gravitas and sense of purpose they hadn't enjoyed since the team's inception. Boyd waited for the holiday season to pass, then exploited the renewed attention with the launch of a solid, year-long national promotional campaign. The *Chicago Defender* ran a front-page photo of the team in its first edition of 1951. The men were pictured gathered at a conference table after having finished their "intensive sales orientation program" in preparation for what would be their biggest, longest on-the-road effort yet as a united team.

The winter training program had also elevated the team's public standing. Boyd continued to tout it as giving the salesmen an education on a par with a business-school course. PEPSI-COLA TRAINS RACE EMPLOYEES was the large headline in the *New Tribune* on January 13. The story stated: "This marks the first instance in the soft beverage field that Negroes have been given an opportunity to obtain the entire fundamentals of the bottling industry." The training was just the sort of experience that the National Urban League and the NAACP had prodded corporations to offer to young, African-American professionals. It showed that Steele, though not as aware as his predecessor of race issues, nevertheless gave the team the same access to employment training as everyone else, and that suited the black community just as well. And Boyd knew how to implement his boss's demands to the greatest benefit of his team as well as for the greater good. Said Wilson: "I knew a lot of guys in the Urban League. They came in with established guidelines and approaches in their mission. It's: How do we improve race relations? How do we get industry to employ? How do we get foundations to give? And it goes on and on. Ed [Boyd] came out of that mold."

The newspaper coverage of the training program was timed for the day before the opening of a four-day annual national convention of Pepsi-Cola bottlers in Chicago. Boyd didn't have to worry about a walkout at the 1951 bottlers' convention. The Negro market wasn't mentioned in the company program, which was filled with the usual discussions of costs, equipment, exports, and national sales. Boyd, however, was given a large exhibition space. He used four partitions to form a spacious corner furnished with café tables, steel chairs, and the metal standing ashtrays ubiquitous at the time. He decorated them with a sign that ran along the top border: "THE NEGRO MARKET . . . IS EVERY TENTH AMERICAN CONSUMER." Smaller signs read: "THIS IS WHAT HAPPENED IN LOUISVILLE, KY . . . 13% INCREASE AMONG ACCOUNTS CALLED." And "VAST, FERTILE, RESPONSIVE . . . BUT UNEXPLORED . . ." Boyd divided exhibit posters into three markets: Youth and Colleges, Social and Civic, and Conventions. The life-size cutout of the black waitress stood among several small pyramids of Pepsi six-packs. Photos taken at the time show Boyd hosting Walter White of the NAACP, and Watson fielding questions from a group of bottlers.

One partition carried a line of national flags and a Pepsi logo written in Arabic script. The black press was intrigued by this newer aspect of the team's domain, and ran a large photo of Boyd with the Cairo bottler exchanging "pertinent facts concerning the soft-drink field in Egypt." Boyd was also pictured with bottlers from Waco, Texas, and Tulsa, Oklahoma. One candid photo taken at the evening festivities is a rare picture of Boyd smiling as he mingled with plant owners and members of his staff. The photographer for these events was usually team member Paul Davis, who had a talent for packaging photos for press consumption.

Boyd also recalled seeing for the first time Joan Crawford, the Hollywood star who would become the wife of Al Steele four years later. Bottlers met with Steele and his management team to talk about problems at the plant—from basic sales strategy to the smallest point-of-sale ad displays—and hash out some solutions. It drove the message home that he wanted a closer relationship with plant managers.

As soon as the convention was over, Boyd gathered the men in New

York to prepare them for the coming campaign. Whenever these road warriors spent time at headquarters, they couldn't help but notice the pace of the work there. One thing was certain: Employees in the white corporate world sure had it easy. Living, as the men did, in communities where they knew former slaves and saw most men and women, and many children, doing thankless, backbreaking jobs for little pay, the routine in Manhattan seemed ideal. It was a revelation to most of the men. They were supposed to be in the office at 10:00, so they arrived at 9:15, Emmons remembered. They would sit around a table, and executives would come in to chat. About 10:30, a shoeshine boy came around to shine their shoes. Then they'd have coffee and rolls. Shortly after that, they'd go to lunch, and in those days, when men had a business lunch, they drank. Meetings would eat up hours in the afternoon. The equation was clear as never before: More education equaled more money for jobs that required less work.

Emmons recalled that every manager he met in the office seemed impressed by the team's work and made each member feel appreciated. "You felt good, walking on cloud nine," he recalled.

Whenever they were in the city the men loved working the Harlem route. It was a lively place with countless clubs and stores lining the streets, and personalities from every walk of life. Wilson recalled how he'd walk into one store with a hearty "Hello!"

"Father is still divine," the owner would respond, incongruously.

Father Divine was a minister whose followers would affirm his standing as a deity with every greeting. He was loved for the free meals and clean rooms he gave to anyone in need. In October 1949, Father Divine and a group of his flock reportedly walked through the crowded streets of Newark carrying half a million dollars in small bills in eight suitcases to buy the Riviera Hotel.

Once, Wilson said, Boyd asked for a sweep from 110th Street all the way up to the Bronx to gain new customers, ahead of a new Pepsi plant opening in the city. Wilson took charge of the clipboard and checked off the number of stores, shoeshine parlors, bodegas, and the like, that sold or might sell Pepsi. The accounting took several days, after which they made some calls and passed the information along to the drivers. "We had on overcoats and suits," Wilson said. At the first big store they finally went into, the men introduced themselves as Pepsi salesmen.

"A choir responded to us: 'Oh, you S.O.B.s! You've been coming up here and we thought you were the feds. We haven't been able to run the numbers for a week!' " Gambling was at an all-time high then, newspapers reported, and police had promised to crack down.

———

Those kinds of experiences, the welcoming public, and their particular place on the front lines of the cola wars turned most of Boyd's men into Pepsi fanatics. "When I'd go down Broadway in Manhattan and see the big Pepsi sign there, or see the big sign across the East River, I'd salute," said Wilson. "Pepsi had that influence on me."

Said Emmons: "All of my friends had to buy Pepsi. I kept stockpiles of Pepsi in my house. All the places I went had to have Pepsi. If I was out with someone and they ordered Coke, I might have thrown a glass of water in their face. I was a son of a gun. If I went to someone's house and they gave me Coke, I'd say, 'How could you pull out that Coke in front of *me?*' My wife would say, 'I think you're going crazy—Pepsi, Pepsi, Pepsi!' "

The family of David Watson remembered the same. "If you had a Coke in the house, you had to hide it when he was around or he'd ream you out," said his niece, Savannah Potter-Miller. "You couldn't even say the name or he'd stop the conversation at the dinner table."

"Loyalty was the difference between then and now," Russell added.

"You developed a loyalty to the product and the company. You just had that feeling that you support the company and support the product."

Their preoccupation was an extension of their routine on the road, where each member had to live and breathe Pepsi. At every opportunity, they had to get their message across. "Every picnic, every party, every bar, every church, every wedding, every social—Pepsi, Pepsi," said Emmons. "You had to see that it was there. You had to know the top, middle, and bottom preachers. You had to know the top, middle, and bottom doctors. You had to know the top undertaker, the big numbers men. All of these people of influence you had to deal with. You had to work the market at all levels to see the product was recognized and accepted, and put in places where it could be delivered."

The men were pumped up for the long campaign ahead, ready to cut a wide swath across the Southern states. A photo in the March 10 issue of the Raleigh *Carolinian* shows a cheerful group dressed in suits, topcoats, and fedoras. "PEPSI-COLA SALESMEN TAKE TO THE ROAD," the headline announced. Another article suggested just how grueling the campaign would be as they prepared their first phase: to "blanket the state of North Carolina," with visits to the counties of Chatham, Orange, Pearson, Johnston, Warren, Granville, Vance, Franklin, Wake, Durham, and Lee, and the cities of Durham, Raleigh, and Henderson.

By March 24, the team was already declaring its initial efforts a success. "In the most elaborate and spectacular banquet and cocktail party given in this area, the Durham Business and Professional Chain presented the members of the National Sales Staff of the Pepsi-Cola Company to the merchants and community leaders of Durham," read the story in the *Carolinian*. More than 150 attended.

Creating a sense of urgency, Boyd told the press that he had cut short his engagement in Nashville, where he was the featured speaker at a three-day session of the Industrial Relations Conference of the

National Urban League, to be with his team. In Durham, he shared his views on the role of black salesmen in corporations. He called the work that his men did efficient and productive, and said the team was the "envy and topic of conversation in top merchandising circles in American 'big businesses.'" In turn, his career was called "brilliant." The *Carolinian* article continued: "Not only has Mr. Boyd been a pioneer in developing top sales jobs for national sales representatives, but also [for] local truck-driver salesmen."

It isn't clear whether Boyd mentioned his work with the truck-driver salesmen to impress Steele, who demanded a renewed focus on drivers as the cornerstone of sales, or to defend his territory against a boss who tended to take credit for himself. What is clear is that the publicity surrounding the team was ratcheted up a notch, giving the sense that the Pepsi salesmen were recognized as more than good role models and successful salesmen; they were community leaders.

Boyd had become more political in his approach to his job. He had gone from a policy of quietly confronting and correcting problems of discrimination on the road to filing lawsuits. He had one pending from a stay in the Bahamas the preceding year, when he was a guest of the Elks during one of their conventions. When he was kicked out of a hotel, he went to the U.S. consulate and, with the help of that office, initiated a local lawsuit. Wilson remembers that Boyd also gave the NAACP the green light Stateside to take another hotel's management to court on the team's behalf after yet another act of discrimination.

By the time Boyd arrived in Durham, he had hired two more team members. One was California native Winston C. Wright, an "All-American football star" from the University of Oregon, who had worked at the Federal Housing Authority and the Los Angeles Bureau of Public Assistance. The other was Julian C. Nicholas, originally from Washington, D.C., a student introduced to Boyd by Pepsi executive Herbert Barnet.

Nicholas was in his junior year at Pace College of Business Administration, now Pace University, in lower Manhattan. As president of the student Marketing Club, Nicholas was in charge of finding corporate executives for a monthly lecture series. In his search for "captains of industry," as he called them, he came across the name of Barnet, who was vice president of operations at Pepsi-Cola. Barnet agreed to talk to the students early in the year. In his speech, he described his job at the company and the type of candidates Pepsi-Cola was interested in hiring: graduates from good schools who were well prepared for business, much like the audience members themselves.

Barnet never mentioned Pepsi-Cola's experiment in special markets in his speech, but apparently it was on his mind while he was being introduced by Nicholas, a confident, mature, twenty-nine-year-old war veteran with a lilting Southern accent. After the talk, Nicholas, as part of his club duties, took the speaker to dinner. That evening, Barnet brought up the subject of Pepsi's sales effort in the African-American market and its hiring policy. Barnet mentioned that the market represented the highest "per-cap consumption" of Pepsi in the country.

Nicholas listened, nodding.

"Per cap," the student repeated to himself. He had no idea what it meant. And he didn't know much about cola drinks, either. His family of dentists, doctors, and intellectuals frowned on the craze for soda pop. "Don't drink soft drinks, drink milk," he was told. "Soft drinks are bad for your teeth."

Nicholas kept his thoughts to himself, of course. Instead, he regaled Barnet with tales of the considerable success of his family's businesses in the nation's capital. Barnet was impressed. He told Nicholas: "I wish you would come to Pepsi. We're trying to do more business in the

Negro market, and you're just the type we're looking for. There are some people I'd like you to meet."

They decided to meet ten days later, which gave Nicholas enough time to learn what *per capita* meant. He wished he had learned more about the company before he arrived at Pepsi-Cola's headquarters. But once inside, he chatted easily with another vice president, Cy Brockway, and then was introduced to Ed Boyd, the only African-American he saw there.

With Mack gone and Steele's culture fully entrenched, the Pepsi executives didn't emphasize the charitable aspects of Pepsi's presence in black communities. They talked dollars and production: where the hottest markets were and who had the best water for mixing Pepsi syrup. "It was all business. They didn't go into the social negatives and positives," Nicholas recalled. "Their business was selling drinks, and they made no bones about it."

Nicholas spoke the same language. Personal success was his primary concern then, he said. "When I heard the word 'national,' that got my attention," he said, echoing the reaction of others on the team. So did the appearance of Boyd's office, which proved to Nicholas that the company was serious about its commitment to the special team. "Boyd's office. Yeah. View of Fifth Avenue," said Nicholas with a smile and a nod. "They started that team off right."

Boyd saw in Nicholas a sincere and conscientious worker with impeccable Washington connections and a solid background in business, both by education and by upbringing. He offered him the job, but didn't pressure Nicholas to quit before his final year of school. Before Nicholas gave an answer to Pepsi-Cola, he did what he often did when facing an important decision: He sought the counsel of the elders of the family, knowing they were the sort of academics the black press was always criticizing for a lack of interest in business. It would be his last chance to change the direction of his career. "I went to Uncle Gene, a philosophy professor at Howard, and Uncle Harold, a history professor there, for advice on whether to go the doctor route or pursue this business route," Nicholas said. "They told me there was a new world coming and this was an area we have not been participating in that might open up, so there was nothing wrong with trying it."

With their permission, Nicholas gave his yes to the company on a Wednesday, and by Friday he was on a plane to Winston-Salem, North Carolina, to join the rest of the team. There, he found a friendly, competent group hard at work, and he was welcomed into the fold.

———————

Finally, Boyd had the twelve-member department he had worked so hard to build over three years, an impressive collection of education and professional know-how—"thoughtful experience," as Steele might have called it. The men were at the peak of their game, and they got there despite the danger, hardship, and obstacles on the road at that time, not to mention a change of regime and corporate culture at the company. The full team was photographed with Boyd and an unidentified bottler that spring, when it was at its peak: David F. Watson, Chuck E. Wilson, Harvey C. Russell, Richard L. Hurt, Allen L. McKellar, Jean F. Emmons, William E. Payne, Paul D. Davis, William R. Simms, Winston C. Wright, and Julian C. Nicholas.

A series of clippings from the weekly newspapers tracked their campaign on duty and off: On April 28, the Baltimore *Afro American* pictured McKellar with his colleague Winston Wright giving out Pepsi, promotional pencils, and literature to hundreds of people packed into the local Afro Cooking School. Three months later, the Houston *Reporter* showed McKellar and Hurt having breakfast in the city with other "hucksters . . . all pushing their wares," including Stokes Marshall of Budweiser, Ralph Ridley of Jax beer, and George Russell of Pabst. George was Harvey Russell's brother, who would later join Pepsi-Cola.

Emmons said of the long campaign: "I was always treated like the ambassador that I was."

Nicholas took detailed orders from Boyd: what he was going to do, where he would do it, which convention he had to service, and the amount of money he could promise local papers for advertising. When they were engaged in these full-staff campaigns, several members of the team would find themselves at the bigger gatherings, and they took turns speaking. For the smaller establishments and bars, the salesmen typically ventured in alone. But the message Nicholas understood was that above all else, he was to place as many vending machines as possible.

The cola industry wasn't the only one infatuated by the so-called silent salesmen. *The Wall Street Journal* reported that by late 1951, the number of vending machines had tripled from one million before the war, dispensing just gum, candy, nuts, cigarettes, and soft drinks, to three million, offering everything from ice cream and soup to a spritz of a dime's worth of expensive perfume. Factory managers were good customers, convinced that the food-and-drink machines made for happier workers. The *Journal* stated that the biggest vending-machine users—Hershey, Coke, Pepsi, Hires, and tobacco companies—reported an increase of up to 20 percent in vending-machine business in 1951, compared with 1950.

The machines were a particularly good way to reach into every corner of a bottler's territory. And they were effective weapons in the race wars because the men could use them to put a definite dent in Coke sales. Ever since the boycott, they would ask their most loyal outlet owners in subtle and not so subtle ways to replace Coke inventory with Pepsi—"get the red machine out," as they put it.

But Woodruff had poured enough money into black colleges to win their loyalty. Harvey Russell complained that some campuses, including those of Morehouse and Spelman, had refused to install Pepsi vending machines in light of Coca-Cola's largesse. "It was really just a dollars-and-cents thing," said Russell, and the bottom line won out over any political consideration.

Nicholas, like the other men, began his work in a territory with a quick market survey, recording the number of black schools, hospitals, retail outlets, and businesses. "They all had Coke machines—all of them," said Nicholas. "Even the black churches had vending machines, because they all had community centers."

Nicholas used whatever pitch would sell Pepsi. "I'd give them the race bit," he admitted. "Pepsi was headquartered in New York; Coke was headquartered in Atlanta; therefore, Coke was a cracker company."

That ploy worked: North Carolina Mutual Life Insurance and Atlanta Life Insurance replaced their Coke machines, he said. At first, they just took the Pepsi machines, too, but as he explained to the business manager that Coke still didn't have a black sales team, they would replace the red with the blue.

"Does Coke have any blacks?" he'd ask a potential client.

"No."

"Well, you see me here," he'd reply.

"I'll take ten cases," the manager would say. "I'll tell the Coke man to come get his damn machine."

Not everyone was that easy a sell, of course. Pepsi was second in everyone's mind, Emmons remembered, and Coca-Cola had the size and clout to command respect in a way that Pepsi could not. "I'm tired of this damn colored water," one gas station dealer told Emmons as he tried to hand him a Pepsi.

"But it wasn't 'damn colored water' with Coke," Emmons added.

Coke looked every bit like the success it was. It had bright, modern trucks and deliverymen dressed in the same uniforms, and acting as professional as they looked. They didn't have the backbreaking jobs Pepsi drivers had, hauling cases that were double the weight of their rival's because of the "twice as much" bottles. Inside the stores, Pepsi was also at a disadvantage because its big bottles took up too much room compared with its rival's. "If they were selling Coke, you wanted space right next to Coke. And you wouldn't want Coke to be at eye level and your drink at knee level. You'd try to reverse it, if possible," Emmons said. "All of these things are important in merchandising."

Race wars aside, the Pepsi team sometimes found the Coke driver-salesmen doing tricks such as wiping the Pepsi bottles with oily rags so they looked dirty. The men didn't despair. They had many victories. And if they had any competition among themselves, it was friendly. "We had pride among us," Wilson said. "If one would accomplish something or come up with a big sale, it was, 'Oh, man, what a sweet deal you pulled off.' "

McKellar agreed. "We were in the same market, but had our own prescribed territory. Everyone had to pull his own weight and do his best job to accomplish something for the day. In the evening, we'd look at our success stories."

During those evening sessions, new team member Bill Simms felt left out. "I'd listen to the other guys bragging at night about how they were able to talk to someone and flip to a deal," said Simms, flipping his hand palm-down in a quick gesture. "I was jealous—not because I didn't have a story, but because I knew I *never* would have a story."

From the start, he had felt the job wasn't quite right for him. He was always paired with a teammate, never achieving the level of independence that the others had. "I remember Allen [McKellar] in particular," he said. "Allen always impressed me as having very good background and experience. He handled himself well."

Even on a nonbusiness level, Simms never joined in on the men's stories. He never had any jokes about a cracker cop or bottler or any tales of fighting prejudice. He was on one end of Boyd's color "rainbow" and able to pass for white. "I must admit that many of the things that happened to *us*, never happened to *me*," he said.

Simms was adopted, as far as he knew, although in his day that wasn't spoken of—especially not to the adopted child. He isn't certain of his parentage or, frankly, even whether he actually is African-American. He doesn't know what informed him of his identity as a black person, except that his adoptive parents considered themselves black, and he has always lived in the black community.

Simms was African-American mostly by choice.

Some distant members of his light-skinned adoptive family tried marrying and living in the white world, and it never seemed to do anything but cause heartache, he thought, so he decided never to try that. He just didn't assert his identity at all, choosing instead to live a color-blind life. "Wherever I went, I was that. With Italians, they thought I was Italian. If I was with Jews, they thought I was Jewish. I had no problem with that," he said. Sometimes he would set them straight, and sometimes not.

For the official censuses he has had to fill out all his life, he has refused to check off any racial identity. "I never put in black; I don't know that I'm black; I don't know what I am," he said. "I put American. I'm an *American*."

———

William Redmond Simms was born on January 23, 1914, in New York City. Nearly ninety years later, he could recall the day he was adopted as a toddler. A woman came, took his hand, and walked him out the front door and onto a city sidewalk. The brownstone they had just left, he remembered, had a long cement shelf with bowls of custard cooling on it, though he couldn't see them and so wasn't sure how he knew the custard was there. All his life, he held that image of that first home—which he came to understand was in an adoption agency.

His new parents were Lena Watkins and David Simms, and his new home was an apartment over a grocery store. One day, his father took his mother and him to the train station and said goodbye, promising that he would send the boy his dog, named Pal, at a later date. He never did. That was the last time Simms ever saw his adoptive father. The three-year-old was riding with his mother in a berth when she told him to look at the big river they were crossing. It was the Mississippi, and the boy was struck by the fabulous image of the moon shining on the dark, moving water.

Lena's Omaha family was big: her mother, three sisters, three brothers, and one sister-in-law. Later, his grandmother's sister arrived with her son, Henry. Simms was the only grandchild in the home. It was a welcoming clan. "Life began for me when we moved in with my grandmother," he said.

Simms attended grammar school in a large, red-brick, integrated school. Few in the family went to school. "Education was not a factor in that household," said Simms. Music, however, was. Simms's mother and grandmother, Lucy Gumm, played in an all-female brass band. Another uncle was a saxophone player in the pre-jazz era.

Simms was closest to his uncle Charles, ten years older, who took him on motorcycle rides, and to Henry, a couple of years younger. Charles was a chauffeur for the prominent Creighton family, for whom Creighton University in Omaha was named. Simms and his uncle occasionally ate dinner at the Creighton family's farm. There would be sixteen people or more—farmhands and family and guests—eating together at one gloriously food-laden table, and Simms loved everything about those meals, down to the plates. "All my life, I have been buying those blue-and-white plates like the ones I remember at those great dinners I enjoyed so much with all those people."

Those gatherings were a comfort to Simms in the years after his mother died of influenza. He was six years old, and from then on, he answered only to his grandmother. "I was treated like an adult. I was never babied. Even with all those women, I wasn't spoiled," Simms recalled.

He was nine years old when he got his first job, attending the ice-house of a farm-goods store on the corner where he lived. The workers cut the ice into blocks of twenty-five to one hundred pounds and loaded them onto a wagon in front of the store. Simms had to drag the pieces to the edge of the cart for each customer and collect the money. In his early teens, he started doing odd jobs at a fruit stand in the local meat market owned by the family of a school friend. "That was a place I could go back to anytime I wanted," he said, adding with a laugh, "It was some years before they found out I wasn't Jewish."

Simms found other odd jobs in Minneapolis after the family moved there in time for him to enter high school. A couple of his aunts had gone there first and had found better employment opportunities than in Omaha. Once there, Simms became a regular at the Phillis Wheatley Settlement House—a combination sports facility, guidance center, and library—run by the indomitable Gertrude Brown. The organization, named for the eighteenth-century woman considered the first African-American poet, helped the community deal with problems big and small, and was the local place for meetings.

The move to Minneapolis changed the course of Simms's life, because of the unique contacts it afforded. His involvement in high-school basketball there led him to meet a player on a rival team, Gordon Parks. Parks would later become one of the nation's foremost artists: filmmaker, photographer, writer, composer. The two became lifelong friends, sharing a love of photography, and one day Parks would participate in a project at Pepsi-Cola.

Simms's exposure to the Settlement House also changed his life. In June 1931, days before his high-school graduation, Simms learned that W. E. B. DuBois was going to speak in town. The internationally renowned scholar was staying with a local family because white hotels wouldn't accommodate him. When Simms asked to meet him, he was invited to the home for a Sunday afternoon.

Simms was introduced to DuBois, and the two strolled alone through the backyard and sat on a wooden swing to have a private chat. DuBois was wearing white suspenders and a white dress shirt, Simms recalled, but hadn't yet fastened his collar. He told DuBois about himself, his adoption, and his interests in life. They spoke for nearly an hour, and Simms was taken with how kind DuBois was, and how generous with his time, considering that Simms was just a high-school senior. Finally, Simms mentioned that he was about to graduate from high school, only the second in his family to do so, and that he was thinking of college.

"You *will* go to college," DuBois responded. The tone of his voice startled Simms. It wasn't tentative, or a recommendation, or the casual remark of a concerned stranger. It sounded like a command that could not be disobeyed. Whenever he felt discouraged, Simms remembered those words. "It was something that stayed with me and had an impact on me when times got tough," he said. Years later, he would have a similar experience with Ralph Bunche when the diplomat had to decline a speaking engagement at an Urban League dinner, but met with Simms to give his regrets in person. "I've always tried to be exemplary in that sense—never too busy to talk to someone. Here they were, so well known and contributing so much—not just to black people but to the world—and I was just a young person, not very important one way or another, and they took the time to see me."

Simms found another guardian angel in the head librarian in the corner library near his new home. Adelaide C. Rood was a constant cheerleader for Simms in all his efforts and dreams. "Sometimes I think of myself as being handed off from one person to another in my career," he said. "People along the way had a sincere interest in helping me."

Simms graduated from high school in 1931 and used contacts he had made working on a country commissioner's election campaign to get a highway-construction job. He made a man's wage—five dollars a day—and in two years' time he had saved more than four hundred dollars for school and had won a tuition grant to Coe College in Cedar Rapids, Iowa. He was nervous about going out into the world, an insecurity he believed stemmed from being adopted, and because of his grandmother's fears. "She said you'll find when you go out there in the world, it won't be very comfortable," Simms remembered. "And I wanted to stay home forever."

Simms spent one year at Coe, then transferred to the University of Minnesota. He had wanted to be a newspaperman, but he decided to enter the field of public relations, making up his own curriculum because of the newness of the field. In a short time, he started doing free PR work for the local National Urban League, beginning a relationship with the group that would last a lifetime. By the time Simms graduated, he had gone from feeling unsure of himself to being proud that he was the first in his family to graduate from college. The truth was that he always found his way to the top, whether it was at school clubs or heading projects. "I had a feeling that there was someone on my shoulder all through my life. I don't know who it was. It could have been my real mother; it could have been anyone. I believe in God, but it's not a religious thing—but it's something good. I had so many breaks in life that I didn't make, they just came to me."

Back at the Settlement House, Simms befriended a professor from Virginia State College, a black school in Ettrick, Virginia, who was working on his PhD. He helped Simms get his first job after college graduation in 1939—in the public-relations department at the school.

The move to the South was something of a culture shock after the friendlier atmosphere in Minnesota. When Simms went on a date with a young woman he had met on campus, he suggested a movie. "Oh no," she said, "I don't go to the movies. I don't like to sit in the balcony."

"We don't have to sit in the balcony," Simms replied, not stating the obvious fact that she didn't necessarily look African-American.

"Oh yes we do!" she shot back.

From then on, Simms always went to the movies alone, and sat anywhere he wanted.

His dating came to an end when he proposed to his hometown girlfriend, the beautiful Hilda Moses, who also had attended the University of Minnesota. They were married in 1941, and his new bride, who dreamed of being an actress, used her married name professionally: Hilda Simms.

The stint at Virginia State proved to Simms that public relations was his calling. He liked his work, and he still prizes a photograph of himself meeting Eleanor Roosevelt there. But his job was cut short when he was drafted in 1942. Simms wasn't too pleased with the turn of events, but characteristically he found a way to land on top. He came to enjoy his time in the army, for several reasons: He was sent to Camp Lee, nearby in Virginia, and there were ties between the camp and the campus, so he felt comfortable. He was a friend of the son of the officer in charge and was treated well. Most of all, he bought a Voigtlander camera, like his friend Gordon's, and was given freedom to photograph his surroundings. "I had this slip that said I could take the camera with me wherever I went, even basic training," Simms said. He started taking portraits, first of the officers, then of the enlisted men, sometimes setting up portrait sessions against a plain wall in the USO building. "I was important; I became the photographer of the group."

Simms learned how to do his own darkroom work, experimenting with the best-quality papers. Once, when he wanted to go on leave to Washington to see his wife, he stood up in the dining hall and announced he needed money and would do portraits for cash. In no time, he raised more money than he needed.

While Simms was stationed on the base, his wife became "starstruck," as he put it, and joined the American Negro Theater in Harlem in 1943. She was given the title role in *Anna Lucasta,* which became a surprise sensation. It moved to the big stage in 1944 and was billed as the first all-black production to be performed on Broadway "without a racial theme." It had an astonishing run of 950 performances. Hilda Simms was a star, one of the first of color on Broadway, and Simms was proud.

Back on base, Simms became a master sergeant, but he never made it overseas because of a freak accident during training, when he seriously damaged his kneecap and leg when he stepped into a foxhole. He was a healthy five-foot-nine and 170 pounds, but when he was discharged three months later, his leg was a half-inch shorter, creating another challenge to overcome.

After his release, Simms went to Chicago, where his wife's play was running. He remembered feeling pressured by some of the activist actors to join leftist organizations, but he declined. He found a job with progressives inside the system and felt comfortable working with them. He worked in public relations for the American Council on Race Relations, a powerful board that included such members as Walter White of the NAACP, adviser and activist Mary McLeod Bethune, and Lester Granger of the Urban League. All worked under Robert C. Weaver, the veteran of the Roosevelt administration. The council was focused on problems of black soldiers returning to civilian life. "They'd strip their uniforms off them and hang them in the South," said Simms of the postwar upsurge in lynchings. "Certain whites at the time hated to see a black face in a uniform."

Simms decided to leave his job with the council when a new director replaced Weaver. Meanwhile, his wife was getting offers to perform on stage and in film. With their careers taking different paths, they divorced. Hilda continued acting, but she never received proper financial reward for her efforts. In the 1960s, she became an activist in fighting discrimination against actors of color.

Simms decided to use money from the GI bill to get a master's degree in public relations from Boston University, the first university to offer such a degree. He founded, and became president of, a graduate chapter of his fraternity, Alpha Phi Alpha. After his studies, he stayed in Boston and did some work for the state Democratic Party. But he wanted to leave the city, where he felt like an outsider.

Boyd, meanwhile, had heard about Simms, who came highly recommended. So the next time Boyd was in Boston, the two met for an interview. Simms was hired on the spot. "I got the idea that this was going to be a great thing," Simms said. "The main thing was that it got me out of Boston and into New York."

———

As it happened, Simms's childhood friend Gordon Parks was tapped to help Boyd launch one of his new series of print advertisements. Boyd planned two splashy campaigns for the year, and the press gave news of their coming big coverage. The special-markets group had ignored the black newspapers throughout 1950, partly due to its tight budget, but also to focus on producing point-of-purchase ads and on stoking the flames of the Coke boycott. The press announcements reminded readers that Pepsi-Cola, "pioneered among large American companies in using Negro subjects and models in advertising," then went on to describe the ten new ads that would be prepared for print: four so-called youth ads and six "Leaders." They'd run in thirty-five leading weeklies, plus *Ebony* and *Our World* magazines, according to the announcement.

Gordon Parks, then thirty-nine years old, would open the third and final "Leaders in Their Fields" series. The text described Parks as the first recipient of the Rosenwald Fellowship in Photography and an "outstanding Life photographer now on leave in Paris." Parks, in fact, was most famous for his 1944 black *American Gothic* photograph that instantly became an icon.

The series was given a new, sleek, airy, 1950s look: big, friendly, professional portraits of the subjects alone against a white background, rather than in a cluttered setting. Alongside the photos was a small, simple sketch illustrating the honoree at work. Gone were the dark pictures and clunky cutout boxes of text. The slogan was shortened to just one line, "Leaders in Their Fields," (leaving out the reference to Pepsi as a "Leader in Its Field") and printed in a thin, modern font. The ads were scheduled to run in black monthly magazines from July through December. Ralph Bunche was back for his final appearance, with an illustration showing him getting his Nobel Peace Prize in Oslo in 1950. "Recognizing a brilliant diplomatic career," the text read. After this ad, Boyd said, Bunche decided Pepsi had used his face enough, and sent a letter insisting the company stop using his name and image.

The company prepared for the special reprint orders expected to pour in, adding a note of appreciation to the "Leaders" package: "No advertising Pepsi-Cola Company has ever run has given us more satisfaction than the group of advertisements reproduced in this folder. To be able to give wider public recognition to the outstanding achievements of these splendid citizens is something for which Pepsi-Cola Company is indeed grateful. We wish to thank all of them for working with us in the preparation of this series."

The ads prepared for the black weeklies were consistent with Mack's appeals to the younger generation, but without adding an element of mission or education. They were about a fanciful, idealized view of middle-class life; the realizing of the American Dream. And African-Americans were portrayed in the same bourgeois comfort that their white counterparts enjoyed. The first of the highly stylized ads showed a young girl in a fashionably wide skirt and peasant blouse on a carousel pony getting ready to sip a bottle of Pepsi. The text was far removed from the inspirational copy of the past. It read: "So *Much* More Fun! . . . So *Much* More Zest! Pepsi sparkles with More Bounce to the Ounce . . . Why take less . . . when Pepsi's Best! *Feel* Smart . . . *Be* Smart . . . Get Pepsi—Livelier—Friendlier—Better!"

Another ad showed a young woman in a swimsuit and bathing cap emerging from a pool, where a well-built man in trunks was waiting with a Pepsi in hand. In another ad, a couple was watching television— on the screen was Faye Emerson, of course. The ads were meant to highlight young African-Americans having fun while "reflecting quality and dignity," the newspaper announcement read. A fourth ad was to complete the series, which started in the weeklies in late May.

Boyd sent off an undated letter to bottlers showing them proofs of the first two ads of the year: the "More Bounce to the Ounce" ad of the woman on the carousel and the Gordon Parks ad. The bottler's driver-salesmen were expected to disperse copies of the two series around their territories.

The newspapers promised considerable support in return for the Pepsi windfall. In a rare letter addressing the press directly, Boyd wrote to the editor of *The Pittsburgh Courier* on June 1 with a reminder that the paper's New York representative had promised help—an unusually generous offer from a news outlet: "This would include the writing of personal letters on your letterhead to certain accounts pointing out the Pepsi-Cola program and soliciting dealer support of Pepsi-Cola; some personal calls by your newspaper representatives to outlets in the Negro segment of the local market; and other merchandising aids which you feel may be of value."

While the Pepsi ads were becoming more "fun," other advertisers aiming at the Negro market were emulating older Pepsi ads featuring role models. Lucky Strike cigarettes, for one, spotlighted business leaders. It also ran splashier ads featuring Dodgers Roy Campanella and Don Newcombe. In 1951, black weeklies could point to a healthy influx of ads from major corporations, sustained throughout the year. Many were selling luxury items for the modern home.

———————

Pepsi-Cola's youth ads reflected Steele's tendency to blur the lines between the Negro market team and the company as a whole. One year after Steele took over, Pepsi-Cola was being transformed, and the team seemed poised to reap the benefits as well. Or was it? Would the team be fully integrated into the company, or were the latest advances just a subtle, albeit more fair-minded, manifestation of a separate-but-equal policy?

The articles announcing the new ad campaigns included another bit of news that meant little to the public but had a big impact on the team. The company was being restructured to include a network of seven regional offices in Atlanta, Chicago, Washington, Dallas, San Francisco, Syracuse, and Columbus, Ohio. The *Omaha Star* reported that when nine of the Pepsi sales staff were working their way through Mississippi,

Louisiana, and Indiana, two others had been given permanent assignments: William Payne had just been sent to the Pepsi-Cola regional office in Chicago, and Jean Emmons was in the Columbus office. "Now, for the first time, our franchise-bottlers will be able to deal directly with responsible company officials in their own geographical areas," Steele wrote in the annual report, released in April 1951.

His moves were part of the latest management theory promulgated by management scholar Peter F. Drucker in his popular writings. The idea was to decentralize, so that employees closest to the business at hand would make the important decisions. Drucker argued in his 1946 best-seller, *The Concept of the Corporation,* a case study of General Motors, that it was crucial to profitability that employees be treated like valuable resources and given more control in the workplace. His theory had so taken hold in the 1950s that Drucker himself would say later that some companies had jumped on his advice without adequately analyzing their situations. It must also be noted that some "average workers" benefited more than others.

The twelve team members learned of the regionalization effort when they suddenly were called off the road to attend a meeting at headquarters. Once they were gathered around a conference table, vice president Cliff Riddle announced abruptly that they would be split up. Most would continue to travel for the time being, but Emmons and Payne were just the first in a full reassignment. The choice of Emmons and Payne was a logical one. They had just completed training and, along with Nicholas, Davis, and Russell, were especially eager to become managers. But the salesmen immediately saw it as a weakening of the team, and particularly of its successful "blanket" strategy. "It was a complete shock to us. We had just come from North Carolina where we had done an exceptional job," McKellar recalled. "So when they decided that, rumors began to fly. You couldn't exactly determine what was coming."

The new system allowed Steele to begin cutting an enormous amount of traveling expenses. Spending for modernization pushed the company's net profit for all of 1950 to another all-time low: a mere $1.62 million, compared with $2.14 million in 1949 (including a one-time profit of nearly $400,000 for the Cuban plant). By comparison, Coca-Cola reported net income of $31 million for the year. The two hardly seemed rivals, and yet Pepsi was pounding Coke in certain small markets in Northern U.S. cities and in some foreign markets.

As usual, the following year was held up as more promising. But this time there was evidence of a real turnaround in progress. Steele pointed out that in the first two months of the year, sales were up 15 percent over the year-ago period. Sales volume at Pepsi was the largest in the company's history, the beginning of a very long period of increasing sales. That was no thanks to Mack, Steele insisted, assessing the start of the decade for a cover story touting his successes in *Business Week*. Steele's judgment of Mack's legacy was scathing, even for a leader trying to erase the memory of a colorful and popular predecessor. He said Mack ran the company on such a frugal budget that employees didn't have the basic tools to do their jobs. He spoke about Mack the way Mack used to speak about his own father: too miserly to use money to make money. As a result, he said, Pepsi-Cola's 650 bottlers worldwide had lost confidence in the company as a viable, permanent business. "You can conserve yourself into bankruptcy, or you can spend your way to prosperity," Steele was quoted in the book *Twelve Full Ounces,* by Milward W. Martin, a former Pepsi-Cola vice president.

Steele told *Business Week* that Mack's advertising innovations were "flamboyant" to the point of looking cheap—and were ultimately unsuccessful. The jingle "Twice as Much for a Nickel, Too" was the downfall of the company, he charged, branding it not only as a poor person's drink but giving the notion that the drink was "twice as bad."

Steele, on the other hand, knew to make the cool beauty of Faye

Emerson the new face of Pepsi through her popular show, telecast three times a week. Steele was making his mark in television the way Mack had in radio—though in a less spectacular way. Pepsi-Cola also sponsored a radio program, *The Phil Regan Armed Services Show*, which had its premiere on March 4, 1951. It was a family program that originated each week from a different military installation or defense plant across the United States.

Steele's annual report for 1950 was a careful review of how he was moving the company into a new era. The changes were considerable; and he took credit for all the important ones started since he joined the company. He invested big in new bottles, new cases, new trucks, and modern loading methods. The twelve-ounce bottle was relegated to home use, and the eight-ounce size, introduced in 1948, was made the standard for public consumption, from restaurants to vending machines. He invested heavily in improved machines and fountain dispensers and gave bottlers the credit to purchase them.

Looking at the bigger picture, Steele returned the company to its core business of making soft drinks, selling the Cuban subsidiary and a shaky bottle-cap-manufacturing venture. He wrote that every salesman would have the equipment he needed to do his job—"the most modern sales devices and material of every description." The budget for advertising for the year would be raised and his "hard-hitting" advertising plan would emphasize the quality of the product, he promised. And the quality of the drink would be guaranteed by the use of other modern machines

Steele bought some of the worst plants in the network and made the company-owned plants bigger, more modern, and more efficient. Overseas sales kept rising. In Nicaragua, Pepsi captured 60 percent of the market in 1950, beating the "principal competitor" four to one; in one Venezuelan market, Pepsi outsold Coke five to one. For 1951, Steele planned twenty new plants in nine countries, including Australia,

Kenya, and Mexico. The Canadian subsidiary swung from a loss to a profit. Finally, in management, James W. Carkner became the new chairman of the board, and four new directors were named.

————————

Boyd missed Mack. For all the improvements in operations, he found that the corporate leadership had gone from Mack's typical, "Is there anything I should know?" to Steele's command, "Don't wear out the rug to my office." Steele certainly wasn't inviting Boyd and his wife out to dinner.

It wasn't the regionalization effort itself that disturbed Boyd. From the start, he had organized promotional activities regionally, centered on bottling plants. That's why he hired men with strong contacts in different cities. But, as he saw it, the experimental team needed a strong central office to smooth its path and coordinate the ad campaigns. Boyd felt that any localized effort should consist of hiring more African-American driver-salesmen for every bottling plant, a plan regarded as important to black professional groups, which saw distribution as increasingly important to the economy.

As the last man through the door, Nicholas made a quick study of the team as it entered its new phase. His first conclusion was that the team was successful, and so much in demand by bottlers that it had more work to do than there were men or hours to handle it. The second was that the driver-salesmen were more driver than salesmen and that Steele's training courses needed to be reinforced. He also noticed that Boyd was very popular in the black community and was able to boost any of the team's efforts whenever he joined the group at a convention or other community event. But Boyd didn't mix well with the Southern bottlers, who considered him a snob. "If you knew any of the soft-drink bottling family, they were hardworking, sleeves-rolled-up types, many not college educated," said Nicholas. "I guess a lot of them thought of Boyd as a smart ass. He was a California guy. He was haughty, and if he saw there was a slight bit of crackerism with the whites, he was even more haughty with them."

By contrast, Nicholas and some of his colleagues felt they could ease tensions and smooth the way to doing business. "I understood the Southern white," said Nicholas.

Boyd knew that in the Steele regime the bottlers ruled, but he didn't mind being cast as "uppity," as he put it. This wasn't the time to play down black status or achievement and the black press was complicit. When Boyd planned a respite at his sister's Mississippi home after an intense campaign through her state and Louisiana, it was reported as a visit to "the palatial Howard estate." Helen Boyd and her husband, Theodore R. M. Howard, lived in the all-black city of Mound Bayou, Mississippi. Dr. Howard was surgeon-in-chief of the Friendship Clinic, but he became better known some four years later when he offered his home to witnesses in the trial of murdered Chicago teenager Emmett Till, earning the wrath of FBI chief J. Edgar Hoover, Boyd recalled.

The tension with the Southern bottlers had a parallel in the team itself. The Northern-born members sometimes felt their Southern colleagues were too submissive to whites. The Northerners were accused of being too integrated into white society. As time went on, and members started to peel away, such divisions among the men widened. They were getting suspicious of Paul Davis, who the salesmen thought was a spy for Boyd because he seemed to ask a lot of questions on the road. Boyd thought he might be a spy for management after he caught him at least once going through papers in one of the desks they used at headquarters. And in those times of political paranoia, rumors spread that he was sending information to Washington, possibly to the FBI. But there was no evidence that Davis was doing anything but his job.

Nicholas also noted the animosity of some—including Wilson,

Simms, and Hurt—about appearing in churches. They believed it was disrespectful, especially because they had to pay the preacher to do it. "I'm not a religious man, but I would resent anyone coming to my church to sell," Wilson said. "It's not my role as a Catholic."

Nicholas, however, sided with his boss. "Boyd was right about the need to go into the churches. I argued about this with Hurt and others on the team until I was blue in the face. We almost had fistfights," he said, adding, "They didn't know Southern life. It wasn't the gospel singing that kept people going to service. It was a total social outlet."

The religious debate seemed a convenient excuse for deeper dissatisfactions with the job on the part of some. Wilson was ready to leave anyway. He had been investigating scholarships as part of a promotional effort in New York. He went into the Swiss Educational Agency looking for undergraduate aid, but ended up discussing how an American could study in Switzerland. Within days, he found himself set to attend medical school in Geneva in the fall and quit the team in July.

Simms, too, felt he had to leave Pepsi-Cola, and Boyd helped him find a new job, a gesture Simms never forgot.

———

At the end of the summer of 1951, Boyd was called into the office of Herbert Barnet. "I have some bad news to report," he began. And so Boyd was told that because the new regional structure would be placing all his men in local offices, his central office wasn't needed anymore.

"I was shocked," said Boyd, who wasn't even aware that Barnet was in a position to fire him and deeply resented him for doing Steele's dirty work. "Barnet was shaking like a leaf," Boyd remembered.

The two sat there for a while and talked, although Boyd had stopped hearing anything coming from Barnet's mouth. Barely four years had passed since Boyd sat in Pepsi-Cola's modest plant in Queens discussing a remarkable job offer with Mack and Houston. The rise of the company to an international brand name, and the role the special-markets department played in that rise, however rocky, allowed Boyd to tell himself that he'd move on to something better.

Back in his own office, he telephoned his wife, Edith, to meet with him at her place of work as he made his way home. She took the bad news in stride. "You'll do what you have to do, and everything will be OK," she comforted her husband. It was upsetting news, but for the both of them there was a certain inevitability in the situation. "I was always thinking I would be fired," Boyd said. "I was walking on eggshells the whole time I was there, especially after my walkout at the Waldorf-Astoria Hotel. So when I *was* fired, I didn't think badly of the company."

Management told Boyd he could stay for a while until he found work. His first move was to go to rival Coca-Cola, which was under new management, so he contacted the New York bottler. The managers were interested enough to invite him to lunch, and then other lunches, Boyd recalled. They asked many questions involving hypothetical situations. He avoided giving details until he was sure he was about to be hired. Then under another line of questioning, he talked about his campaign strategy and the thinking behind it. "And I never heard from them again," Boyd said, certain they had all the information they needed, free of charge.

Boyd had to leave Pepsi-Cola without having a job lined up. He turned to his first two allies in the corporate world—Mack and Houston—who had moved on since their departure from Pepsi-Cola. They promised they would help him find another job.

Ultimately, Boyd blamed Steele alone for his dismissal. But Boyd never got a satisfactory answer from the new regime as to why he was fired. Was it because he was Mack's protégé? Was it because the bottlers didn't like him? Was it a cost-cutting measure? Boyd wondered if it was the several discrimination suits that the team had brought against seg-regated hotels that really bothered Pepsi-Cola.

The political climate in the country at the time was intense. In the Chicago area, for example, some four thousand white youths were rioting, with impunity, to keep one black family from moving to an apartment in Cicero, ultimately driving them from their home. DuBois went on trial with four others for not having registered their since-defunct Peace Information Center as a foreign agent; the case was finally dropped at the end of the year, and an embattled DuBois reportedly wept with relief. A man and woman were dragged from their beds and brutally beaten by a white mob in Georgia. A prominent educator in the New Orleans area died of injuries received the preced-ing year while working to register blacks. Whites picketed a theater in Macon, Georgia, for allowing blacks in for the first time, even though they were relegated to a segregated balcony.

Overseas was another matter. Pepsi-Cola and its rivals were getting a lesson in the downside to global business. In Egypt, the gem of their worldwide expansion effort, sales were falling. Anti-Americanism was being fueled by animosity over the presence of British troops in the coun-try. "We're sick of Pepsi-Cola and Chevrolet imperialism," a member of Egypt's parliament declared. The nationalists told Egyptians that Pepsi was made from the blood of pigs, a religious taboo as well as a preposter-ous notion. Despite vehement denials by local Pepsi distributors, thou-sands steered clear of the drink, and Coke as well. Pepsi-Cola's management later countered rumors with the help of Muslim leaders. That incident told managers that minority employees might better serve the company outside U.S. borders.

Again, the national sales team was brought into a conference room by Clifford Riddle, who gave them the news of their boss's departure.

They were just as shocked as Boyd. Shortly after the announcement, the team members were reassigned one-by-one, and both print advertising series came to an abrupt halt. "There was a lot of loyalty from the black team, but Pepsi wasn't loyal to us," Russell lamented. "They seemed to be saying, 'We don't care what you black guys are doing, just don't get in the way and stay out of trouble.'"

Russell, Watson, and Davis were to work in headquarters in New York. Most of the others were sent to their home-state areas. Nicholas was assigned to work in the Washington, D.C., region under vice president Carl Saltz, along with William J. Curtis, who earlier had helped the team on the road. Wright was sent to California to report to the San Francisco regional office. McKellar was sent on the road for the remainder of the year, then was assigned to join Payne in Chicago, where he lived. But McKellar, like many of his colleagues, was skeptical about his future prospects. "I was worried I'd lose my job, so I started to look elsewhere," he said.

Once in their regional offices, the men had very different experiences. Nicholas was happy under Saltz. He remembered an early chat with his new boss in which the white Alabaman told him that when he was a boy, his parents took him in a buggy to hear Booker T. Washington lecture at Tuskegee Institute. Nicholas wasn't about to argue that his family leaned more toward the politics of DuBois. He appreciated the gesture. "From then on, we got along like two peas in a pod," Nicholas said.

Likewise, Bill Payne thrived in Chicago. He didn't live long enough to recount his story here, but he achieved brisk sales amid brutal competition. In early 1951, Dr Pepper had sued Coca-Cola on charges of trade restraint, claiming that Coca-Cola pressured retailers to sell five-cent bottles by advertising that no soft drink should cost more. Yet Coke was being sold for a dime in places outside of Chicago at that time. Lawyers charged Coca-Cola kept prices below cost to force other bottlers out of the market.

But Emmons was unhappy with his manager in Columbus. "As far as I'm concerned, I was thrown out to William Durkee and the umbilical cord was cut," he said. He felt communication with New York had been skimpy from the start; and now was nonexistent. He missed his camaraderie with Payne. "Bill Payne was the only one that I could really sit down and talk with," he said. "He was educated and mature, and from a successful family. He had an intellectual bearing; he saw things. Otherwise, you never got into the kind of conversations that would really have helped us."

Emmons tried to fit in, but he found that when the men got together to drink and swap stories, they weren't comfortable with Emmons on the scene. Worse, Emmons felt he had no management support when things went wrong on the road. He told of one incident in Kentucky when he was doing promotional work at a convention hall, one of two situated close together. He figured he'd visit the other when he was finished, to cover more ground. As he approached the building, he was surrounded by some white youths. He was too big to beat up, he said, but the usual racial name-calling ensued. The police broke it up. Emmons wrote a letter to the management of the center, and to his surprise his boss wouldn't support him. "You're messing up," was the message he got. No one spoke with the management at the Kentucky Convention Center as Boyd, or even Mack himself, might have done.

Emmons did, however, enjoy the support of the local black community and also found the white bottlers of Columbus, Ohio, and South Bend and Terre Haute, Indiana, to be welcoming and cooperative.

McKellar went right back out on the road. Harvey Russell joined him in Tulsa in November. The two wrote a narrative report and sent it to their supervisors at headquarters.

It was one of the final narratives written, and McKellar held on to it. The new regional system didn't require them. The details of this one, dated November 5–21, 1951, sum up the nearly four years of achievements of Pepsi's experimental Negro-market department under Boyd, and how his team left its mark. They pioneered black advertising, black modeling, market research, and forced greater recognition—and measurement—of the power of niche marketing, particularly to African-Americans. It also suggests the greater context in which their work was carried out in the black community.

In the report, the two found that 15 percent of Tulsa's thirty thousand residents were black, and that a remarkable 95 percent of the retail outlets in the black community were black-owned and thus responsive to the team's work. "Our bottler and all competitive companies, including Coca-Cola, Royal Crown, Seven Up, Hires, the milk, beer and bread companies, hire Negro driver-salesmen in Tulsa due to a concentrated campaign put on by the Negro Chamber of Commerce some years ago," it stated. The chamber worked hard to help Russell and McKellar make contacts in the community.

The two found that Pepsi already accounted for 75 percent of the coolers in town. The largest black-owned drugstore in the city, however, had refused to carry Pepsi because of a feud with the bottler that dated to 1945. The men persuaded him to reopen his account with a healthy ten-case-per-week order. The men got a plug for Pepsi at a Duke Ellington concert that drew five thousand fans. They also addressed the NAACP's state convention; were permitted to present Pepsi-Cola's history to the entire student body of Booker T. Washington High School and Carver Junior High School; got the Retail Grocers and Tavern Owners Association to promise support; got the six largest churches to introduce them to the congregation; attended five fraternity or sorority events; and serviced a gathering of two hundred at a library art exhibit and held events at the YMCA and YWCA. They also were given a promise to install one or two vending machines at a new, $300,000 Carver Community Center housing various kids' organizations.

Because the men found carton sales low, they held a Silver Dollar Promotion—where a dollar coin was hidden in a carton at the largest supermarket in the area. To prepare, they distributed a remarkable three thousand handbills door-to-door—twice!—arranged for the leading black disc jockey to play up the treasure hunt, had the local paper run a note, and had schools announce the contest to students. Meanwhile, some twenty-five hundred people were given samples of Pepsi at the store itself.

The report showed the hard work and dedication to the company that McKellar and Russell maintained over a rigorous schedule that never let up. But they were never convinced that it was appreciated. Harvey Russell said, shortly before his death, that he always wanted to write a book about his experiences and those of his generation of colleagues. So many doors were opened, he said, yet they always seemed to get stuck at the entrance. "I wanted to name it 'View from the Threshold,'" he said, "because you never really went past the threshold of the door."

Even Nicholas can remember when he was disabused of any romantic notion of his mission at Pepsi. On one road trip, he went out early one morning to play golf and saw the local Pepsi bottler and Coke bottler teeing off together. "Here we are fighting a damn war in the street and in the stores, and here they are teeing off together. That was a lesson," Nicholas remembered. From then on in his career, it would be strictly about business.

Simms, too, felt disillusioned and that the team's efforts were underappreciated by headquarters. For him, the bad fit was with Corporate America in general. "Selling Pepsi, selling anything really, is no kind of life," he concluded. "A life should be spent helping others, making some sort of a difference in this world—that's what a life should be."

— Chapter Eight —

Crossing the Threshold

IT WAS A DIFFERENT EXPERIENCE BEING A SALESMAN FOR Pepsi-Cola's Negro market once Boyd was gone and the men were reporting to regional office managers. The salesmen were no longer part of a team or organized at the national level, but they still shared their specialized training—and the objective to increase sales in the African-American population.

From 1952 on, if the team members were going to blaze any more trails, it was going to be as individuals helping their new bosses—all of whom were white and typically vice presidents—make their local sales goals. Ties to black communities through national organizations like the National Urban League and the NAACP were loosened, and each salesman focused on his own career.

Ironically, just as Pepsi-Cola dispersed the team, African-American salesmen were achieving a new level of recognition in American business. *The Wall Street Journal* used the term *Negro market* in a major news article for the first time in a front-page story on February 23, 1952. "Negro Market has become part of business vocabulary," the story stated, as the clout of the black consumer rose sharply on improved wages in the cities. It estimated the income of the black population at fifteen billion dollars a year, with average family income climbing 132 percent from 1940 to 1950, and college enrollment up 2,500 percent. In the story, *Ebony* publisher John H. Johnson claimed twelve new advertisers in its next issue. The magazine was showing a promotional film called *Selling the Negro Market,* which still gave advice such as remembering to call African-American men Mr. and not to "talk down to him or patronize him." It also warned: "Don't mention Joe Louis or Jackie Robinson, unless you know he's interested in sports."

The long list of products reported to be advertised in black periodicals included Philco, Morton salt, Van Camp's, Nunn Bush, Magic Chef, Pillsbury Mills, and the Quaker Oats Company, which was sponsoring two radio programs in Harlem. Surprisingly, neither Pepsi-Cola nor its historical efforts were even mentioned in the *Journal* story—an omission that would have been unthinkable just one year earlier.

Steele had no plans to abandon the market altogether—his rival Coca-Cola, after all, was continuing to advertise in the black press, using generic ads showing bottles and caps. But his previous preoccupation with image in the domestic market lost its urgency. Faye Emerson, "of plunging neckline fame," as *The Wall Street Journal* put it, was shown the door in the spring of 1952. Pepsi said the $43,000-a-show tab to sponsor her Saturday-night series was too expensive. Many other TV advertisers also fled the soaring production costs.

Pepsi-Cola had a new focus: overseas markets with their remarkable per capita consumption of colas. Specialized ads would begin to signify advertising in different languages, rather than African-American models. The overall advertising budget for 1953 surged 40 percent, but advertising geared toward black-owned media had virtually disappeared. After the "Leader" series stopped in August 1951, no Pepsi-Cola ads appeared in the major black papers for all of 1952 or 1953. The salesmen, instead, offered bottlers a choice of discounted novelty items: pens (a marketing craze since the late 1940s), a choice of pencils, a tiny

Pepsi tractor-trailer keychain and flashlight, a small lighter in the shape of a bottle, umbrellas for hot-dog stands, paper cook's caps, stationery, illuminated clocks; and the popular Dow Company Whirl-Away ashtrays, where you push a plunger at the top and ashes spin into a bottom receptacle. Vending machines became available in more styles to buy or rent from the parent company.

Within two years of Boyd's departure, most of his salesmen had left, discouraged by the team's breakup and feeling a lack of support from the central office as well as from individual regional bosses. Emmons, Hurt, McKellar, and Wright were the next to go. They found few comparable jobs at other major firms; only McKellar stuck with beverage sales, finding a job with the Falstaff Brewing Corporation. Emmons took his MBA from the University of Chicago and his successful record in public relations and sales for a major company, and grabbed the first job he could find immediately to support his growing family—mopping floors at an insurance company in Columbus, Ohio.

Just five of the original twelve members stayed with the company: Harvey Russell, David Watson, and Paul Davis in New York; Bill Payne in Chicago; and Julian Nicholas in Washington. Russell remained a staff coordinator and took over some of Boyd's duties on a national level, which included making frequent trips into the field around the country. Like Boyd, he worked well with upper management. But he was not given the assistant-sales-manager title and there were no direct reports under him.

The salesmen found that their day-to-day routine under the new regional system didn't change much at first. The foundation laid under Boyd's direction—sales technique, proper use of displays and materials, identifying potential customers—proved a consistently solid model for building consumer loyalty to the brand. Unfortunately, the daily obstacles didn't change much either, despite the rise of an increasingly more affluent and modern society. Harvey Russell later told an interviewer from *The New York Times* that he hadn't encountered any business problems because of his race, but "after business, it is something else."

"We still slept in some lady's guest house, or in the few places they had rinky-dink black hotels," said Nicholas. "I'd go into places where the store owner, white, had a shotgun hanging on the wall and pistols in the register. I'm talking the South before integration."

But Nicholas and his colleagues who stayed on sensed one important difference in their newly defined jobs: opportunity. They believed that working at their own desk in one manageable region, where their successes were more easily measured and so more obvious, was a way to rise through the corporate ranks. "We had to jump right into the direct-sales thing, or we might have never gotten off first base," said Nicholas. "I was without any doubt that the regional approach was the best move that Pepsi made because it increased the bottlers' sales best."

The salesmen could hammer away at a single area over a period of time—an improvement over the here-today, gone-tomorrow strategy of before, when a few men were spread thin over the entire country. Their task: If an outlet takes five cases, get the manager to take ten; if a campus has two vending machines, install two more, and two more after that; if a place has a Coke machine, put in a Pepsi one for now and edge out the red machine later. Door-to-door campaigns like the one McKellar and Russell did in Tulsa were a thing of the past. The salesmen continued to do every sort of public-relations work to win more customers, but now they returned week after week, year after year. Sometimes, the salesmen even took the local bottler along with them to a big event. In addition to building bonds with outlets, the new arrangement was strengthening relations between the salesmen and the area plant owners. Even the most intransigent bottlers began to see the salesmen as individuals and as colleagues—and competent ones at that—whereas before, many felt uncomfortable when the whole team of black men arrived. "If you help the bottler ring the cash register that was a plus, whether you were black, white, green, or grizzly," said Nicholas, using a favorite expression.

The new regional bosses—at least the good ones—helped build those bonds. Carl Saltz, for example, called bottlers and recommended Nicholas in glowing terms. That allowed Nicholas to develop a relationship with Saltz that wasn't possible with Boyd, whom he didn't see on a daily basis. Just as Steele had hoped, bottlers warmed up to the white regional managers, who were showering them with attention. Pepsi-Cola was, as Boyd predicted, developing into more of a good ol' boy network, but the result was more accommodating for the salesmen than anyone might have expected.

It was still the era of the large black college, and Nicholas estimated he placed hundreds of vending machines on campuses as well as in high schools in the Washington region, which included bottlers from South Carolina to Pennsylvania. He put about one hundred thousand miles a year on each of the five Fords he drove in the 1950s while a regional salesman.

One improvement the regional salesmen worked to implement was the hiring of more black driver-salesmen. The drivers were the backbone of sales for the bottler, and the regional office needed their clout to keep increasing orders from outlets. The salesmen had to find candidates themselves, and they turned to the same organizations—the NAACP and the National Urban League—that had always helped the team, thereby reestablishing ties. The driver-salesmen were paid well and were highly visible connections to companies—working as they did in uniforms and trucks emblazoned with corporate logos. Integrating the delivery fleet was seen as a significant contribution to the integration of commerce as a whole.

These sales and marketing jobs were so appealing to the underemployed African-American population, that when Langston Hughes, in his *Defender* column, gave his recommendations for gift books for Christmas 1952, first on his list was *The Potential Negro Market*, a how-to for salesmen. The author, Lincoln University professor Joseph T. Johnson, gave a full picture of the market—sales techniques, advertising, customer reactions, tips for white hucksters, and examples of actual campaigns, including a look at Pepsi-Cola's marketing team. The Christmas list also included Ralph Ellison's *Invisible Man*, "the race's best-seller of the year"; Carl T. Rowan's account of his return to his native South as a journalist "to ask dangerous questions"; and W. E. B. DuBois's *In Battle for Peace*.

When the local Pepsi-Cola offices began looking for driver-salesmen, a surprising number of applications came from teachers, clerks and other candidates ready to switch from the traditional jobs open to minorities. They had to be trained, and the regional salesmen picked up that task, too. "That put me in a blue uniform and training them on their rounds for a week or two at a time. I couldn't leave the bottler with a dud. So there would be three of us in a cab: the white driver, the guy I'd hired, and me—all riding the routes," Nicholas said. "If he could learn to be a driver-salesman, he was given a truck full of Pepsi and he served the black area."

A good salesmen was a good salesman and those with talent, training, and a solid track record would eventually handle accounts at white-managed outlets, too. The same was true at the regional level. Nicholas and Payne, for example, began to handle accounts outside the special-markets outlets. "It was a normal progression," Nicholas said.

———

The company was on an upward trajectory that lasted the whole decade. Net profit for 1951 more than doubled from the year before, soaring to $2.63 million from $1.27 million; for 1952, it was $3.88 million; for 1953, it hit $5.48 million. The company posted fifty straight months of gains compared with their year-earlier months. Dozens of plants opened worldwide. Steele planned a new showcase headquarters more befitting a world-class competitor—a $7.8 million, eleven-story, glass-and-steel building at 500 Park Avenue in Manhattan, to be occupied in 1960.

Steele's success helped him to ride out some potential career-damaging scandals. In May 1953, he was forced to respond to a Senate report that the company gave the highly controversial, red-baiting Republican Senator Joseph McCarthy of Wisconsin a loan, through its Alexandria, Virginia, bottling plant, to curry favor during the sugar-control battles. More bad news followed that summer when Steele was accused by a stockholder of not filing proper expense vouchers and getting a kickback on vending machines. An investigation by the board of directors could turn up no wrongdoing.

Meanwhile, Walter S. Mack grabbed some favorable publicity for himself. In a string of news stories beginning in April 1953, Mack, as president of National Phoenix Industries, announced he was rolling out five flavors of soft drinks in New York City stores—in cans! *The Wall Street Journal* predicted a soda-pop "revolution," a word Mack would have insisted upon. Mack had been eager to move to cans ever since his failed experiment with Pepsi in 1950, when the cans exploded from the carbonation. The new, stronger cans, sold under the name of Cantrell & Cochrane Corporation, could hold carbonation and were flat-topped to reduce shipping space and costs. And they were disposable. By mid-decade, the beverage industries were test-marketing all manner of cans, and so Mack ushered in the throwaway era in consumerism—as always, by putting a fresh twist on an existing practice.

A truer revolution in business was afoot the following year due to political upheavals. Any notion that business was neither black nor white but green gave way to a demand that companies declare where they stood in matters of race. At the start of 1954, *The Wall Street Journal* noted that "even white businessmen below the Mason-Dixon Line" were starting to get up the courage to pursue black customers, even though "prejudices dating back to Reconstruction days are still strong and tradesmen have feared they'd alienate their white customers."

The story noted that the advertising agency Batten, Barton, Durstine & Osborn, Inc., had just hired a second black marketing man on plans to make its Negro consumer-marketing section permanent. Meanwhile, the number of radio stations in the United States aimed at a black audience had surged from 4 stations in 1943, when they were pursuing interviews with the Pepsi-Cola marketing interns McKellar and Maund, to about 270 by 1954. That was out of a total 2,500 stations, a greater percentage than its population share. "All this interest in the Negro market doesn't mean that Negroes have attained anything approaching economic parity with the white population," the article warned. Negroes made up 9 percent of the total population, but only 5 percent of total U.S. income.

Coca-Cola, which had been hesitant to create ads geared toward African-American consumers, changed policy. In June 1954, Harvey Russell found a letter on his desk from a Wilmington, North Carolina, bottler. "The attached is an advertisement of the Coca-Cola Company appearing in the local Negro newspaper," wrote J. W. Jackson. "The Coca-Cola Company is running an advertisement each week in this newspaper and each advertisement carries the picture of a well-known Negro character. We thought perhaps you might be interested."

Russell was definitely interested. The attached Coke ad featured ballplayer Larry Doby of the Cleveland Indians—a full six years after Pepsi-Cola launched its "Leaders in Their Fields" campaign. Coca-Cola had hired on retainer pioneer black adman Moss Kendrix to handle its campaign, and Kendrix stayed with the company for twenty years, according to the Museum of Public Relations Web site. He went on to acquire the accounts of Ford Motor, Carnation, and other big companies in the 1950s. In 1954, he and a handful of other admen—including representatives of Esso Standard Oil and American Telephone and Telegraph—helped launch in Washington, D.C., the National Alliance of Market Developers for minorities in the marketing and public-relations field, which was still going strong at the close of the century.

Pepsi-Cola also had returned to the black weeklies in 1954. This time, it was Pepsi that ignored the readership, running ads created for mainstream publications. The six-part series, much larger than the black-press ads that the company typically ran, featured very elegant, very slim white women who might worry about fitting into their exceptional wardrobes. "Refreshing—Not Filling" was the slogan. Sam Hall, the Philadelphia special-sales representative, remembered that for some time after he joined the company in 1955, many managers remained stubbornly certain that African-American women would never care about calories. And so those ads soon ended.

Just as Coca-Cola was embracing marketing to the African-American population, racial politics again took center stage. On May 17, 1954, the U.S. Supreme Court ruled on *Brown v. Board of Education*, ending school segregation by striking down the doctrine of separate but equal. The segregationists dubbed the day Black Monday and provoked the inevitable backlash against the growing economic clout of African-Americans.

Militant Citizens' Councils were formed to fight integration, gaining enormous support among a broad spectrum of whites in the South. The members' weapon of choice was the business boycott, which had developed into a far more sophisticated weapon than in the days when the team faced down rumors about blacks falling into vats of cola. Leaflets, books, and newspapers denouncing white-owned businesses that sold to blacks passed into the hands of hundreds of thousands. The movement, the *Journal* reported, stemmed from "a determination to use almost any means of preventing white and Negro students from attending the same public schools."

By March 1956, another *Wall Street Journal* story portrayed Southern businesses as squeezed between the lucrative African-American market they had come to rely on for added income and the white customers—many of them hostile to integration—who made up their core customers.

"Buy a Ford and Help Destroy Segregation in Georgia and Help Communize America," one leaflet read. The action was justified by a perceived link between the automaker and the liberal Ford Foundation in New York.

"The owners of Philip Morris may discover that their cigarettes are just for Negro consumption," a segregationist newspaper article chided after noting the company's use of black models in ads in African-American weeklies.

"When you drink Falstaff beer, you are aiding the integration and mongrelization of America," wrote another after the brewery bought one of its African-American salesmen a membership in the NAACP.

McKellar remembered the panic the boycott sent through Falstaff when he worked there. "They were hit hard and had to get the company's name off the NAACP roster and wait out the boycott," he said.

One wholesaler was boycotted for using a radio ad on a black station; a Memphis baker was targeted for donating to the NAACP, even though he denied it. J. C. McCrory, vice president of Hart's Bakery, said housewives quit buying his products in grocery stores. "They catch one of our men in the store and really unload on him," he said.

The *Journal* concluded: "It is clear that some individual merchants have been hurt, and the reluctance of big companies to talk about boy-cotts of their products indicates their fears about the explosive mixture of race and business."

As an example of the split in the country, the *Journal* did an article later that same month about fifty merchants getting together in New York for a "first of its kind in the U.S." exhibition with white-owned companies going all out to get the city's 1.2 million blacks to buy their products. The Standard Oil Company of New Jersey distributed thou-sands of copies of "The Negro Travelers Green Book."

A year after *Brown*, the country again was sharply divided over race in the aftermath of two more incidents: the brutal murder in August 1955 of Chicago teenager Emmett Till in Mississippi for allegedly speaking in a familiar tone to a white woman, and one hundred days after that, the refusal of Rosa Parks to sit at the back of a bus, sparking a bus boycott in Montgomery, Alabama, that lasted more than a year. The whole world followed the Till trial and was outraged when half brothers Roy Bryant and J. W. Milam were found not guilty. A grand jury also refused to indict the two on kidnapping charges, and the men again went free. Alabama journalist William Bradford Huie, writing for *Look* magazine, paid one of the men to give his account of the mur-der. In the end, Huie wrote, the only justice served was when blacks boycotted the stores owned by the families of Milam and Bryant, which put them out of business.

The Southern marketplace again became a battlefield. Roy Wilkins, executive secretary of the NAACP, demanded that big national corpo-rations keep an eye on their franchises to ensure that none participated in what the *Defender* called in an October 1955 story, "a reign of terror against Negroes in the South." The paper reported that deliveries were cut off to black merchants from many big companies, beginning with Coca-Cola and spreading to Pepsi-Cola, Dr Pepper, Royal Crown Cola, and various bread, milk, and medicine distributors to intimidate black voting registration and school enrollment. Car dealers, it said, were refusing to extend monthly payment plans to black customers. The list was long. Wilkins warned that what a big company might dismiss as a local problem had much bigger implications. He and other leaders threatened a boycott by black customers against participating dealers and merchants, and their parent companies. The paper quoted an unidentified "white citizen" as saying a 90 percent compliance with a black-consumer boycott "would close 80 percent of the white locally owned businesses" in many areas.

It was in this atmosphere that the Pepsi-Cola salesmen worked harder still for integration of their staffs. To fully realize the potential of the African-American market, they insisted, the plants would have to hire more black employees in the front office as salesmen. "I told them they needed their own Julian," Julian Nicholas said.

The regional salesmen began to recruit, hire, and train staff for sales jobs in the plants. Nicholas hired men for the bottlers in Washington, D.C., Richmond, Virginia, Charlotte, North Carolina, and Charleston, South Carolina. In 1955, Sam Hall became the first black sales manager at the Philadelphia plant. Harvey Russell hired Hydel White, a thirty-four-year-old Tuskegee-trained Schenley liquor salesman for New Orleans. White liked the culture of the cola company. "There were certain things I could do with Pepsi I couldn't do with Schenley—like go to churches, school, religious conventions. I could bring Pepsi much further," he said in a 2005 interview.

Russell thought it was time to reestablish the team on a national level. While the regionalization was successful, there was a limit to the expansion of the local programs. After being sent "for the umpteenth time" to the same Southern cities to work with the same bottlers, he felt he had done all he could to increase sales locally. The task had become one of maintaining purchase orders. Russell sent a letter in 1957 to his boss Clifford Riddle in New York, complaining that his talents weren't being put to good use. "I don't think this is the proper use of anyone," he recalled writing. "You know we had the highest-trained group of salespeople in the whole company. Everyone we had was a college graduate, you know. It's a shame not to utilize this group of men, who were trained to a greater advantage."

He got a letter back asking him to report to Riddle's office the following Monday. "I knew I was going to be fired," Russell said, with a smirk. Instead, Riddle told him: "If you think you know so much about it, I want you to run it."

Russell was made director of the group. The first thing he did was to insist the term *Negro market* not be used any longer. (None of the salesmen on the Boyd team had ever used the term *Negro* in their official titles.) Instead, the department was renamed "special markets." More than six years after Ed Boyd was fired, the company was reinstating the division. "It took them that long to realize what they had, or else they would have replaced us right away," Emmons said.

By that time, the Kenyon & Eckhardt Company had the six-million-dollar Pepsi account. Pepsi-Cola had dismissed Biow, then called Biow-Beirn-Toigo, Inc., in 1956, with no reason given, although newspapers reported that Steele had felt the agency was giving better treatment and more talent to Philip Morris's campaign than to Pepsi's. By 1958, Russell, Pepsi-Cola's Al Goetz, and the agency representatives had restarted print-ad campaigns in the black press. Russell also used Spanish-language ads in domestic newspapers, and added a second Spanish-speaking manager to his department.

It had been nearly three years since the black weeklies had a Pepsi campaign. The new five-ad series was a direct counterpart to the 1954 "Refresh Without Filling" series. It featured young, attractive African-American women—slim and modern, though less elegantly dressed. "Look at the modern buffet. You'll find the lighter food and drink that active men and women prefer," the ad text began. A bylined article that ran alongside the first of the series on March 8, 1958, featured Harvey Russell's brother. "Our introduction to the new 'less weight for mother' Pepsi-Cola came about through a personable and energetic young gentleman, George Russell, who has served as special representative with the Pepsi-Cola Company for the past two years," wrote Betty Granger of the New York *Amsterdam News*. George, the article said, had two certificates from the Pepsi-Cola Route Managers' School.

The models in this latest series were a new group of professionals. Barbara Watson Models, formerly Brandford Models, had closed in 1956, victim of new licensing regulations. Watson said the agency would focus on its charm school, and admitted that it had spent more on getting assignments for its models than it could ever earn back. Barbara Watson got a law degree and began an impressive second career, ending up in the Johnson Administration. It is because of her hard work that the U.S. Post Office now processes passports.

But the black weeklies themselves were beginning to weaken. The civil rights movement overtaking the news of the decade, as well as the lure of the daily newsroom to top black reporters, undermined the role of the black press.

After Harvey Russell's promotion was decided, Nicholas was called to headquarters and promoted to another New York post as head of the entire Eastern Division, which was comprised of bottlers from South Carolina to Maine and had the highest per capita consumption figures for the African-American market. When Nicholas went to New York, Sam Hall of Philadelphia took his place heading the Washington region.

Russell and Nicholas had a friendly rivalry that devolved one night into a drinking contest, for bragging rights, in the ballroom of a small black-owned hotel in Asheville, North Carolina. They were knocking back shots of vodka, one for one, into the wee hours of the morning. Nicholas sat at one of the café tables while Russell played the upright piano in the room—empty except for the amused hotel owner. "Harvey won," Nicholas conceded. "He didn't drink more than I did but he sat there and played the piano the whole time while I just about passed out."

The two were climbing the corporate ladder in tandem. They had the same philosophy to work hard, to be as successful as possible, and to benefit yourself, your family, and your community. For Nicholas, it was the realization of his family's creed.

———

Julian Cardozo Nicholas was the son of two very successful small-business owners from Washington, D.C., where a whole neighborhood and a school still bear the name of his maternal great-grandfather, Francis Lewis Cardozo. Nicholas was born February 1, 1921, to Elizabeth Cardozo Nicholas. She had a second son, Francis Lewis, eighteen months later, and soon thereafter divorced. Nicholas was about twelve years old when his mother remarried, and he loved and admired Beltran Barker. His stepfather was one of the first African-Americans in the district to own a gas station. Taking advantage of Esso Standard Oil's earliest efforts to establish minority-owned franchises to serve black communities, Barker cornered the Washington neighborhood markets with three stations. He bought his first station in the 1920s, when gasoline was pumped with a lever, and when it was still possible for a government worker to save enough money to purchase a franchise. "My father ran his stations and auto-repair shops all during Prohibition," Nicholas said, and repaired trucks for the bootleggers coming from Canada. After Prohibition, he sold only gas.

The work ethic was instilled with a passion in the Nicholas-Barker household, and Julian's stepfather drafted him immediately to pump gasoline on weekends. Nicholas remembers meeting the famous Billboard Jackson, Esso's pioneer black public-relations man whose territory included the 186 Negro-operated gas stations that opened in nineteen Eastern states. Jackson, always promoting the home office's new products, was one of the men who liked to gather at the Barker stations, particularly the newest one at Eighth Street and Florida Avenue NW. "My father held squash sessions, as they called them. All the black leaders bought gas at my father's station. One would get out and go sit and talk to him, then another would come, then another. Before you'd know it, there would be five civil-rights leaders in there talking," Nicholas recalled. Chief NAACP counsel Thurgood Marshall and his cadre of sharp lawyers—including George E. C. Hayes, William R. Ming, Jr., and James Nabrit, Jr.—were among the regulars. They'd discuss details of their preparations for the big court cases. On weekends, Nicholas's mother would invite these distinguished customers to their home in the Brookland district, an exclusive black neighborhood in Washington.

By the time Nicholas had joined Pepsi-Cola, his stepfather also had become the first African-American in Washington to own a home-appliance store, selling RCA television sets, Norge refrigerators, Bendix washing machines, "always the top-of-the-line items," Nicholas recalled. "My father lived and breathed for his businesses—and his golf."

But Nicholas's mother, Elizabeth, had an even more successful business than her husband's. She and her four sisters owned the nationally known hair salon The Cardozo Sisters. The salon had an extraordinary fifty-two-year run, into the 1970s. It employed thirty-five stylists at its peak, the largest hair salon in Washington, D.C.—"black, white, green, or grizzly," as Nicholas put it.

The sisters were trained by cousins who owned barbershops and beauty salons on the Boardwalk in Atlantic City, New Jersey. The eldest sister, Margaret, was made the chief stylist after she went to study in Paris salons. Another sister, Emmeta, joined the venture after starting her own business in Harlem with Rose Morgan. She was the Meta of Rose Meta Cosmetics, one of the most famous black-owned cosmetics companies flourishing at the time. She had gone to New York seeking a career in entertainment, and was a Ziegfield Follies showgirl before starting the business venture. Duke Ellington was a friend of hers and sometimes visited the Nicholas home.

So, even before her marriage to Barker, Elizabeth Cardozo Nicholas was able to afford a comfortable life for her two sons. She hired the domestic help she needed to run her households as a single mother working six long days a week at the salon. In addition to their home in Washington, the family had a summer place at Highland Beach, Maryland, the exclusive Chesapeake Bay enclave settled by the family of Frederick Douglass. Later, they bought another summer home on Cape Cod.

Despite the family's lifestyle, Nicholas said he never felt pampered. "Everybody worked. My brother and I had jobs since we were twelve or thirteen, and we had to give my mother a certain amount of money each month," he said. "That was part of our training."

While in junior high school, Nicholas also started caddying at the Chevy Chase Country Club, where his stepfather had caddied as a youth. He soon was promoted to the club's dining room, which gave him his first inside look at the affluent lifestyle of whites in the segregated capital.

For all its focus on hard work, Nicholas described his family as funloving. The whole family enjoyed music, and Nicholas fell in love with jazz, especially after meeting Ellington. Other visitors to the home included the boxer Joe Louis and the activist actor Paul Robeson, whose wife, Eslanda "Essie" Goode, was a Cardozo. When these luminaries would gather for dinner, the talk would turn to art and culture, business, and the plight of blacks. The children were taught that although they were shielded from much, they would always have to battle prejudice. "All you had to do was walk down the street and prejudice slapped you in the face—all the places you couldn't go," Nicholas said. He remembered his well-dressed, light-skinned mother having white salespeople from the city's finer shops bring dresses to her home for her to buy.

Nicholas's parents kept their coffee table covered with reading material: the major local daily; the Baltimore *Afro American* and *The Pittsburgh Courier* weeklies, *The New Yorker* magazine, *Good Housekeeping,* and *Fortune.* The mix showed him various sides of life. "There were always possibilities of rising above the turmoil that you read about or heard about—not just racial turmoil, mainly economic turmoil, the difference between the poor and the rich," Nicholas said. "You always knew that with education and a trade, you could live in a better house or move to a better area."

Many in his family had—for generations. Nicholas's maternal grandmother was Blanche Warrick, from the Philadelphia family that had operated businesses in catering, barbering, and hair styling since before the Civil War. Subsequent generations produced doctors and dentists. Blanche married Francis Lewis Cardozo, Jr., and had five daughters, including Nicholas's mother, and a son. When Blanche died young, her husband sent the children to Catholic boarding schools. Nicholas's mother, Elizabeth, practiced Catholicism until she tired of the segregated parishes in Washington. She then joined the All Souls Church, a progressive Unitarian congregation that advocated equal rights for blacks and women.

In the 1960s, Elizabeth was made chairwoman of the cosmetology board in Washington. She helped pass a law that anyone with a cosmetologist's license had to show efficiency in doing all types of hair. "Before that, we had a lot of beauty shops all over Washington that blacks couldn't go to," Nicholas remembered. "Yet a number of my mother's customers were white."

Elizabeth Cardozo's famous grandfather was the educator Francis Lewis Cardozo, son of a free black woman and a man of Portuguese Jewish decent whose family immigrated to Charleston, South Carolina, before the Civil War, according to an unpublished family history. Francis L. Cardozo was sent overseas to be educated, first to the University of Glasgow and then to the University of Edinburgh, in Scotland, and finally to England to the London Theological Seminary. He returned to America in 1864 to be pastor of a church in New Haven, Connecticut. There, he began to see the salvation of his people in terms of education rather than of formal religion.

Cardozo moved back to South Carolina and opened the Avery Institute to train a cadre of teachers whom he envisioned educating the freed slaves. During Reconstruction, he also served as secretary of state of South Carolina, then secretary of the treasury. He faced charges of misuse of funds—all trumped up, the family says—but was pardoned by the governor. He moved to Washington, D.C., penniless, but taught at a succession of local black high schools until he worked his way up to principal. One senior high school still bears his name.

His son, Francis L., Jr., Elizabeth's father, inherited the same love of teaching. But Elizabeth wanted her sons to own their own businesses. She was the only sister to marry a businessman; the others mostly married Howard University professors. The women's only brother, William, was a doctor. "The family always argued about which was better, business or the professions," Nicholas said.

His uncles won him over. Nicholas entered Howard University with plans to become a doctor. But in 1942, in his sophomore year, he decided to enlist in the army. Assigned to Camp Lee in Virginia, he was sent to officer training school for a thirteen-week course. When he had finished his training and was ready to get measured for his officer's uniform, he was called in to his superior's office. The officer had a question:

"Mr. Nicholas, does the name The Bookshop sound familiar to you?" the officer asked.

"Yes."

"Were you a member?"

"Yes."

"Well, we're going to have to transfer you. The Bookshop is a Communist front. You were a member, and on that basis we're not going to let you graduate."

Nicholas couldn't believe he wasn't going to be an officer. The Washington Bookshop was an actual bookstore and de facto social club on Connecticut Avenue in Washington that also sold art and regularly featured big-name jazz artists. It was a haunt of the Ertegun brothers, Nesuhi and Ahmet, sons of the Turkish ambassador to the United States who went on to found Atlantic Records. Nesuhi was a friend of Nicholas's uncles Harold Lewis and Eugene Holmes, Howard professors who were charter members of the club. The Erteguns also would invite Nicholas and his uncles to hear Sunday jazz performances at the Turkish embassy. "The Bookshop was just a place where liberals and artists went, so they welcomed blacks. We were students. We couldn't spell communism. We went for jazz, to see Count Basie and Duke Ellington," said Nicholas.

Later, that same membership roster was used in the House Un-American Activities Committee's hunt for Communists, and the FBI questioned both of Nicholas's uncles, but they never went before the committee, Nicholas recalled. "They were all liberals with leftist leanings, but we were all about Americanism," he said.

Nicholas instead was sent to the 92nd Infantry Division, in Fort Huachuca, Arizona, part of the famed Buffalo unit of African-American fighters. Nicholas became a platoon sergeant and went to Italy with this fifteen-thousand-man division. "Most black outfits were trucking companies or service companies that worked in the rear, but they were sent into combat," Nicholas said. The group fought shoulder to shoulder in Italy with an international group of front-line fighters of color. Nicholas's division suffered heavy casualties, and was reinforced with fighters from a Japanese-American Nisei 100th Battalion, nicknamed the Purple Heart Battalion for its own tremendous losses. Alongside them, under the British Eighth Army, was a battalion of Gurkhas and Sikhs. These battalions cut a wide swath up Italy's boot to the Franco-Italian border, from its western shore to deep inside the country.

Nicholas was in a rifle company on the front lines when he joined Sherman's Raiders, an all-black volunteer reconnaissance unit. Part of his reason for volunteering, he said, was to separate from the inexperienced white officers sent in as replacements amid the heavy fatalities. "They were ill-trained for combat, and that messed up your head!" Nicholas remembered. "A wrong order could send you to your death. So after all the degradation we suffered in the military, we came up with this all-volunteer outfit that was fierce and combat-ready. We protected ourselves and advanced the regiments with few casualties."

The famed Tuskegee Airmen, black aviators of the 99th Pursuit Squadron, which later combined with the 332nd Fighter Group, gave cover to the ground troops in Italy. Nicholas remembered being on night patrol once when he was nearly spotted by the Germans. "The Lord decided they wouldn't find me," he said. "I was hiding right under a Madonna statue in the field, like there were in the fields all over Italy."

In Lucca, the Ruspoli family, Italian nobility whose older sons were partisan fighters, asked to meet some of the black soldiers who had liberated the area. Nicholas and some others stayed in their palace for a month. To his delight, they had a collection of jazz records by Louis Armstrong and Duke Ellington. As Nicholas was leaving, the Princess Ruspoli gave him a lace cloth she had made. "She said it was for my mother; that was one of the nicer experiences," Nicholas said.

By the time the men reached the Alps, the war in Europe had ended. "We had our big parade in Genoa, then shortly after, I had enough points to come home," said Nicholas, who for decades after attended reunions of the division's alumni group.

Nicholas returned to Howard as a junior in 1947, and soon met the woman who would become his wife, Bettina "Tina" Amonitti, from a Philadelphia family of African-American and Italian-American descent. Nicholas's stepfather insisted his son attend the same college to which white, middle-class business owners sent their children, so Nicholas left Howard and took his new wife to New York City to enroll in Pace College of Business Administration. He was one of about five African-Americans at the school. Loyal to his family's work ethic, he attended classes while holding a job at a Harlem appliance store.

———————

Nicholas knew as soon as he arrived at Pepsi-Cola what his personal goal was: to become the first African-American Pepsi bottler. He was glad of the opportunity to work in headquarters after his 1958 promotion. He was learning the business from the ground up. The timing was right for him to make a move to New York. After nine years of marriage, Nicholas was divorced; his ex-wife and daughter moved to Philadelphia.

Nicholas was plotting his next move when the company hierarchy was shaken by the death of its top executive. On April 19, 1959, Alfred N. Steele died of a heart attack, days shy of his fifty-eighth birthday. Some twelve hundred mourners attended his rites at St. Thomas Church in Manhattan, with another two thousand lining the streets— as much to catch a glimpse of his famous third wife, Joan Crawford, as to honor Steele.

Crawford was elected to Pepsi's board of directors the following month in a surprise move at the annual meeting. Pepsi President Herbert Barnet had credited her with helping her husband build the brand. (Pepsi posted net profit of $11.55 million for 1959.) In addition to her director's fees, she had a six-year contract and a $50,000 annual salary. The special-market salesmen were pleased with the news. Ever since Steele married Crawford in 1955, they had identified the frank-spoken actress as an ally. Barnet succeeded Steele as CEO and was given the power to preside at board meetings. The chairman's seat was left empty for the time being, in memory of Steele. This change in leadership would have far-reaching consequences for the special-markets department.

BBD&O set the tone for the post-Steele regime by replacing his "Be Sociable" slogan with one that again focused on youth. The wildly popular new slogan, "Pepsi—for those who think young," captured the zeitgeist of the baby boomers in their teen years, and the nation as a whole under the administration of John F. Kennedy. The agency, which had established the permanent Negro-market department, assigned Tom Sims to work with Harvey Russell's domestic account.

Amid the push into global markets, many black professionals became excited about the prospects of participating in the economic transformation of Africa. All along, Harvey Russell had been pushing Pepsi-Cola's efforts on the continent. He saw the move into the international arena as a new, wide-open frontier for his group. After Pepsi-Cola won government approval for franchises in Western Nigeria in 1959, he sent "three aces," as the press called them—George Russell, Bill Payne and Hydel White—to open four plants there and stay on as temporary plant managers. Paul Davis was sent to Ghana. The men reported to the president of Pepsi International, Don Kendall.

In this rush into Africa, *Ebony* worried that the domestic Negro market was being abandoned, even though its value had reached twenty billion dollars. The magazine quoted a British publication's calculation that the average income for the American Negro topped the income of the average Briton.

There was good reason for concern. Companies were being criticized for falling behind on their fair-hire practices. In the fall of 1960, civic groups called a boycott against Pepsi-Cola in Philadelphia until it made more African-American hires. "We were surprised to be included in the boycotts," Russell told the press. In two days, the local plant promised to hire more driver-salesmen and a secretary. To further placate locals, Joan Crawford was sent to open a black debutante ball. But the local hiring started by the former regional salesmen was slow to progress.

Russell was preoccupied with the African venture. A photo of Russell in his office from that period shows a large poster announcing that trumpeter Louis Armstrong would be playing at a stadium in Lagos, Nigeria, as part of a "jazz safari" on behalf of Pepsi-Cola. In 1961, Russell went on a seven-week investigation of the African market, estimated to have 230 million potential customers. He visited Nigeria, Ghana, Sierra Leone, Liberia, and Senegal. "Sending a Negro over is an extra plus for Americans who want to open markets in West Africa," Russell told the *Times*. "There is room for American business in West Africa now, as long as it does not enter on a basis of exploitation."

Nicholas figured his best chance of being a bottler was to go to Africa, where the company was expanding and where a black American could make contacts and get a large bank loan. He planned to start by getting an assignment as temporary plant manager, and announced to his superiors in late 1961 that he was ready to be sent overseas.

He was surprised and disappointed when he was told he had to stay Stateside. The rejection didn't make sense until January 1962. Then, Pepsi-Cola president Herbert Barnet dropped a bombshell on American business: Harvey C. Russell was elevated to vice president in charge of special markets, the first black American to earn such a seat at a major international company. Nicholas, in turn, would be promoted to national public-relations director for special markets, with a million-dollar budget. Nicholas was glad for the opportunity to take an important national post, but it derailed his dreams of making his fortune.

Ebony called Russell the top Negro in American big business—a "$20,000-plus a year man"—barely mentioning Jackie Robinson, who had been named vice president at a smaller company, Chock full o'Nuts, in 1957. "It was in recognition of the great job Harvey has done. He got it strictly on merit," Barnet felt compelled to explain to the press after giving Russell one of twenty-eight vice president posts at the company.

Russell responded: "The problem facing my race is getting to a spot in which to prove ability. Once in a position where ability counts, there are few problems." He also reminded reporters that they were "overlooking the companies that are owned by Negroes."

Russell remembered management being careful about his promotion, and worried about how the Southern bottlers would take the news. He suggested they speak to a New Orleans bottler who happened to be in the coast guard with him. The bottler gave a stellar recommendation. But after the announcement, when Russell proudly had reprints made of his six-page spread in *Ebony,* he was prevented by top management from handing them out at the next bottlers' convention. "They didn't mind that I had been made a vice president, but they didn't want me to go hawking it to the world," Russell recalled later.

He was also frustrated that his vice president's post had to be tied to special markets even though he had, as *Ebony* pointed out, "handled many companywide, nonracial assignments, including the campaign for acceptance of the firm's new twenty-six-ounce bottle."

Other companies were slow to follow suit in elevating minority employees. Some eighteen months later, Charles T. Williams, Jackie

Robinson's brother-in-law, was named vice president at the Schenley Distillers Company of Schenley Industries, Inc. Some small local concerns also made moves. Yolande H. Chambers became vice president of Davidson Brothers, Inc., a Detroit department store, and Kenneth Sherwood was appointed vice president of the Fleetwood Furniture Company in New York City. Three years later, the press noted a handful more: E. Frederic Morrow, assistant vice president of Bank of America International (and former staffer in the Eisenhower administration, the first black executive in the White House); Spencer Robinson, head of the Advanced Space Engineering Division of the Douglas Aircraft Company; and Cage S. Johnson, vice president, public relations, for the Schick Safety Razor Company.

Ebony noted the progress but derided it as "piddling" compared with the more than two hundred thousand white executives and directors in American business. Russell told the magazine that he believed full equality for blacks would benefit business and vice versa, but added: "There are no moral issues here. This is business entirely."

Once in the vice president's post, however, Russell behaved with an awareness of the various implications of his new role. He sought to reestablish the importance of segment marketing at the company. He created the post of national coordinator of activities for the Spanish market in 1964 for a Spanish-speaking executive. But he emphasized that the African-American market was the more important because blacks comprised the one ethnic group that didn't lose customers— Spanish-speakers assimilated after some years.

Just how big a deal Russell's promotion was is evidenced by how closely even the major media covered his career over the decade. Like it or not, Russell had to be the spokesman for all matters of business and race. He was in constant demand. He received countless honors from civic groups. In 1964, he became co-chairman with Rodman Rockefeller, son of then-governor of New York Nelson Rockefeller, of the

Interracial Council for Business Opportunity. Governor Rockefeller later named Russell to a committee to study the surge in welfare costs in times of prosperity. Russell also championed the Office of Economic Opportunity. In 1971, he was a pallbearer at the New York City funeral of Whitney M. Young, Jr., executive director of the National Urban League.

Russell was ready for the spotlight. The six-foot-two-inch, forty-four-year-old "looking every bit the football player he was," as the *Times* described him, was a talented speechwriter and public speaker.

When Pepsi executive Herbert L. Barnet died at age sixty-one at the end of 1970, the year after he retired, his obituary, of course, told of his career at Pepsi-Cola—from his appointment as a vice president in 1949 to his rise to president in 1955 and his role as board chairman in 1963. A full one-third of his obituary in *The New York Times,* however, was dedicated to his decision to make Russell a vice president.

———

As race and the civil rights movement remained center stage in American politics, the African-American executives were forced to think about the role they would play. Nicholas remembered a teachers' convention in North Carolina where he had set up a booth. He hired students to hand out Pepsi. When they told Nicholas they wanted to join a sit-in for civil rights at Shaw University, a black college in Raleigh, Nicholas used the students in shifts, driving the ones who had finished working at the booth to the protest.

For the executives, the contrasts between their experiences in Corporate America and the problems facing the communities they targeted exposed one inarguable truth: Companies weren't doing enough to help African-Americans achieve equality. The executives were stung when some of the new generation of activists saw them as sellouts to the big, white corporations, rather than the trailblazers that they were. They worked harder to make their pioneering efforts more meaningful in the highly charged atmosphere. Russell returned to the origins of the special-markets group with a new approach to celebrating black achievement. He had read about how thoroughly black history had been left out of schools nationwide. Russell wanted to create a packaged minicourse in black history, complete with film strip, record albums, and a booklet. In a campaign reminiscent of the "Leaders" series of the late 1940s, he created a three-LP series called "Adventures in Negro History," released 1963–1969. It included the stories of Frederick Douglass, Marian Anderson, Dr. Ralph Bunche, Phillis Wheatley, Jesse Owens, Jackie Robinson, W. C. Handy, and some forty others. Noted historians participated, including John Hope Franklin, who narrated the second album. An African-American record company added music. Pepsi-Cola sold or gave out close to half a million copies. Some bottlers sold the albums for one dollar with a six-pack of Pepsi. "But some places wouldn't take it," Russell said. In New Orleans, he was told they would sell it only if he X-ed out the name of Paul Robeson, "because he was a communist."

It was too much too soon for some. After all, it wasn't until Christmas 1963 that Schenley Industries Inc. felt brave enough to make "a forthright, uninhibited 'pitch' for the female market" in its advertising, according to a *New York Times* story ahead of the holiday campaign. This was despite the fact that surveys showed women represented almost half of all distilled liquor sales in the United States.

Russell also decided it was time to put an African-American in a general-media ad. He chose popular football star Jim Brown of the Cleveland Browns, whom he had hired as a Pepsi spokesman, to pose for the new piece ("10,882 yards for Cleveland . . . 168,427 miles for Pepsi"). "It was a beautiful ad," Russell recalled of the full-page, four-color ad that ran in *Sports Illustrated* on March 8, 1965, "but it was used just one time because we got complaints from bottlers. They objected to our having Jim Brown in the white media."

Pepsi-Cola was criticized another time when Joan Crawford was on a television program and Sammy Davis, Jr. walked up and kissed her after his introduction. "The howls that came from bottlers around the country!" said Russell.

He would give them another reason to howl. When Russell was named vice president, he told *Ebony*: "Negro advancement in American business is an evolutionary thing. In 1945 you could count the companies with one or two Negro representatives on one hand; soon practically all companies had one or two. Now there's been a breakthrough toward the executive level. The next step is to appoint officers not in direct connection with the Negro market."

That next step happened for Russell in 1965, when he was named vice-president, corporate planning, of the newly formed PepsiCo Inc., founded through the merger of Pepsi-Cola and Frito-Lay, with headquarters in Purchase, N.Y. To take his place as head of special markets, he lured H. Naylor Fitzhugh to Pepsi-Cola from Howard University, where Fitzhugh taught marketing. Fitzhugh, known as the first African-American to earn a Harvard MBA (in 1933), brought improved marketing-research techniques to the special-markets division. He served as vice president there until his retirement in 1974, after which he became a consultant for Pepsi-Cola until his death in 1992.

As bad as it was at times, Russell never expected the attacks that followed his promotions to be directed at him personally. But in the summer of 1965, the Ku Klux Klan decided to take action against his promotion. Russell saved one of the two hundred thousand flyers handed out on the streets of South Carolina, North Carolina, Georgia, and Florida. It showed Russell, his wife, Jackie, and black company salesman Bob Logan at a podium during a New York dinner ceremony. "Below, Picture of Negro Vice President of Pepsi-Cola, At Left, And His

White Wife, In Center; Let the Pepsi People Know What You Think Of Their Vice President And His White Wife."

Without using the word *boycott,* it was a call to action. The second page of the leaflet was a fifty-six-line poem titled "The Saddest Story Ever Told," written by a Klansman based in North Carolina. The poem was a maniacal rant against mixing races that begins, "When a white girl marries a negro, her sun of life goes down."

"Isn't that poem awful?" Russell asked, rereading it years later. "You get furious, but what do you do? If you quit, they say, 'Good, we never thought you'd leave.'"

JET magazine responded by noting Pepsi-Cola's dismay at the attack, and identified Jacqueline Russell as "a light complexioned Negro woman," daughter of the late Colonel Franklin Denison of Chicago, commander of the all-black Eighth Illinois Regiment in World War I.

The special-markets department discreetly resorted to tactics it hadn't used since the cola race wars some fifteen years earlier. It started an unofficial campaign: "Fight the Klan, Drink Pepsi."

In October of that year, the KKK's anti-Pepsi leaflet was used as evidence in a belated investigation of the Klan by HUAC, which had been ordered by President Johnson to curb racial violence across the South. The committee identified the two culprits involved in the anti-Pepsi leafleting as drifters trying to bilk the KKK. The two invoked their right not to incriminate themselves some two hundred times in their appearances before the committee. Leafleting was identified as one of the sixteen types of harassment recommended by the Klan against its enemies; others included the use of mad dogs, itching powder, stink bombs, and slingshots, and putting dead rats in mail boxes, and nails, sugar, and molasses in gasoline tanks.

In the 1960s, the hiring and promotion of black employees in white-owned companies continued at a brisk enough pace that

African-American businesses began to suffer. The best employees were leaving for better-paying jobs and career opportunities at the larger, white-owned corporations. Black-owned businesses tried to woo white workers to fill their ranks, but met with little success. North Carolina Mutual Life Insurance, among others, reportedly banned white recruiters from its conventions to prevent further raiding.

Harvey Russell's final promotion came in March 1968, when he was made vice president in charge of community affairs for PepsiCo, where he stayed until his retirement in 1983.

———————

Harvey Russell once complained of feeling stuck at the threshold of success and acceptance. In fact, he and the Pepsi team made it well through the door in terms of the legacy they established at one of America's iconic companies. By the time of Russell's retirement, Pepsi-Cola counted dozens of African-American managers. The team had established a legacy in minority hiring. The team members could hardly have imagined how far their legacy would go, until they heard the news that half a century after they blazed a trail at the company, Indra K. Nooyi, born in India, was named the new head of PepsiCo. Ed Boyd was sitting at home that day in August 2006 when his wife came up to him and read from a newspaper about the appointment.

"I was so surprised and delighted, I didn't know what to do," said Boyd. He thought back to when he sat in that front row in the Waldorf-Astoria as Walter Mack, then head of the company, made his speech— and his slip of the tongue. Back then, Boyd said, he could never have envisioned himself, or any person of color, in Mack's place on the podium.

"When I think of how the odds were against us; the way in which we had to work to outdo others," he said, taking a deep breath. "I never would have thought a woman could take Mack's place, and even less that a person of color could—and certainly not in my lifetime. It makes me happy to think about her and people like Ken Chenault [at American Express]. It means a lot to me."

Epilogue

THE SIX SURVIVING MEMBERS OF BOYD'S TEAM OFTEN expressed how sorry they were that their parents couldn't have seen all the advances African-Americans made in the workforce and in society at large, let alone their sons' contributions to that radical change. But their parents' generation seems to have had no doubt whatsoever that those accomplishments were at hand, or that their children would play a role.

The Pepsi-Cola experiment was a beginning—for the company, for American businesses just evolving into modern organizations, and for the pioneer sales-team members. After they left the Pepsi-Cola Company, most of the men went on to careers outside the corporate world, in fields that directly helped improve people's lives or that advocated change. Not one, however, regretted the time spent at the company.

Edward F. Boyd took a job alongside Bryan Houston at the Sherman & Marquette, Inc. ad agency. Mack kept in touch, persuading Boyd to be active on some of the many public-service boards he supported. Through those contacts, Boyd was introduced to managers at the international aid agency CARE. In 1954, he was offered a position as mission chief, responsible for setting up an office in Cairo, supervising an international staff, and negotiating contracts between the Egyptian and U.S. governments to provide aid. He helped disburse some ninety-two million tons of food to needy Egyptians and to Palestinians in refugee camps in Gaza during the first year of operation. It was the largest peacetime food-aid program ever undertaken by the agency at that time, Boyd recalled.

He left CARE to work for the Society of Ethical Culture in New York, joining its Encampment for Citizenship plan to establish leadership-training programs for high-school seniors and college students. Boyd helped establish one at the University of California at Berkeley. In the 1960s, he went to work for Wyeth International, a unit of American Home Products, based in Radnor, Pennsylvania. The company was one of many big manufacturers rushing to establish a presence in Africa as countries there began to win their independence. "It took on a great significance to me because of what was happening on the continent," said Boyd.

Wyeth was marketing a new baby formula overseas. Boyd made several trips yearly to Africa, and established a base office in Accra, Ghana, where he hired, trained, and supervised a staff. While on a trip to scout plant sites in Lagos, Nigeria, he crossed paths with William Payne of Pepsi-Cola. Payne spent several years helping to manage the Lagos plant until it could be turned over to local control.

Boyd was unhappy living away from his wife and four children, who had remained in New York City, and left to do consulting work. In the 1970s, he began working in the Washington, D.C., area, first with a computer-marketing firm, then establishing his own market-research consultancy, Resources Management Ltd.

Some thirty years after Mack first called Boyd to offer him a job, he called him again. This time, Mack was gathering former cola executives together to form a new venture, King Cola. He had waited until Tom Elmezzi, his trusted Pepsi-Cola chemist, was out of his contract in 1978 to start the new business. He envisioned the country divided into twenty-nine marketing "kingdoms," and wanted Boyd to help plot strategy. Mack was eighty-three, and walking with a cane, Boyd remembered, but still an energetic businessman. Boyd declined the offer. He had his own ideas about his last career move.

Boyd retired in 1981, and remained in the Manhattan apartment he first moved into after he joined Pepsi-Cola. He developed an alpaca farm with his children at his second home, in Bethel, New York.

Julian C. Nicholas left Pepsi-Cola in 1963. After more than twelve years' traveling the country for Pepsi, he wanted to travel the world. By the end of his tenure as head of public relations, he often worked with Pepsi International on promotional campaigns. Through connections made with that group, he was introduced to Angier Biddle Duke, then chief of protocol for the U.S. State Department. He hired Nicholas as one of a handful of protocol officers for the Johnson administration, in charge of orchestrating high-level state visits. You can pick out Nicholas in many official photos of President Lyndon B. Johnson and his foreign guests, from the Pope to various heads of state. Nicholas escorted the distinguished visitors around the United States, whether they were interested in visiting a steel mill, farms, factories, NASA, or, as one African delegation insisted, the filming of a movie starring the Rat Pack. Several dignitaries stand out in his memory, including Princess Margaret. "Julian, where can we go afterwards?" she asked, happy to find she was being escorted by a jazz aficionado. Imelda Marcos wanted to hire him away from his government post to work in the Philippines.

Eager to work in Africa, Nicholas passed the exam to become a Foreign Service officer. He was assigned to Nigeria just as the spreading civil war reached the capital in 1968. As the transportation specialist, he was put in charge of evacuating three thousand American citizens from Lagos. His following assignments were in the U.S. embassies in Togo and Senegal. He left government work during the Nixon administration, but returned to head protocol for Jimmy Carter's presidential inauguration. In all, he spent fourteen years with the federal government. "My finest hours of my three careers were with the Foreign Service; no question it was the most gratifying and the most interesting, traveling all over the world," said Nicholas, who also remarried during this time.

Nicholas's third career began when he joined the administration of Washington D.C.'s first elected mayor (and first black mayor of a major U.S. city), Walter Washington, as the appointed deputy for the office of business and economic development. He stayed on when Marion Barry defeated Washington in 1979 and served more than twenty years in local government.

Nicholas retired in 2000 to his home in Highland Beach, Maryland.

Allen L. McKellar had been keeping an eye on the Falstaff Brewing Company for some time before he left Pepsi. The marketing jobs in breweries paid better and afforded a better chance for advancement than in the soft-drink industry. In 1953, he became regional sales representative for Falstaff's Southern markets. His job took him first to Birmingham, then to Atlanta, and finally to St. Louis, where he was promoted to vice president of marketing.

McKellar was successful in boosting sales and in hiring more African-Americans as driver-salesmen. He stayed with the company for more than twenty-one years before it collapsed, partly from the consequences of the infamous boycott led by the White Citizen's Council. He retired to his St. Louis home in 1975 with his wife, Ernestine. It wasn't long, however, before he returned briefly to school to study the import-export business and launched a trading company, Senrenella Enterprises, Inc., dealing mostly with African clients.

As soon as William R. Simms left Pepsi, he contacted the New York Urban League and was hired immediately. "Can you start tomorrow?" the telegram asked. He made the office wait until he made a visit home to Minnesota, then began a twenty-seven-year career with the organization. His success in fund-raising got him promoted from the state to the national office, also based in New York. He then rose from assistant director of fund-raising to director, and by the end of his career had helped raise millions of dollars for the organization.

Simms was working at the Urban League when an informal dinner with some friends led to what he sees as his most lasting contribution to his field. In 1960, Simms started a fund-raising organization with Benjamin Sklar of Brandeis University, Harry Rosen of the Federation of Jewish Philanthropy, and Abel Hanson, who became the first chairman of the group. Their aim was to set standards for ethical fund-raising. By 1979, the National Association of Fundraising Professionals had about nineteen hundred members. Some twenty years later, the group dropped the "National" from its name as it grew to twenty-seven thousand members with chapters in six countries, becoming the largest fund-raising group in the world. Such was its impact that Canada's Labour Party, for one, adopted its code of ethics for fund-raising. In 2005, the AFP honored the legacy of its last surviving founder with the presentation of the first annual William R. Simms Award for Outstanding Youth in Philanthropy. The award is given out in two categories: candidates ages eighteen to twenty-three, and those under eighteen.

Simms retired from the Urban League in 1979, when he turned sixty-five years old. He left his office on a Friday, and by Monday had started a four-year project to help organize the centennial celebration of Tuskegee University, the Alabama college founded on the Fourth of July in 1881 by Booker T. Washington.

Simms retired in earnest in 2003, to Great Barrington, Massachusetts, where his second wife and their two children had a summer home. Simms was delighted when the town in 2005 finally voted after years of debate to officially recognize its role as the birthplace of W. E. B. DuBois, the man Simms had once met and admired his entire life.

Charles E. Wilson arrived in Geneva in 1951 and entered a rigorous five-year program at the University School of Medicine—in French. He became so proficient in the language—and so well known—that he was asked by the U.S. consulate in Geneva to participate in the United Nation's First International Conference on the Peaceful Uses of Nuclear Energy. That 1955 gathering of more than fifteen hundred delegates is considered a landmark scientific meeting. Wilson was assigned to give lectures to visitors to an exhibition hall on a variety of topics, including agriculture, food irradiation, factory-machine calibration, and portable emergency generators. His presentations were aired on Swiss radio.

The year after he arrived at school, his fiancée, Mary Shelton, joined him and they were married in a civil ceremony. "A representative from the American consul told us when to say, *Oui*," Wilson recalled. While Wilson studied, his wife worked for the United Nations in its refugee division. During the summers, Wilson attended schools in France.

Wilson relished his years abroad. He thought about his reputation when he was a child for being a dreamer, "building air castles," as his teachers complained. But it paid to have dreams, he said. "Geneva was my pearl in the oyster, and for five years I was able to get out from under the yoke of racism," he said. European youth at that time were "Americanophiles," he said, and many sought Wilson out for conversation. He recalled countless acts of kindness from citizens, including the policeman who greeted him with, "Enjoy my country!" And the train conductor who, instead of relegating him to a separate cabin, noted his mixed group of friends and said, "We must mix the races."

But he didn't leave American race politics behind. The brutal murder of Emmett Till in 1955 prompted Wilson to get the hundreds of students who had been following the trial in the international press to sign a petition. He sent the Eisenhower administration the petition, which denounced racism and demanded that justice be served.

After Wilson earned his medical degree in 1956, he was offered a residency in a Geneva hospital. But by then he missed his family, so he planned his return home. His wife, pregnant with the second of their three children, went to live with relatives in Atlantic City while he became the only black intern at the Martland Medical Center in Newark.

The first thing he did when he got back to the States was go for a haircut. "I went to this barbershop and the fellow told me he didn't cut black people's hair," said Dr. Wilson. "It hit me like a ton of bricks. I had been away from this for five years and here I was returning to face it again. . . . But I knew what I wanted to do."

After two years, he joined his family in Atlantic City, where he opened his private practice, and was a general practitioner for the community from 1958 to 1997. In 1970, he was called to Washington by the Nixon administration to participate in its national campaign to combat drug addiction as it affected thousands of Vietnam veterans, he said. He commuted to Washington for six months, helping devise addiction therapies; his specialty was methadone dependence. He was asked to continue his work full-time, and closed his practice for one year to work in Washington.

When he opened the doors to his New Jersey practice after his absence, "there was a line around the block," he said. "That was heart-warming."

Once settled in, Wilson entered politics to help his party after the Watergate scandal, winning a seat as county freeholder for two terms before being defeated. He was active in other organizations, becoming a member of the board of education in Atlantic City, trustee of Hampton University, trustee of Atlantic Community College, cofounder and director of a convalescent center, and medical director of a treatment program for the aged called CARING. For nineteen years, he served as chief medical director for the New Jersey State Athletic Association. He also cofounded a bank, Atlantic National, which promised to employ blacks and not redline African-American applicants for car and home loans. It was bought out by Mid-Atlantic Bank.

He retired with his wife to homes in Atlantic City, Delaware, and St. Maarten island, devoting time to sailing.

Jean F. Emmons worked only briefly cleaning floors before entering the insurance business in Columbus, Ohio. It proved to be a lucrative job, and he was promoted to manager. But Emmons found the work "soul-deadening," he said. He quit to return to graduate school and earn a master's degree in education, the field he thought could effect the most social change. During his studies, he taught seventh grade in a black suburb. (He wanted to start with younger children but that was seen as a woman's job.) After graduation, he moved to a teaching job in the city. He stayed three years, entering training for principals.

To supplement his income, he ran two gas stations until a worker on a night shift was shot and killed by police in what Emmons believed was an unprovoked attack. He quit the business soon after and focused solely on education. He considered himself a strict disciplinarian who demanded high achievement from his students. After his training was completed, he landed a principal's job at one of the city's predominantly white elementary schools, with more than eight hundred pupils. "That was the best job I ever had in my life," he remembered. "The kids loved me, the teachers loved me, the parents loved me, and we had high academic achievement."

He stayed only two years, unable to refuse an offer from the Dean of Education at Ohio State University to become his assistant and earn a doctorate in education. In an odd twist of fate, that dean died within a month, and Emmons found his plans partly derailed. But he graduated with a PhD by 1971, and went to Evanston, Illinois, to be director of personnel for the public-school system. He also worked as a consultant at Procter & Gamble in Cincinnati, while his wife taught at Northwestern. All along the way, he broke color barriers.

But Emmons wanted a number-one position. After seven years in Evanston, that chance came when he took the superintendent's job in Trenton, New Jersey. In 1975, he moved his wife and two children to Trenton to become superintendent of public schools, which had 80 percent African-American students. He was in charge of thirty elementary schools, five junior high schools, and one senior high school. He found the system in a shambles, he said, but was determined to turn it around. He left in 1981, declaring his tenure a mixed success. He knew it wasn't popular to say so, but he felt the African-American parents were too reluctant to allow ranking of the students. No one was marked for success or excellence, and it served to bring down the top students, rather than encourage the lower achievers, he felt.

He left education and retired in Ocala, Florida, with his wife.

Richard L. Hurt left Pepsi-Cola shortly after the breakup of the team and received a master's degree in public relations from Syracuse University. He went to work in Washington as a public-information specialist in the Office of Personnel Management. He eventually joined the staff of the *Boston Globe.* In 1962 he won honorable mention in the American Newspaper Guild's Heywood Broun Award, meant to reflect "the growing social conscience of the press." He wrote a series on the shameful living conditions at the Columbia Point housing project in Boston. He lived in the development for two weeks, centering his story on a fight by Columbia Point residents to close two dumps at the edge the project where a six-year-old girl was killed. The dumps were eventually closed. Hurt left the paper to join the Peace Corps, and continued to write, including book reviews. He never married.

Harvey C. Russell retired to Yonkers and his summer home in Oak Bluffs, Martha's Vineyard. Today, PepsiCo Inc. presents the Inclusion

Award for outstanding work toward a diverse working environment, in honor of Russell's groundbreaking career at the company.

The résumés of those team members who didn't live to retell their stories here are beyond the scope of this book. But relatives of Maund and Watson told the following in interviews for this book and with employees at PepsiCo:

David F. Watson spent his entire career at the Pepsi-Cola Company, living in Elmhurst, Queens. He retired in the late 1970s and died in 1983.

Jeanette Maund got her master's degree in social work from Columbia University in 1945. She subsequently distinguished herself as a social worker in New York City and in Utica, New York, in Los Angeles, and, finally, in Cambridge, Massachusetts. In Utica, she was selected to be that city's Ambassador of Good Will to Sweden and to Denmark, according to information gathered from relatives for Pepsi-Cola. She died in 1990.

Because the men began their careers at a time when opportunity was severely limited, they felt strongly about what it takes to succeed, regardless of your background. Above all is an education. And not just in business, Nicholas added, but a well-rounded education and knowledge of the world and how it works—and how we got to where we are today. "We all, black and white America alike, should know what the past was so we can determine what the future should and shouldn't be," Emmons added.

Next, travel. Getting an international perspective on your career, they advised, allows greater economic opportunity and a chance at a richer life. Finally, for balance and a sense of contributing to something beyond yourself, interest in community activities. "You've got to be involved civically," said Nicholas. "Don't just vote, do something more than that, for the community, for the church, for poor people—something!"

Mack lived to see African-American professionals promoted to the highest echelons of Corporate America, and was both humbled by his own efforts some forty years before and in awe of the possibilities. "We are moving into one world—in the end, a new and better one for all," he said. He promised at the end of his book never to stop helping others, and challenged American business leaders to do the same, much as he did in 1940 when he asked companies to hire young interns of every background.

The real Pepsi challenge is the same for every corporation—to recognize that diversity is good for business and that business should be good for diversity. "All of us have a role to play, and we all could be doing more," Emmons said.

The experiment of Pepsi-Cola, in which a white executive with a vision opened the door to ambitious and optimistic black pioneers, didn't in itself change the business world. It was a snapshot in time. It is up to another generation to achieve a fully diverse American workplace.

"If at the end of a day, after everything that happened to you—and some of you understand what I'm saying—you still have some of the love inside of you that you started out with that morning, that's what I call 'Love Remains.' "

—Bobby Watson, saxophonist, composer, educator,
Dizzy's Club Coca-Cola, March 12, 2005
("Love Remains," Red Records, 1986)

Acknowledgments

This book was researched and written with the thoughtful and tireless participation of six surviving members of the original Pepsi special-markets teams: Edward F. Boyd, Jean F. Emmons, Allen L. McKellar, Julian C. Nicholas, William R. Simms, and Charles E. Wilson. They not only made possible the retelling of this important episode of business history—they made the whole writing of the book enjoyable.

I am grateful to Rebecca Boyd, daughter of Ed Boyd, for introducing me to this story back in 1997, from which I wrote a column in *The Wall Street Journal*. Becky Boyd has a keen eye for the stories behind a story. Thanks to her, interviews with the late PepsiCo vice president, Harvey C. Russell, and Wilson were saved on tape, though other material, including an interview with Richard L. Hurt, was lost in the paper cleanup after the September 11, 2001, attack, which damaged the *Journal*'s headquarters in Manhattan.

Much-needed accounts of the broader history and personalities at Pepsi-Cola were garnered in several other interviews. Sam Hall and Hydel White told of their own post-team sales careers. And Hall's photographs and copies of ad campaigns were most helpful. Also, I am lucky to have met Thomas A. Elmezzi, the last surviving staff member of the first modern incarnation of Pepsi-Cola Co. and one of the chemists who created the Pepsi formula, who shared stories of the early days of the company. At ninety-one years of age, he was in the Queens office of the Thomas and Jeanne Elmezzi Foundation every day, impeccably dressed and full of good humor and good will, working to the end of his life for his charity. I had another pleasant surprise when I found Adrian Hirschhorn of Connecticut, a retired adman, who recalled interviewing Boyd in the late 1940s, and then handed me his well-preserved master's degree thesis on early advertising in the black press.

Throughout the process, I was aided—and invited to many fine corporate functions—by Maurice Cox, PepsiCo vice president in charge of corporate development and diversity. For years, Cox, members of the company's Black Employees Association, and a group of staffers—black and white—gathered oral histories and materials from the African-American pioneers at Pepsi-Cola to chart minority participation in the building of the company. They did this despite a dearth of corporate archives. Cox and the association first reunited two of the original special-markets team in 1996, and have orchestrated several meaningful celebrations since. Mr. Boyd later hosted an important gathering of team members and their memorabilia.

I had help from many corners in expanding on the specific recollections of the team members. Ahmet Ertegun, who founded Atlantic Records the same month Boyd entered Pepsi-Cola, shared colorful stories of the public and private gatherings of jazz musicians and their fans in Washington, D.C., before World War II, and of his friendship with members of the extended Nicholas family. And he, in turn, offered up more contacts to help with long-forgotten names. Other wonderful anecdotes were told by Glenda "Kandee" Watson, daughter of David Watson; Watson's niece Savannah Potter-Miller; Mary Shelton Wilson, wife of Charles Wilson; Edith Jones Boyd, wife of Edward Boyd; and Ernestine Jones McKellar, wife of Allen McKellar. And Lori Gusdorf and Walter Sczudlo, of the Association of Fundraising Professionals, gave details of Simms's post-Pepsi activities on behalf of career fundraisers.

An interview with Dr. john a powell, professor at the Moritz College of Law, the Ohio State University, helped me to outline the political history of the book's time period.

Gina Cotter, my niece, saved valuable time by transcribing many hours of recorded interviews with lightning speed and impressive accuracy, and reviewing archival material. Mary McGlynn also helped early on by gathering articles on advertising history from the international press. Later, Aresta Alemayehu plowed through a mountain of microfilms to review many years' worth of newspaper advertisements at the Schomburg Center for Research in Black Culture in Harlem.

Acknowledgments

The quality of the photographs in this book was made possible by veteran photojournalist Marcelo Montealegre, who managed expert reproduction of the Pepsi-Cola advertisements from the 1940s, often reviving them from a battered piece of microfilm. Maryanne Murray of the *Journal* art department advised on the final photo layout.

As always, I am indebted to my mentor and former colleague Ellen Graham, a pioneer in her own right as a female business reporter at *The Wall Street Journal*, who offered her editing expertise in the first read of the manuscript. The book reached its final shape thanks to the editing of Martin Beiser at Simon & Schuster's Free Press imprint, and to the copyediting of Celia Knight and Fran Fisher. From the start, Dominick Anfuso lent his enthusiastic support and marketing acumen to the project, and Kate Harris Jay led the final publicity campaign for the Free Press. At WSJ Books, Roe D'Angelo was an original champion of the project, and coordinated marketing and promotion for the *Journal* side. I also benefited from the constant friendly encouragement and professional advice of Marti Gallardo, of the *Journal*'s advertising department.

I also am grateful for the input, as the manuscript progressed, of my friend Larry Worth; of my family, Neva Capparell, Bill Cotter, Susan Cotter, and Roz DiCuccio, all talented editors; of my colleagues Cynthia Crossen, Christopher Farley, and Tim Carroll; and of Hasan Jeffries, professor of history at the Kirwan Institute of Ohio State University. Professor Jeffries brought a deep knowledge of African-American history to his review of the manuscript.

Any creative endeavor takes the hard work of many staff members and an important core of solid supporters who decide to commit to a project to the bitter end. That core is especially vital when dealing with a topic as controversial as race and business. For getting the book over its many hurdles, I'd like to thank Paul Steiger, Jim Pensiero, Fred Kempe, and Alan Anspaugh at *The Wall Street Journal*. Melinda Beck and my colleagues on the *Journal*'s Marketplace page enabled me to take leave from the paper.

Finally, it is a godsend to have a writer's retreat, especially one filled with ardent supporters of the project. The staff of the Wainwright Inn in Great Barrington, Massachusetts, under the generous direction of Marja Tepper Grader, and the hospitality of her husband, Robert, afforded a perfect gathering place for a long-awaited reunion of the Pepsi-Cola team—the first, in 2004, of every surviving member. Later, the inn became a refuge for long and fruitful writing sessions.

In the end, I feel tremendously indebted to a whole generation of editors and writers of the African-American press, who were asked to tackle some of the most daunting issues of the twentieth century and did so with remarkable intellectual depth, commitment, and most important, a vision for a better future.

Bibliography

Material for this book was gathered from books, Web sites, documentaries, movies, newspapers and magazines, and the business ephemera collected by Edward Boyd and Allen McKellar. Microfilms of African-American weekly newspapers, including the Norfolk *Journal and Guide,* the New York *Amsterdam News,* the *Chicago Defender,* and *The Pittsburgh Courier* were scanned from 1939 to 1959 for advertisements and stories, and a page-by-page reading of the *Defender* and *Courier* was done for the years 1947 through 1951. *Ebony* and *Fortune* magazines were scanned from 1945 through 1953. The entire publication archives of *The Wall Street Journal* and *The New York Times* were searched online by topic using ProQuest.

All of the data shaped a particular understanding of the cultural and political world inhabited by the original Pepsi-Cola sales teams. The following bibliography is intended to list only items specifically quoted or offering essential supplemental information. It is divided into chapters to facilitate identification of sources and means of deduction, and to give a historical overview, although material was shared throughout without repeating the listings.

Introduction

BOOKS

Mack, Walter, with Buckley, Peter. *No Time Lost: The Autobiography of Walter Mack.* New York: Atheneum, 1982.

Tye, Larry. *Rising from the Rails: Pullman Porters and the Making of the Black Middle Class.* New York: Henry Holt and Company, 2004.

DuBois, W. E. B. *The Souls of Black Folk*. With introduction and notes by Farah Jasmine Griffin. New York: Barnes & Noble Classics, 2003. (Originally published in 1903)

Pendergrast, Mark. *For God, Country and Coca-Cola*. New York: Basic Books, 2000.

NEWSPAPERS, PERIODICALS, AND BUSINESS EPHEMERA

"For God, Country and Coca-Cola," book review, *Washington Monthly*, June 1993.

"Negro Market: It Expands Sharply as Economic Welfare of Negro People Improves," *The Wall Street Journal*, Feb. 23, 1952.

"Pepsi-Cola Elevates Special Markets Aid," *The New York Times*, Jan. 30, 1962.

"Pepsi's New CEO Doesn't Keep Her Opinions Bottled Up," *The Wall Street Journal*, Aug. 15, 2006.

Radio interview with Allen McKellar and Jeanette Maund by "Mr. Durr," transcript, *Age-Herald News*, Denver Carlton Hotel, Allen L. McKellar Collection.

WEB SITES AND DVDS

National Baseball Hall of Fame and Museum, "Jackie Robinson," baseballhalloffame.org/hofers_and_honorees/hofer_bios/Robinson_Jackie.

Chapter 1: The High Road to Profit

BOOKS

Drucker, Peter F. *Adventures of a Bystander*. New York: Harper & Row, 1978.

NEWSPAPERS, PERIODICALS, AND BUSINESS EPHEMERA

"Advertising Dips: Goods Cut by Strikes, Some Firms Trim Copy; But Big Year Is Forecast," *The Wall Street Journal*, Feb. 18, 1946.

"Advertising News and Notes," *The New York Times*, Aug. 23, 1945, p. 27.

"America's Two Smartest Graduates," *The Weekly Review*, newspaper clipping, n.d., McKellar Collection.

"Anna Hedgeman, Sinatra on CIO Race Amity Honor Roll," *Chicago Defender*, Feb. 2, 1946.

"Atom Bomb and the Colored World," The Winds of Time column by W. E. B. DuBois, *Chicago Defender*, Mar. 26, 1946.

"Big City Crowds 'Go Small Town' at Parks' Giant Dancing Parties," *The New York Times*, July 22, 1949.

"Body of Man Who Led Fight for Race Found in River," *The Pittsburgh Courier*, July 6, 1940.

"Bottling Representatives Visit Here," unidentified newspaper clipping, McKellar Collection.

"The Brown Hucksters," *Ebony*, May 1948.

"Business Interns Have Been Chosen; Mrs. Roosevelt, the Mayor and Other Leaders to Be at the Naming Tomorrow," *The New York Times*, July 7, 1940.

"Business Notes," *The New York Times*, Mar. 18, 1940.

"Color Lines: They Are Being Erased in War Industries, Ten Key Cities Report," *The Wall Street Journal*, Oct. 19, 1942.

"Congratulates Winners," photo of two new interns, *Chicago Defender*, Aug. 2, 1941.

"Contest Spurs Pepsi-Cola Sales," *The New York Times*, Sept. 1, 1939.

"Continued Heat Wave Slows Down Industry in East, Midwest; Store Sales Slump; Mercury in High 90s," *The Wall Street Journal*, Aug. 28, 1948.

"Court Asked to Halt Loft Stock Sales," *The Wall Street Journal*, Jan. 6, 1937.

"Court Decision Gives 91% of Pepsi-Cola Stock to Loft, Inc.," *The Wall Street Journal*, Sept. 20, 1938.

"Court Rules Cola a Generic Name," *The Wall Street Journal*, Jan. 6, 1944.

"Enigma," Herman Smith item in Adventures in Race Relations column, *Chicago Defender*, Sept. 20, 1947.

"Ethnology of Jim Crow," *Chicago Defender*, Feb. 9, 1946.

"Festival to Show U.S. 'Spirit' Urged," *The New York Times*, June, 27, 1941.

"Fiery KKK Crosses Warn South of New Terror," *Chicago Defender*, Apr. 4, 1946.

"Find No 'Eleanor Clubs,'" *The New York Times*, Sept. 23, 1942.

"For Business Men Who Listen In," radio program schedule, *The Wall Street Journal*, Feb. 26, 1941.

"$4,915,000 Cleared by Pepsi-Cola Co.," *The New York Times*, Oct. 27, 1942.

"14 1/2 Million of U.S. Population Colored: Census," *Chicago Defender*, Feb. 16, 1946.

"Georgia Meet Ruled by White Supremacy," *Chicago Defender*, Oct. 19, 1946.

"The Great Game of Politics; The Negroes in 1940," *The Wall Street Journal*, July 15, 1940.

"Harlem Night Club Boon," *Ebony*, Nov. 1946.

"High Court Agrees to Review Rail Jim Crow Laws," *Chicago Defender*, Jan. 26, 1946.

"How American Youth Faces Its Future," essay submitted to Pepsi-Cola contest, in press release from desk of Ruth R. Maier, Pepsi-Cola press representative, McKellar Collection.

"Industry in Drive to Get War Scrap," *The New York Times,* May 26, 1942.

"Interracial Radio Station to Open," *Chicago Defender,* Nov. 14, 1946.

Itemized budget, Pepsi-Cola expense account form, January 1943, McKellar Collection.

"Job Award Plan for Youth to be Told by Walter Mack," unidentified newspaper clipping, McKellar Collection.

"Job Winners," *NEWSPIC,* Apr. 1941.

"Jobs for Youth Called Urgent," unidentified newspaper clipping, Allen L. McKellar Collection.

Letter, "Dear Mr. McKellar," signed by Walter S. Mack, Jr., July 1, 1940, McKellar Collection.

Letter, "To Whom It May Concern," signed by Olin D. Johnston, governor of South Carolina, Nov. 30, 1943.

"Local Pepsi-Cola Co. Joins with Mr. Allen L. McKellar to Fete Meridian Business Men and Women," *The Echo,* Dec. 5, 1941.

"Mother Describes 'Streamlined' Lynching of Son in Mississippi," *The Pittsburgh Courier,* July 13, 1940.

"Move to Eradicate Racial Frictions," *The New York Times,* June 30, 1943.

"Mrs. Paul Robeson Says Negroes Making Progress," *Chicago Defender,* Feb. 16, 1946.

"NAACP Bureau to Advise on Negro Film Portrayals," *Chicago Defender,* Dec. 7, 1946.

"Negro Actors Cheered, Then Barred at Hotels Restaurants," *Chicago Defender,* June 15, 1947.

"Negro Employment Is Rising Fast in War Industries," *The Wall Street Journal,* Oct. 8, 1942.

"Negro Will Get $3,200 Car Denied in Raffle; Kiwanis Head Forces Action After Protest," *The New York Times,* July 17, 1947.

"Negro Workers: West Coast Asks: What Can We Do with Them? Jobs End But They Stay," *The Wall Street Journal,* Dec. 8, 1945.

"Negroes Enlist Because of Civilian Job Shortage," *The Pittsburgh Courier,* Mar. 23, 1940.

"Negro Market Study Urged," New York *Amsterdam News,* March 16, 1940.

" 'New' Negro Replacing Stereotype, Says White," *The Pittsburgh Courier,* Aug. 23, 1947.

"New Youth Center Opened in Harlem," *The New York Times*, Apr. 21, 1945.

"N.Y. Anti-Bias Law Lauded," *Chicago Defender*, Jan. 12, 1946.

"Officers Honored at Gala Navy Ball," *The New York Times*, Oct. 30, 1945.

"OPA Dies; NAACP Urges Buyer Boycott in Mass Protest," *Chicago Defender*, July 6, 1946.

"Over 600,000 Negroes Left Dixie Before '39; What Will '40 Figures Be?" *The Pittsburgh Courier*, Feb. 24, 1940.

"Paul K. Edwards of Rutgers Dead," *The New York Times*, Dec. 8, 1959.

"Pepper and Salt," *The Wall Street Journal*.

"Pepsi-Cola and Black Americans: A Long, Intensive Effort Linked Soft Drink Manufacturer to Blacks and Gave the Business World Lessons in 'Target Marketing,'" PPHST92.A.doc., unpublished interviews with former employees and families of Pepsi salesmen compiled at PepsiCo.

"Pepsi-Cola Co. Appoints Herman T. Smith to New Sales Promotion Position," Norfolk *Journal and Guide*, March 23, 1940.

"Pepsi-Cola Co. Hires Hall to Inform Holders of Problems, Outlook," *The Wall Street Journal*, Apr. 7, 1949.

"Pepsi-Cola Co. Shows $3,240,333 Net for Year Ended December 31, 1938," *The Wall Street Journal*, Apr. 22, 1939.

"Pepsi-Cola Defends Syrup Importation," *The New York Times*, Nov. 18, 1943.

"Pepsi-Cola Fetes Greek Fraternities," *Chicago Defender*, Jan. 17, 1942.

"Pepsi-Cola Gives Jobs to Negroes," *Chicago Defender*, Jan. 30, 1943.

"Pepsi-Cola Co. Hires Hall to Inform Holder of Problems, Outlooks," *The Wall Street Journal*, April 17, 1949.

"Pepsi-Cola, Loft Boards Approve Merger Program," *The Wall Street Journal*, Apr. 29, 1941.

"Pepsi-Cola Names H. T. Smith to Negro Market Sales Post," *The Pittsburgh Courier*, Mar. 23, 1940.

"Pepsi-Cola Profit $5,821,853 in 1940," *The New York Times*, Mar. 11, 1941.

"Pepsi-Cola Profit Put at $6,274,776," *The New York Times*, Mar. 13, 1943.

"Pepsi-Cola Reports Record Sales Rise," *The New York Times*, Oct. 28, 1941.

"Pepsi-Cola Representative Here," *The Forum Sun*, May 7, 1943.

"Pepsi-Cola Representative Visits City," *The Forum Sun*, June 1942.

"Pepsi-Cola Representative Visits City," *The Miami Times*, Apr. 17, 1943.

"Pepsi-Cola Sales Down in First Quarter," *The Wall Street Journal*, Apr. 9, 1949.

"Pepsi-Cola 'Scholars' Visit Us," unidentified newspaper clipping, McKellar Collection.

"Pepsi-Cola Status Explained by Loft," *The New York Times*, Oct. 21, 1938.

"Pepsi-Cola Vice President to Head Franchise Work," *The New York Times*, item of Major Talbot O. Freeman, Oct. 5, 1940.

"Pepsi-Cola's Walter Mack," *Fortune*, Nov. 1947.

"Pepsi-Cola Well Supplied with Ingredients, Mack Says," *The Wall Street Journal*, May 17, 1940.

"Polishing Brown Diamonds: African American Women, Popular Magazines, and the Advent of Modeling in Early Postwar America," by Laila Haidarali, *Journal of Women's History* 17, no. 1 (2005), pp. 10–37.

"Powell's 'Marching Blacks,'" Off the Book Shelf column by Ben Burns, *Chicago Defender*, Jan. 26, 1946.

"Race Engineer Employed by Douglas Corporation," *The Pittsburgh Courier*, June 8, 1940.

"Recent Slur on Joe Louis by Radio Announcer," *Chicago Defender*, Feb. 2, 1946.

"Red Cross Gets $20,525," *The New York Times*, Feb. 1, 1941, p. 20.

"Regal Beer Employs National Negro Salesman," *The Pittsburgh Courier*, June 29, 1940.

"Repairing Senate's Record on Lynching; 'Long Overdue' Apology Would Be Congress's First on Treatment of Blacks," *The Washington Post*, June 11, 2005.

"Returning GI's Arrested After Clash with Police," *Chicago Defender*, Sept. 21, 1946.

"Rockefeller Sees More Concern by Industry over the Negro's Lot," *The New York Times*, May 27, 1944.

"Romeo and Juliet Lead to Hilda Simms," *Chicago Defender*, Mar. 2, 1946.

"Salesmanship," Adventures in Race Relations column, *Chicago Defender*, Aug. 18, 1945.

"San Bernardino Gets First Negro Deputy," *Chicago Defender*, Sept. 21, 1946.

"Senate Disturbed over Bilbo's Race Ravings," *Chicago Defender*, July 6, 1946.

"Service Center Host to Two Million Men," *The New York Times*, July 22, 1943.

"Should I Sacrifice to Live Half-American? Birth of the 'Double V,'" *The Pittsburgh Courier*, 1942 brochure, McKellar Collection.

"Sinatra's Program Takes in Schools," *Chicago Defender*, Feb. 23, 1946.

"Soft Drink Industry's Sales, Profits Up But Raw Materials Pinch Ahead," *The Wall Street Journal*, July 18, 1941.

"Soft Drinks Found Vital for Morale," *The New York Times*, Jan. 3, 1943.

"Soft Drinks: Supply Will Depend on Sugar; Customer Rationing Under Way," *The Wall Street Journal*, Jan. 30, 1942.

"The South: Regional Impressions; Cotton Is No Longer King But Southerners

See Opportunity in Future Economic Growth of Nation," *The Wall Street Journal*, Nov. 28, 1945.

Success Story, booklet distributed by the Pepsi-Cola Company, circa 1961.

"Sugar Trouble: Candy, Cake, Ice Cream to Be Harder to Get; Some Flavors Are Out," *The Wall Street Journal*, Feb. 13, 1942.

"Talmadge Attacks Negroes; Carmichael Lashes KKK," *Chicago Defender*, June 1, 1946.

"2 Chicago A.F.L. Unions Ordered to Cease Discrimination Against Negroes," *The Wall Street Journal*, June 15, 1942.

"2 Race Students Win Mack Job Award Scholarships," Norfolk *Journal and Guide*, July 20, 1940.

"Unions Down South: Industry There Girds for Hot Campaigns by Both AFL and CIO; Fears Revival of Negro Problem (and Ku Klux Klan); Seeks a Better Press," *The Wall Street Journal*, May 3, 1946.

"W. L. B. Abolishes Pay Differentials Between Negro, White Workers," *The Wall Street Journal*, June 7, 1943.

"W. S. Mack Jr., Loft Chairman, Elected President of Pepsi-Cola," *The New York Times*, Aug. 2, 1939.

Walter Mack Job Awards Luncheon, program for thirty-five-year celebration of the Bottling of Pepsi-Cola, July 8, 1940, McKellar Collection.

"Walter Mack Job Awards for Youth to Start Today," *The Wall Street Journal*, July 8, 1940.

"Walter S. Mack, Jr. Named President of Pepsi-Cola," *The Wall Street Journal*, Oct. 17, 1938.

"Walter S. Mack, Who Made Pepsi the No. 2 Cola Maker, Dies at 94," *The New York Times*, Mar. 19, 1990.

"War Industry Executives to Discuss Factory Problems," *The Wall Street Journal*, Nov. 10, 1942.

"Washington Wire," item on African-American reporter admitted to presidential press conference, *The Wall Street Journal*, Feb. 11, 1944.

"Western Electric Gives $12,000, Pepsi-Cola Co. $10,000 to Red Cross," *The Wall Street Journal*, Dec. 31, 1941.

"When Cotton Goes Up, Lynchings Go Down!" *The Pittsburgh Courier*, Apr. 20, 1940.

"White American Thinking; Half Call Negro Mental Equal," *Chicago Defender*, Sept. 28, 1946.

"White, Negro GIs Clash; U.S. Troops in Italy Returned Home," *Chicago Defender*, Nov. 30, 1946.

"Whites Favor Housing Covenants, Poll Reveals," *Chicago Defender*, Feb. 2, 1946.

"Whites Quit When U.S. Agency Integrates Staff," *Chicago Defender*, Mar. 20, 1946.

"Worker at Phillip Morris Tells of Company's Progress," *Chicago Defender*, Apr. 12, 1947.

"Youths Begin Career; 13 Awarded Jobs by Pepsi-Cola Co. Take Up Duties," unidentified newspaper clipping, McKellar Collection.

WEB SITES AND DVDS

The Black Collegian online, "African-American Pioneers in the Corporate Sector," www.black-collegian.com/african/avery, June 2005.

PBS.org, "The Pittsburgh Courier," www.pbs.org/blackpress/news_bios/courier, June 2005.

United Nations, "History of the United Nations," www.un.org/aboutun/unhistory, July 2005.

Wikipedia, "Robert C. Weaver," http://en.wikipedia.org/wiki/Robert_C._Weaver, July 2006.

Chapter 2: Black, White, and Green

BOOKS

Hays, Constance, L. *The Real Thing: Truth and Power at the Coca-Cola Company*. New York: Random House, 2004.

Mills, Robert Lockwood with Harry Maurer. *Thomas Elmezzi: The Man Who Kept the Secret*. JET Foundation Press, Great Neck, NY, 2004.

NEWSPAPERS, PERIODICALS, AND BUSINESS EPHEMERA

"Applied Democracy," book review of *Investment in People: The Story of the Rosenwald Fund*, *The New York Times*, Mar. 20, 1949.

"Biography of Barbara M. Watson," The Barbara M. Watson Papers, The New York Public Library, Schomburg Center for Research in Black Culture.

"Black Press Brought Needed Change," *Quill*, May 2003.

"Bob Woodruff of Coca-Cola," *Fortune*, Sept. 1945.

"Café Bars Negroes, Closed by Pastor's Picket Line," *Chicago Defender*, Mar. 2, 1946.

"Coca-Cola Counter Suit Filed Against Pepsi-Cola," *The Wall Street Journal*, Sept. 20, 1938.

"Coca-Cola Enjoys Big Volume of Sales," *The Wall Street Journal*, Mar. 1, 1924.

"Coca-Cola's Foreign Expansion," *The Wall Street Journal*, May 4, 1925.

Bibliography

"Coca-Cola Freed in Pepsi-Cola Suits," *The Wall Street Journal,* Oct. 12, 1932.

"Credo of the Negro Press," *Wilmington Journal,* June 5, 1954.

"Davies Is Opposed in Republican Club; Committee Formed to Back W. S. Mack, Jr. for Presidency of National Organization," *The New York Times,* Apr. 6, 1939.

"First Negro Model Agency Opened in New York," *Advertising Age,* Aug. 5, 1948, Barbara M. Watson Papers, Box 9, Schomburg Center.

"Glamorous Harlem Girls Become Professional Models," *Chicago Defender,* Nov. 30, 1946.

"Group to Run Pepsi-Cola," *The New York Times,* Mar. 14, 1939.

"No Uncle Toms or Aunt Jemimas," *The AFRO Feature Page,* Nov. 30, 1946, Watson papers, Box 9.

"Pepsi Parties: In Four Cities, They 'Hit the Spot' with Hitherto Unseen Stockholder," *Life,* 1947.

"Robert Woodruff Dies; Built Coca-Cola Empire," *The New York Times,* Mar. 8, 1985.

"Six New Pepsi-Cola Directors Are Elected; Court to Name Neutral Member of Board," *The New York Times,* Oct. 15, 1938.

"Soft Drink Business Yields Big Profits," *The Wall Street Journal,* June 7, 1918.

"The Theatre: Carmen Jones in Town," *The Wall Street Journal,* May 7, 1945.

"The Theatre: *Deep Are the Roots,*" *The Wall Street Journal,* Sept. 28, 1945.

"The Theatre: *Jeb,*" *The Wall Street Journal,* Feb. 26, 1946.

"The Theatre: *On Whitman Ave,*" *The Wall Street Journal,* May 10, 1946.

"The Theatre: *Strange Fruit,*" *The Wall Street Journal,* Dec. 3, 1945.

"Think Ostracism by Other Whites Cause of Suicide," *The Pittsburgh Courier,* Apr. 6, 1940.

"Tolerance Award Given to Driscoll," *The New York Times,* Mar. 24, 1949.

"27 Negro Colleges in $1,500,000 Drive," *The New York Times,* May 4, 1944.

"Unions Must Represent All Workers in a Craft, Supreme Court Declares," *The Wall Street Journal,* Dec. 19, 1944.

WEB SITES AND DVDS

The Hucksters. DVD. Directed by Jack Conway. MGM/UA, 1947.

"The New Negro; Alain Locke" (1925); Prof. Casey Nelson Blake on The Harlem Renaissance. Columbia250; www.c250.columbia.edu/c250_celebrates/harlem_history/blake

Chapter 3: How Big Is Your Negro Market?

BOOKS

Navasky, Victor S. *Naming Names*. New York: Hill and Wang, 1980.

Smith, Mona Z. *Becoming Something: The Story of Canada Lee*. New York, Faber and Faber, 2004.

NEWSPAPERS, PERIODICALS, AND BUSINESS EPHEMERA

"Advertising Company Specializing in Negro Market," *The New York Times*, classifieds, Nov. 30, 1928.

"Advertising News and Notes," item on American Marketing Association, *The New York Times*, May 8, 1946.

"Advertising News and Notes," item on American Marketing Association panel, *The New York Times*, Nov. 20, 1942.

"Advertising News and Notes," Item on Interstate United Newspapers. *The New York Times*, Aug. 16, 1946.

"Anderson Opposes End of Sugar Curb," *The New York Times*, June 5, 1947.

"Archbishop Warns Catholics Seeking to Bar Negro Pupils, Letter Read at Masses in St. Louis, Serious Penalty of Excommunication Is Pointed Out," *The Pittsburgh Courier*, Sept. 27, 1947.

"Auto Workers Elect First Negro to International Union Office," *Chicago Defender*," Nov. 22, 1947.

"Big Bankers Aid South's Racist Politicians," *Chicago Defender*, Jan. 4, 1947.

"Bill Drafted to Outlaw Race Label in Crime News Story," *Chicago Defender*, Feb. 15, 1947.

" 'Body and Soul,' Starring Canada Lee, Gets 'A' Rating from Broadway," *Chicago Defender*, Aug. 30, 1947.

"Book Boom for Negro Authors," *Ebony*, Nov. 1945.

"Broadway Glitter Opens New Center; City Gets Pepsi-Cola Quarters in West 47th Street for Information Services," *The New York Times*, Oct. 29, 1947.

"Broadway Witnesses Two Pictures on the Treatment of Minority Groups," *Chicago Defender*, Nov. 15, 1947.

"Brooklyn Appoints 1st Negro Probation Officer," *Chicago Defender*, Feb. 8, 1947.

"Buffalo Gets Its First Negro Owned Department Store," *Chicago Defender*, Mar. 22, 1947.

"Burned Out Vet to Defy West Coast Racists, Plans to Rebuild Home," *Chicago Defender*, July 26, 1947.

"Canada Lee in White Face," *Ebony*, Jan. 1947.

"Case History of an Ex-White Man," *Ebony*, Dec. 1946.

"Chicago Defender Honor Roll of 1946," *Chicago Defender*, Jan. 4, 1947.

"College Grants Go to 2 New York Boys," *The New York Times*, Apr. 11, 1947.

"Consumer Advertising to the Baltimore Negro Market," thesis submitted by Adrian Hirschhorn toward MBA degree, School of Business and Civic Administration of the City College of New York, June 1949.

"Courier Attends Big Klan Meeting, Exposes Names of Kluxers Who Run Ga. Town," by Stetson Kennedy, *The Pittsburgh Courier*, Nov. 29, 1947.

"Cutbacks Start, Whites Replace 30 Negro Workers in Restaurant Jobs," *Chicago Defender*, May 24, 1947.

"The Death of Bilbo," Here to Yonder column, Langston Hughes, *Chicago Defender*, Aug. 30, 1947.

"Defender Show Grads Join Pepsi-Cola Show," *Chicago Defender*, n.d. (summer 1947).

"Defies Dixie Diner Jim Crow Six Hours, Wins Passengers' Sympathy," *Chicago Defender*, Oct. 4, 1947, p. 1.

"Demands Arrest in Test of Va. Bus Jim Crow Law," *Chicago Defender*, Aug. 30, 1947.

"Dining Car 'Curtains' Opened Before ICC; Decision Pending," *Chicago Defender*, Feb. 8, 1947.

"Divorces W. S. Mack Jr." *The New York Times*, Aug. 19, 1945, p. 24.

"Dr. Bunche Named UN Palestine Chief," *The Pittsburgh Courier*, Dec. 13, 1947.

"Ed Boyd, Grandson of Calif. Pioneers, Gets Big Job with Pepsi-Cola Co.," *The Lost Angeles Tribune*, Oct. 11, 1947.

"Ed Boyd Tore Down Race Barriers to Build a Market for Pepsi," *The Wall Street Journal*, Aug. 29, 1997.

"$11,000 Is Given to Art Winners; Waldo Pierce Gets First Prize," *The New York Times*, July 26, 1944.

"Erskine Sought by Old Tobacco Firm in South," *Chicago Defender*, May 24, 1947.

"Executive Vice President Added to Pepsi-Cola Board," *The New York Times*, Apr. 3, 1947.

"Ex-Slave Marks 100th Year Recalls Days of Civil War," *Chicago Defender*, July 19, 1947.

"Ex-Slave Woman Dies at 107 in North Carolina," *Chicago Defender*, May 31, 1947.

"Family Man Jackie Robinson," *Ebony*, Sept. 1947.

"Five Men Go on Trial in Lynching of Veteran," *Chicago Defender*, Feb. 22, 1947.

Bibliography

"5 Million U.S. White Negroes," *Ebony*, Mar. 1948.

"5,900 Officers Commissioned, Only 32 Negro," *Chicago Defender*, Oct. 25, 1947.

"Fortune Survey Reveals, Few 'Unprejudiced' Persons in Nation," *The Pittsburgh Courier*, Oct. 18, 1947.

"Free Pepsi-Cola, Cream, Candy and Cookies to Billiken Picnic Guests," *Chicago Defender*, Aug. 9, 1947.

"Georgia Ex-Slave Became a Leading Banker," *Chicago Defender*, July 19, 1947.

"Guild Girds to Save Negro Film Positions, Committee Formed to Set Up Policy; Asks Industry's Aid," *The Pittsburgh Courier*, Nov. 29, 1947.

"Hawaii, Which May Be 49th State, Is Larger Than Connecticut," *Chicago Defender*, Aug. 30, 1947.

"Henry Luce Lauds Urban League as He Presses Drive for $450,000," *Chicago Defender*, Apr. 5, 1947.

"Honor Roll of Democracy, 1947," *Chicago Defender*, Jan. 3, 1948.

"Indict Thirty-One in S. C. Lynching," *Chicago Defender*, Mar. 22, 1947.

"Induct Dr. Johnson at Fisk U.; 3-Day Ceremony Ushers in First Negro President," *Chicago Defender*, Nov. 15, 1947.

"Introduce Negro Air Commercial," *Chicago Defender*, Sept. 12, 1947.

"Inventory Curbs Set Up as Industrial Sugar Rationing Is Ended; Price Controls Retained," *The Wall Street Journal*, July 29, 1947.

"Jackie Mobbed by Fans, 'Rookie of the Year' in Spotlight on Eve of Series," *The Pittsburgh Courier*, Sept. 27, 1947.

"Jivin' with Jackson," *Ebony*, Nov. 1945.

"Job Discrimination Called Major Problem of Workers," *Chicago Defender*, Feb. 1, 1947.

"Knights of Columbus Accept Negro Member," *Chicago Defender*, May 17, 1947.

"Legal Test Looms for Jim Crow Travel Laws in North Carolina," *Chicago Defender*, May 10, 1947.

Lionel Hampton and LouisTurner photo, no title, *Chicago Defender*, July 19, 1947.

"Macy's Training First Negro Woman as Large-Scale Buyer," *Chicago Defender*, Oct. 18, 1947.

"Making Hollywood Reform," *Ebony*, Feb. 1947, p. 36.

"Matt Henson," *Ebony*, July 1947.

"May Use Loyalty Test as Cover for Negro Hater," *Chicago Defender*, Sept. 13, 1947.

"Movie Maids; Eight New Hollywood Films Backtrack to Hack Racial Stereotypes in Casting Negro Actors as Usual Maids and Menials," *Ebony,* Aug. 1948.

"Movie Moguls Sue to End Color Ban," *Chicago Defender,* Sept. 27, 1947.

"Msgr. Sheen Flays Bias on Mobile Hospital Site," *Chicago Defender,* May 3, 1947.

"NAACP Presents Petition to UN Exposing Treatment of Negroes," *Chicago Defender,* Oct. 25, 1947.

"Negro GIs Dread Return to U.S. as Duty in Italy Comes to End," *Chicago Defender,* July 19, 1947.

"Negro Staff to Be Integrated in Pepsi-Cola Field Organzation," *Journal and Guide,* n.d., Boyd Collection.

"Neither Big Gains Nor Great Losses Witnessed in 1946," *Chicago Defender,* Jan. 4, 1947.

" 'New Red Probe Is Aimed at Negroes,' Thomas Says," *The Pittsburgh Courier,* Oct. 4, 1947.

"News and Notes of the Advertising Field," item on "A Survey of the Negro Market," *The New York Times,* Feb. 6, 1939.

"NNPA Forms Advertising and Editorial Societies," *Chicago Defender,* Jan. 25, 1947.

"Norman Granz and Jazz Stars Make It Hot for Michigan Restaurant," *Chicago Defender,* Oct.18, 1947.

"Norman Granz to Receive New Award for His Campaign on Discrimination," *Chicago Defender,* May 17, 1947.

"North Pole Explorer Honored in New York," *Chicago Defender,* Apr. 19, 1947.

"100 Gridiron Stars Guests at a Dance," *The New York Times,* Nov. 30 1947.

"1,018,000 Donated to Negro Colleges," *The New York Times,* Dec. 14, 1947.

" 'Paintings of Year' Plans 4th Awards," *The New York Times,* Feb. 7, 1947.

"Passengers Jim Crowed in New York's Penn Station; Fight 'Gentlemen's Agreement' to Segregate Travelers to Dixie," *Chicago Defender,* Aug. 16, 1947.

"Passive Resistance Sit Down Cracks St. Paul Hotel Bias," *Chicago Defender,* Jan. 25, 1947.

"Pepsi-Cola Appoints Man to High Sales Post," *Chicago Defender,* Oct. 11, 1947.

"Pepsi-Cola Awards: 119 Scholarships Await Prep Grads," *The Pittsburgh Courier,* Oct. 4, 1947.

"Pepsi-Cola Is the Drink," photo, *Chicago Defender,* July 26, 1947.

"Pepsi-Cola Names Young Educator to Scholarship Board," *Chicago Defender,* Aug. 30, 1947.

"Pepsi-Cola Plans Negro Field Staff, Edward F. Boyd Is Named Assistant Sales Manager," *The Pittsburgh Courier,* Oct. 11, 1947.

Bibliography

"Pepsi-Cola President Asks End to Sugar Rationing March 31," *The Wall Street Journal*, Mar. 4, 1947.

"Pepsi-Cola President Endorses Price Plea," *The New York Times*, Apr. 13, 1947.

"Pepsi-Cola Rents Office Building," *The New York Times*, Dec. 1, 1947.

"Pepsi-Cola Scholarship Student Begins 3rd Year at Northwestern," *Chicago Defender*, Oct. 11, 1947.

"Pepsi Marketers Faced Rebuffs in the Field and in Home Office," *The Wall Street Journal*, Sept. 5, 1997.

"Personnel Notes," item on Bryan Houston appointment, *The Wall Street Journal*, Feb. 11, 1946.

"Phone Company to Use Negro 'Hello' Girls," *Chicago Defender*, Oct. 11, 1947.

"Picnic Guests Will Get Pepsi-Cola and Evervess; 14,400 Cups of Cold Drinks for Kiddies," *Chicago Defender*, July 5, 1947.

"Plants Drop Jim Crow Policy; Hire More Negroes," *Chicago Defender*, Jan. 2, 1947.

"Race Equality Pays Off Big Dividend in Hawaii," *Chicago Defender*, July 19, 1947.

"Randolph Rips Sen. Ellender at FEPC Probe; Demand Southerner Show Some Dignity, Call Him 'Mister,' " *Chicago Defender*, June 21, 1947.

"Real Estate; Housing Boom Skyrockets Annual Sales to over Billion for 5,000 Colored Brokers," *Ebony*, Nov. 1948.

"Record of UN on Racial Discrimination Shocking," *The Pittsburgh Courier*, Dec. 6, 1947.

"Red Probe Blocks Sepia Film Roles," *The Pittsburgh Courier*, Dec. 27, 1947.

"Regular Army Now Includes 1,569 Officers, 43 Negroes," *Chicago Defender*, Feb. 1, 1947.

"Remington-Rand Co. Hires Chicagoan as Representative," *Chicago Defender*, Oct. 25, 1947.

"Resists Train Jim Crow—Slain," *Chicago Defender*, Apr. 19, 1947.

"See Labor Drives in South Nullifying Hate Group Action," *Chicago Defender*, Feb. 22, 1947.

"See Talmadge Senators Forcing White Primary," *Chicago Defender*, Feb. 8, 1947.

"Skywriters Mass Today," *The New York Times*, Nov. 21, 1946.

"Southern Railway to Dine Its Negro Passenger in 'Bull Pen,' " *Chicago Defender*, Jan. 11, 1947.

"Stockholders Visit Here," *The New York Times*, Apr. 12, 1947.

"Success Poll Won by 5 Business Men," *The New York Times*, July 3, 1947.

"Sugar Prices May Rise After Decontrol, Mack of Pepsi-Cola Says," *The Wall Street Journal,* May 9, 1947.

"Sugar Rationing Ends Urged as Price Curb," *The New York Times,* Mar. 4, 1947.

"Summary Shows Race at Stand-Still During 1946," *Chicago Defender,* Jan. 4, 1947.

"Takes All Kinds of People," Herman Smith item in National Grapevine column, *Chicago Defender,* July 19, 1947.

"Talmadge Is Dead at 62 in Georgia," *The New York Times,* Dec. 22, 1946.

"The Negro's Share in America," *The New York Times,* July 31, 1949.

"3 Birmingham NAACP Officers Warned by Klan," *Chicago Defender,* Jan. 25, 1947.

"Tired of Being White, Wisconsin Pastor Heareafter Will Be Colored," *Chicago Defender,* Sept. 20, 1947.

"Tired of Jim Crow, Negro Changes Race," *Chicago Defender,* Oct. 4, 1947.

"Top Cabarets in Harlem Close as Smaller Clubs Grab the Spotlight," *Chicago Defender,* Mar. 25, 1947.

"Trial Date Set for 31 Lynchers," *Chicago Defender,* Apr. 26, 1947.

"Tuskegee Figures Show 1946 Tops Lynch Record," *Chicago Defender,* Jan. 4, 1947.

" 'Twelve Full Ounces, That's a Lot,' " *Fortune,* Jan. 1947.

"Twelve Students Get Awards for '47–'48," *The Pittsburgh Courier,* Aug. 23, 1947.

"23 Southern Students Win Scholarships from Pepsi-Cola," *Chicago Defender,* Apr. 12, 1947.

"$21,250 in Prizes Awarded for Art," *The New York Times,* Oct. 1, 1947.

"Urban League Publishes Comic Book of Heroes," *Chicago Defender,* Mar. 25, 1947.

"Urban League to Hold Closed Confab; Gears for City Population Increases," *Chicago Defender,* Aug. 16, 1947.

"Walter Mack Divorced," *The New York Times,* Feb. 15, 1945.

"We Negro Americans . . ." political advertisement signed by Paul Robeson and W. E. B. DuBois, *Chicago Defender,* Apr. 26, 1947.

"What Happened to the War Workers? Negro Pioneers on West Coast Building New Communities, " *Ebony,* Dec. 1946.

"What's Ahead for the Negro in '47," *Ebony,* Jan. 1948, p. 40.

"When Joe Louis Fought, the Country Came to a Halt," *The Detroit Free Press online,* Oct. 22, 1999.

"White Churches Draft Edict to Ban Jim Crow," *Chicago Defender,* Jan. 18, 1947.

"White Man's Views," *The Pittsburgh Courier,* Sept. 20, 1947.

Bibliography

Bibliography

Bibliography

"Whites Arrested for Aiding Negro," *Chicago Defender*, Oct. 25, 1947.
"Whites March with Negroes on Dixie Labor Day," *Chicago Defender*, Sept. 13, 1947.
"Worker at Phillip Morris Tells of Company's Progress," *Chicago Defender*, Apr. 12, 1947.

WEB SITES AND DVDS
Alpha Phi Alpha Fraternity, "Eugene Kinckle Jones," www3.baylor.edu/Alpha_Phi_Alpha/jones, June 2005.
Answers.com, "1947," www.answers.com/main/ntquery, July 2005.
The City Review Book review: *It Happened on Broadway: An Oral History of the Great White Way*. www.thecityreview.com/bway, Aug. 2005.
Harvard Square Library, "Norman Cousins: Editor and Writer, 1915–1990," www.harvardsquarelibrary.org/unitarians/cousins, June 2005.
Johnny Roventini, www.bellhop.org/johnny, June 2005.
Mission Inn, "Explore Our History of the Hotel," www.missioninn.com/hotel-history.php.
The Museum of Public Relations, "Edward L. Bernays, www.prmuseum.com/bernays/bernays_1915, June 2005.
W. E. B. DuBois Learning Center, "A Biographical Sketch of W. E. B. Du Bois," www.duboislc.org, May 2005.

Chapter 4: Leaders in Their Fields
BOOKS
Whitfield, Stephen J. *The Culture of the Cold War*. The Johns Hopkins University Press, Baltimore, 1996.

NEWSPAPERS, PERIODICALS, AND BUSINESS EPHEMERA
"Advance of Negroes in Business," *Chicago Defender*, Apr. 10, 1948.
"Advertising News," item on Biow Co. Inc. winning Pepsi account, *The New York Times*, May 19, 1948.
"American Airlines Drops Slur Ad After Protest," *Chicago Defender*, Feb. 23, 1946.
"The American Bazaar," *Fortune*, Nov. 1947.
"Anti-Red Bill Called Threat to Civil Rights," *Chicago Defender*, May 29, 1948.
"*The Atlanta Constitution*, Georgia's Bugle of White Supremacy, Attacks the *Chicago Defender*—And Gets Spanked," Apr. 17, 1948, p. 1.
"Attends College on Scholarship Award," unidentified and undated newspaper clipping. Boyd Collection.

Bibliography

"Atwater Camp Brings Fond Memories to Campers," *The Pittsburgh Courier*, Sept. 3, 1949.

"'Billboard' Jackson Tells Strides Made in Business," *Chicago Defender*, Aug. 19, 1950.

"Billikens to Get Free Pepsi-Cola at Picnic," *Chicago Defender*, June 12, 1948.

"Booker T. Washington High School Seniors Enter Pepsi-Cola Contest," unidentified and undated newspaper clipping, Boyd Collection.

"Brewing Company Hires Public Relations Man," *Chicago Defender*, Apr. 17, 1948.

"Business Bulletin," item on booming souvenir-pen business, *The Wall Street Journal*, Mar. 11, 1948.

"Business Bulletin," item on *Ebony* sales, *The Wall Street Journal*, Jan. 27, 1949.

"Café Refuses Service to Negroes; Closes as 50 Patrons Await Food," *Chicago Defender*, Nov. 27, 1948.

"Canada Lee, R. Taylor Quit Political Race," *Chicago Defender*, Aug. 28, 1948.

"Canada Lee Shines in Another 'Must,'" *Chicago Defender*, Feb. 7, 1948.

"Cattle Broker; Negro Trader Is President of Big Buffalo Livestock Exchange," *Ebony*, Nov. 1947.

"CBS Takes Over Phil Harris–Alice Faye Program from NBC," *The Wall Street Journal*, Dec. 10, 1948.

"A Celebration of the Life of Harvey C. Russell, Apr. 14, 1918-February 20, 1998," unpublished tribute written by Russell family, Feb. 1998.

"Chicagoans Honor Negro Co-Discoverer of North Pole," *Chicago Defender*, Mar. 28, 1948.

"Cuban Government Seizes Coca-Cola, Pepsi-Cola Bottling Plans in Havana," *The Wall Street Journal*, Sept. 25, 1948.

"Customer Lures; Businessmen Trying New Promotion Ideas in Drive for Sales," *The Wall Street Journal*, Apr. 7, 1948.

"Defender Show Grads Join Pepsi-Cola Show," *Chicago Defender*, July 3, 1948.

"Dixie Court Upholds Sentences of Anti-Bias Bus Passengers," *Chicago Defender*, Mar. 27, 1948.

"Drop Racial Designation in New Draft," *Chicago Defender*, July 3, 1948.

"F. J. Jacobs Boosts Output of Bottle Vending Machines," *The Wall Street Journal*, May 28, 1948.

"The First Line of Defense," political advertisement signed by DuBois and Robeson, *Chicago Defender*, Aug. 28, 1948.

"First Negro Since Reconstruction on Mississippi Jury," *Chicago Defender*, July 17, 1948.

"First Pepsi-Cola Scholar Winds Degree in 3 Years," *Chicago Defender*, May 22, 1948.

"500 Negroes Watch Game from Levee 'Outside' Wall; Others Are Jim Crowed," *Chicago Defender*, Apr. 17, 1948.

"Florida White Students Rap Uprising of Rebel Governors," *Chicago Defender*, Mar. 13, 1948.

"Frisco's First Negro High School Teacher," *Chicago Defender*, Feb. 28, 1948.

"Gary Gets First Negro Referee; Judges Next," *Chicago Defender*, Feb. 7, 1948.

"Gen. Bradley Shocks NAACP on Army Bias," *Chicago Defender*, Aug. 7, 1948.

"Georgia Negroes Appeal to Courts as Dixiecrats Purge Voting Lists," *Chicago Defender*, Aug. 14, 1948.

"Hires Co. Will Seek Extra Business with New 8-Ounce Bottles," *The Wall Street Journal*, Oct. 13, 1948.

"Hopping the Rails," Pepsi-team item in Along Celebrity Row, *Chicago Defender*, March 20, 1948.

"How Big Is Your Negro Market?" *Modern Industry*, Apr. 15, 1948.

Jay Jackson Pepsi-Cola advertisement cartoon, "Mmm, Daddy! Now that's art," *Ebony*, June 1948.

Jay Jackson Pepsi-Cola advertisement cartoon, "What's Pepsi got that we haven't?" *Ebony*, July 1948.

Jay Jackson Pepsi-Cola advertisement cartoon, "Don't be silly, Miss Sweet,—I'm not chasing you, I'm running to the cooler for a couple of Pepsi-Colas!" *Ebony*, Aug. 1948.

Jay Jackson Pepsi-Cola advertisement cartoon, "Any you gals got bottle openers?" *Ebony*, Sept. 1948.

Jay Jackson Pepsi-Cola advertisement cartoon, "Now I'm sure this is the right address," *Ebony*, Oct. 1948.

Jay Jackson Pepsi-Cola advertisement cartoon, "Party? Smarty! Pepsi," *Ebony*, Nov. 1948.

Jay Jackson Pepsi-Cola advertisement cartoon, "Twice as Many, Ice as Many, Pepsi," *Ebony*, Dec. 1948.

"Job Training Needed as Business Booms," *Chicago Defender*, Aug. 21, 1948.

"Joe Louis Punch Sales Soaring as Loyal Fans Predict Walcott Kayo," *Chicago Defender*, June 12, 1948.

"Leader in Her Field: Mrs. Mildred Blount, Pepsi advertisement," *The Pittsburgh Courier*, Oct. 30, 1948.

"Leader in Her Field: Mrs. Rachel Ratcliffe Wilson, Pepsi advertisement," *The Pittsburgh Courier*, July 10, 1948.

Bibliography

"Leader in His Field: Cornelius E. Ford," Pepsi advertisement, *Chicago Defender*, May 8, 1948.

"Leader in His Field: Dr. Paul B. Cornely," Pepsi advertisement, *Chicago Defender*, June 19, 1948.

"Leader in His Field: Dr. Percy L. Julian," Pepsi advertisement, *Chicago Defender*, Sept. 25, 1948.

"Leader in His Field: Dr. Ralph J. Bunche," Pepsi advertisement, *Chicago Defender*, Apr. 24, 1948.

"Leader in His Field: Dr. Theodore R. M. Howard," Pepsi advertisement, *Chicago Defender*, Aug. 28, 1948.

"Leader in His Field: Jesse H. Mitchell," Pepsi advertisement, *Chicago Defender*, Aug. 14, 1948.

"Leader in His Field: Joseph S. Dunning," Pepsi advertisement, *Chicago Defender*, Oct. 16, 1948.

"Leader in His Field: P. Bernard Young, Jr.," Pepsi advertisement, *The Pittsburgh Courier*, June 5, 1948.

"Leader in His Field: Walter Franklin Anderson," Pepsi advertisement, *The Pittsburgh Courier*, May 22, 1948.

"Lest We Forget . . . Negro History Week . . . 1948," *Chicago Defender*, Feb. 14, 1948.

Letter, "Dear Sir," sent to African-American educators to encourage cooperation with local bottlers, signed by Edward F. Boyd, Sept. 21, 1948.

"Local Patter," item in Along Celebrity Row, *Chicago Defender*, Oct. 2, 1948.

"Memphis Ousts 'Boss' Crump; Negroes Swell Vote to Overthrow 'Machine,' " *Chicago Defender*, Aug. 14, 1948.

"Methodist Aid Group Names 1st Negro Head," *Chicago Defender*, Jan. 10, 1948.

"The NAACP," *Ebony*, Aug. 1946.

"NAACP Wins 21 of 23 Cases Taken Before U.S. Supreme Court," *Ebony*, Aug. 1946, p. 38.

"Nat'l Urban League Places 25,000 in Jobs in 1947," *Chicago Defender*, Jan. 3, 1948.

"Negro Executive Finds There Is Room at the Top, New Vice President at Pepsi-Cola Sees Gain for His Race," *The New York Times*, July 1, 1962.

"Negro Fans in Reserve Seats in Dallas Park," *Chicago Defender*, Apr. 17, 1948.

"Negro Prodigy to Plug Pabst Beer This Fall," *Chicago Defender*, July 10, 1948.

"Negroes in Georgia Threatened by New Talmadge," *The Pittsburgh Courier*, Mar. 6, 1948.

"New Joe Louis Drink Faces Problem Tougher Than His Ring Opponents," *Chicago Defender*, Dec. 21, 1946.

"New Moves in the South to Restrict Negro Voting," *The New York Times*, Apr. 25, 1948.

"New York Urban League Sees More Job Openings," *Chicago Defender*, Sept. 25, 1948.

"No Cigarette Hangover," first Philip Morris ad in series, *The Pittsburgh Courier*, June 5, 1948.

"On the Line," item in Along Celebrity Row, *Chicago Defender*, July 17, 1948.

"Pepsi-Cola Adds 4 Negroes to Marketing Staff," *The New York Age*, Feb. 28, 1948, Boyd Collection.

"Pepsi-Cola Cites Georgia Student," *Chicago Defender*, Apr. 10, 1948.

"Pepsi-Cola Contest Winner," unidentified newspaper, August 1948, Boyd Collection.

"Pepsi-Cola Fellowship Announced by Board," unidentified newspaper, February 1948, Boyd Collection.

"Pepsi-Cola to Launch Two Advertising Campaigns in Negro Publications," press release distributed by the Pepsi-Cola Company in May 1948, Boyd Collection.

"Pepsi-Cola Offers 8-Ounce Bottle," *The Wall Street Journal*, Apr. 30, 1948.

"Pepsi-Cola Plans Expansion Through Two Sales Outlets," *The Wall Street Journal*, May 6, 1948.

"Pepsi-Cola Profit Sets a New Mark," *The New York Times*, Mar. 20, 1948.

"Pepsi-Cola Scholarships Go to 17 Southern Negro Pupils," newspaper clipping, n.d., Boyd Collection.

"Pepsi-Cola Winner Chooses M'house," unidentified and undated newspaper, Boyd Collection.

"Praises Lucky Strike Educational Campaign," *The Pittsburgh Courier*, Oct. 2, 1948.

"President Truman Wipes Out Segregation in Armed Forces," *Chicago Defender*, July 31, 1948, p. 1.

"Ralph Bunche Heads Mission to Palestine; Replaces Bernadotte," *Chicago Defender*, Sept. 25, 1948.

"Remove Jim-Crow Toilet Signs at Site of Truman Inaugural," *Chicago Defender*, Dec. 4, 1948

"Rickey Warns Against Special Days for Jackie," *The Pittsburgh Courier*, Mar. 27, 1948.

"See Store Trend in Upgrading of Negro Employees," *Chicago Defender*, Mar. 27, 1948.

"St. Louis Girl Wins Pepsi-Cola Scholarship," *Chicago Defender,* Mar. 27, 1948.

"Store Broadcasting: New Ad Industry Grows But Food Chains Debate Value of 'Salescasts,'" *The Wall Street Journal,* June 8, 1948.

"The Social Swirl," item in Along Celebrity Row, *Chicago Defender,* Feb. 5, 1949.

"Third Confab on Negro Business Opens in D.C.," *Chicago Defender,* Apr. 3, 1948.

"Time Table Blues," item in Along Celebrity Row, *Chicago Defender,* Sept. 4, 1948.

"Tussle over Jim Crow Screen Nets Woman Police Beating," *Chicago Defender,* Dec. 18, 1948.

"2 College Seniors Given Three-Year Scholarships for Graduate Study," unidentified and undated newspaper, Boyd Collection.

"Urban League Places 1,440 Since January," *Chicago Defender,* June 12, 1948.

"Vending Machine in Rising Demand; Paper Cut Drink Dispensers Hit $19,000,000 in Volume and Are Still Growing," *The Wall Street Journal,* Nov. 8, 1948.

"Vet Is First Negro to Enroll in Realty School," *Chicago Defender,* July 3, 1948.

"Virginia Censors Ban Anti-Ku Klux Klan Movie," *The Pittsburgh Courier,* Oct. 4, 1947.

"Wanted: Jobs for a Million Vets," *Ebony,* Sept. 1946.

"War of the Nickel; Fatalities Likely Among Soft Drink Bottlers as Competition Rages," *The Wall Street Journal,* Feb. 19, 1948.

"Widow, 25, Tells Courier How Husband Was Slain in Ga. . . . Because He Voted," *The Pittsburgh Courier,* Oct. 9, 1948.

WEB SITES AND DVDS

The African America Registry, "Kenneth B. Clark, Activist, Psychologist and Author!" www.aaregistry.com/african_american_history/283/Kennth_B_Clark_activist_psychologist_and_author.

The New Georgia Encyclopedia, "National Association for the Advancement of Colored People (NAACP)," www.georgiaencyclopedia.org/nge/Article, June 2005.

Salute to Pioneering Cartoonists of Color, "Jack Jackson, www.clstoons.com/paoc/jjackson, Apr. 2005.

Scandalize My Name: Stories from the Blacklist. DVD. Directed by Alexandra Isles. Urban Works, 2004.

Bibliography

Chapter 5: The Brown Hucksters

BOOKS

Bennett, Tony, with Friedwald, Will. *The Good Life.* New York: Pocket Books, 1998.

Bentley, Eric. *Thirty Years of Treason.* New York: Thunder's Mouth Press/ Nation's Books, 2002.

Jerome, Fred, and Taylor, Rodger. *Einstein on Race and Racism.* New Brunswick, N.J.: Rutgers University Press, 2005.

Washington, Booker, T. *Up from Slavery.* New York: Signet Classic, 2000.

NEWSPAPERS, PERIODICALS, AND BUSINESS EPHEMERA

"AAUW Votes to Admit Negro Women," *Chicago Defender,* July 2, 1949.

"Advertising News and Notes," item on Samuel A. Alter of Biow Company, *The New York Times,* Apr. 4, 1949.

"Air Corps Drops Jim Crow," *Chicago Defender,* Jan. 22, 1949, p. 1.

"Airport Cafe Drops Race Bars," *Chicago Defender,* Jan. 15, 1949.

"Alfred N. Steele, Official of Coca-Cola, Named Pepsi-Cola Vice President," *The Wall Street Journal,* Mar. 24, 1949.

"Armstrong Field's Electric Scoreboard," unidentified and undated newspaper clipping, Boyd Collection.

"Bottlers Advised on Higher Prices," *The New York Times,* Apr. 5, 1949.

"Business Bulletin: Torrid Temperatures Catch Brewers and Soft-Drink Bottlers Short," *The Wall Street Journal,* July 7, 1949.

"Business Is Still in Trouble," *Fortune,* May 1949.

"Canada Lee: 'Not a Red,' Actor Says," *The Pittsburgh Courier.* June 15, 1949.

"Canada Lee Sees 'Blue' as Winchell Hint of 'Red' Speech," *Chicago Defender,* Oct. 29, 1949.

"Catholics Ask Democrats to Pass Anti-Lynch Law," *The Pittsburgh Courier,* July 20, 1940.

"CBS to Get McCarthy Show," *The Wall Street Journal,* Feb. 12, 1949.

"The Chicago Defender Honor Roll for 1949," *Chicago Defender,* Dec. 31, 1949.

"CIO's Drive Called 'Crusade' in South," *The New York Times,* June 29, 1949.

Classified ad, item on David J. Sullivan, *The New York Times,* Apr. 4, 1949.

"Coca-Cola's State Street Plant Good Example of Company's Fairplay Plan," *Chicago Defender,* Oct. 1, 1949.

"Colgate's Negro Market Expanding," *The Pittsburgh Courier,* Mar. 12, 1949.

"Communists' Trial Marked by Sharp Clashes, Tension," *The Pittsburgh Courier,* Jan. 22, 1949.

"Converts of Color, Catholic Church Finds Equality Policy Wins Negro Followers," *Ebony*, Mar. 1946.

"Cotton Club Kept Negro Guests Out," *Ebony*, Apr. 1949.

"Dixie Court Upholds Sentences of Anti-Bias Bus Passengers," *Chicago Defender*, Mar. 27, 1948.

"Dixie Railroads Defy Move to End Jim Crow," *Chicago Defender*, Oct. 29, 1949.

"Don't Look Now But That Dixie Censor's on the Loose Again," *Chicago Defender*, Jan. 15, 1949.

"Etiquette of Race Relations," *Ebony*, Dec. 1949.

"Extra: Jackie Hits Homer at Red Probe," *Chicago Defender*, July 23, 1949.

"Father Divine on Trial in Legacy Case," *Chicago Defender*, Mar. 12, 1949.

"Fight Hate Law to Disfranchise 125,000 Negro Voters in Georgia," *Chicago Defender*, Feb. 5, 1949.

"Fine Woman in Jim Crow Bus Case," *Chicago Defender*, June 1, 1949.

"Five Lynch Well-to-Do Ga. Farmer," *Chicago Defender*, Sept. 10, 1949.

"5 Negroes Receive Degrees at Ohio U.," *Chicago Defender*, Jan. 1, 1949.

"5 Racial Awards Listed; Driscoll and W. S. Mack Jr. Are Among Those Honored," *The New York Times*, Mar. 22, 1949.

"5 Win Democracy Prizes," *The New York Times*," Feb. 7, 1949.

"Fortune Press Analysis: Negroes," *Fortune*, May, 1945, p. 233.

"4 Who Defied Jim Crow Ready for Sentences on Chain Gang," *Chicago Defender*, Mar. 26, 1949.

"Hamp to Play on Inaugural Program," *Chicago Defender*, Jan. 8, 1949.

"Hampton Installs 1st Negro Prexy," *Chicago Defender*, Oct. 29, 1949.

"Hampton Was First to Ban 'Race' Discs," *Chicago Defender*, Feb. 5, 1949.

"Heat Wave Sends Soft Drink Sales Spurting Above Last Year's Level; Costs Come Down from 1948 High," *The Wall Street Journal*, Aug. 22, 1949.

"Henson Never Had Cold in Arctic, Now Plagued by Lumbago," *Ebony*, 1948.

"High Court Agrees to Review Rail Jim Crow Laws," *Chicago Defender*, Jan. 26, 1946.

"Integration to Dissolve 332nd Unit," *Chicago Defender*, Apr. 16, 1949.

"Is Negro Baseball Doomed?" *Chicago Defender*, Apr. 23, 1949.

"Klan Attacks White Woman, Warns Catholics, Negroes," *Chicago Defender*, June 18, 1949.

"Leader in His Field: Dean Dixon," Pepsi advertisement, *Chicago Defender*, July 2, 1949.

Bibliography

"Leader in His Field: Dr. Harold D. West," Pepsi advertisement, *Chicago Defender*, May 14, 1949.

"Leader in His Field: Dr. John W. Davis," Pepsi advertisement, *Chicago Defender*, Aug. 13, 1949.

"Leader in His Field: Dr. Percy L. Julian," *Chicago Defender*, Oct. 29, 1949.

"Leader in His Field, Dr. Ralph J. Bunche," Pepsi advertisement, *Chicago Defender*, July 39, 1949.

"Leader in His Field: James J. Johnson," Pepsi advertisement, *Chicago Defender*, July 16, 1949.

"Leader in His Field: Mathew A. Henson," Pepsi advertisement, *The Pittsburgh Courier*, Mar. 16, 1949.

"Leader in His Field: Mr. A. A. Alexander," Pepsi advertisement, *The Pittsburgh Courier*, Oct. 15, 1949.

"Leader in His Field: Mr. Fred Jones," Pepsi advertisement, *Chicago Defender*, Oct. 1, 1949.

"Leader in His Field! Mr. J. Finley Wilson," Pepsi advertisement, *Chicago Defender*, Sept. 10, 24, 1949.

"Leader in His Field: Mr. Walter A. Gordon," Pepsi advertisement, *Chicago Defender*, Sept. 3, 1949.

"Lee and Lena Deny Red Charge," *Chicago Defender*, June 18, 1949.

"Lena 'Clipped' by Memphis Censor," *The Pittsburgh Courier*, Jan. 15, 1949.

Letter, "Dear Customer," signed by Edward F. Boyd, Aug. 8, 1949, Boyd Collection.

"Market Detectives: Researchers Rushed by Orders to Ferret Out Nation's Buying Habits," *The Wall Street Journal*, Sept. 24, 1947.

"Matt Henson, Long Ignored to Get Medal for North Pole Discovery," March 13, 1948.

"Military Order Shakes Color Bar; New Army Policy Falls Short of Truman Goal," *Chicago Defender*, Oct. 8, 1949.

"Mob Flogs Aged Man in Wild Midnight Raid," *Chicago Defender*, May 21, 1949.

"More Bounce to the Ounce!" Pepsi advertisement with Marian Jeffreys, *Ebony*, Nov. 1949.

"More Bounce to the Ounce!" Pepsi advertisement with Virginia Radcliffe, *Ebony*, Oct. 1949.

"Most Hampton Grads Get Jobs," *The Pittsburgh Courier*, Apr. 6, 1940.

" 'Mr. Anna Lucasta' Sees Hope for the Negro in Theatre's Changes," *Chicago Defender*, Aug. 20, 1949.

"The Negro and American Industry," *Chicago Defender*, Jan. 15, 1949.

Bibliography

"Negro Attorney Electrifies 'Red Trial' Opening," *The Pittsburgh Courier,* Jan. 29, 1949.

"Negro Investments Prove . . . There Are No Jim Crow Dollars," *Chicago Defender,* Aug. 6, 1949.

"Negroes' Buying Power Stated Above $3 Billion," *The Pittsburgh Courier,* May 14, 1949.

"New 'Boom' Seen in Numbers Racket, Kingpins of Digit Games Cleaning Up," *Chicago Defender,* June 4, 1949.

"1948—Honor Roll—1948," *Chicago Defender,* Jan. 8, 1949.

"No Cigarette Hangover," advertisement in Philip Morris series, *Chicago Defender,* May 7, 1949.

"No Negroes Under Contract to Major Studio Scribe Says," *Chicago Defender,* Dec. 31, 1949.

"North Carolina NAACP Units Back Bus Cases," *The Pittsburgh Courier,* Aug. 30, 1947.

" 'Not Mad at Jackie'—Robeson Tells Press, *Chicago Defender,* July 30, 1949.

"Notre Dame Lists 5 Negro Students," *The Pittsburgh Courier,* Mar. 12, 1949.

"Only 1,400 Negro Reds in U.S., Report Shows; Leaders Question Cause of Loyalty Probe Within Race," *The Pittsburgh Courier,* July 23, 1949.

"Opposition Candidates for Directors Defeated at Pepsi-Cola Meeting," *The Wall Street Journal,* May 5, 1949.

"Our Opinions: Jackie and the Klan," *Chicago Defender,* Apr. 23, 1949.

"Outdoor Ads: Another Big Year for Billboards Expected in 1950 as Orders Mount," *The Wall Street Journal,* July 18, 1949.

"Pepsi: Trouble in Large Size," *Newsweek,* Apr. 4, 1949.

"Pepsi-Cola Opposition Loses," *The New York Times,* May 6, 1949.

"Pepsi-Cola's Campaign to the Negro Market," by Adrian Hirschhorn, *Printers' Ink,* Sept. 9, 1949.

"Pepsi-Cola's '49 Sales Are Estimated Near Last Year's Levels," *The Wall Street Journal,* Nov. 28, 1949.

"Pepsi-Cola's 3-Year Contract with Steele Sets $85,000 Annual Pay," *The Wall Street Journal,* Apr. 12, 1949.

"Philip Morris Co. to Launch Bigger Press Campaign," *The Pittsburgh Courier,* Apr. 2, 1949.

"Philip Morris Gives Urban League $1,000," *Chicago Defender,* Oct. 29, 1949.

"Postal Workers Vote to Launch Full Scale Attack on U.S. Loyalty Probe," *Chicago Defender,* Aug. 27, 1949.

"The Promise of '49," *Chicago Defender,* Jan. 1, 1949.

"Publishers: Owners of Negro Newspapers Are Hard-Headed, Far-Sighted, Race-Conscious Businessmen," *Ebony*, Nov. 1949.

"Quiz Masters: Industry Pays Millions to Market Researchers Finding Public's Taste," *The Wall Street Journal*, Mar. 15, 19454.

"Race Loyal, Say Leaders," *Chicago Defender*, July 23, 1949.

"Race Pioneers in Television Field Compete with Top Production Lines," *Chicago Defender*, Mar. 5, 1949.

"Recruit Called 'Darky' by U.S. Army Officer," *The Pittsburgh Courier*, July 20, 1940.

"Red Scare Haunts Show Business; Our Stars Hit as Nation Quakes at Communist Yells," *The Pittsburgh Courier*, June 18, 1949.

"Red Smear Hurts Actor Canada Lee," *Chicago Defender*, July 16, 1949.

"Reporter Looks In on Pet Milk Families in Rural Communities," *Chicago Defender*, Dec. 17, 1949.

" 'Ripe Old Age' No Longer a Dream; Race Health Better, Says Survey," *Chicago Defender*, Aug. 6, 1949.

"Robeson Blasted for Paris Speech," *Chicago Defender*, Apr. 30, 1949.

"A Salesman Is Everybody," *Fortune*, May 1949.

"75,000 Negroes Witness Inauguration," *The Pittsburgh Courier*, Jan. 22, 1949.

"S.C. Whites Razz Klan Klowns; Governor Folsom Warns Them," *Chicago Defender*, Mar. 5, 1949.

"Showdown Set on Red Probe," *Chicago Defender*, July 16, 1949.

"Silence of Educated Negroes Slants Sex Report, Kinsey Says," *Chicago Defender*, Nov. 27, 1948.

" 'South Pacific' Is Sterling Story That Broadway Likes," *Chicago Defender*, Sept. 3, 1949.

"Talmadge Calls for Disfranchisement," *Chicago Defender*, Jan. 22, 1949.

"There'll Be No Discrimination at Harry Truman's Inauguration," *Chicago Defender*, Jan. 22, 1949.

"They Made It . . . Breaks Job Ban with Urban League Help, Then Makes Jobs for Others," Nov. 12, 1949.

"They Made it . . . Here Is Good Example of What One Must Possess to Land Topflight Job," *Chicago Defender*, Nov. 5, 1949.

"Think This Picture Ugly? Well, So Is Lynching!" *Chicago Defender*, June 11, 1949.

"Third of Million Negroes in America Are Catholic," *Chicago Defender*, Feb. 14, 1948.

"30 States Ban Mixed Marriages," *The Pittsburgh Courier*, Apr. 30, 1949.

"This Is What Jackie Told Congress," *Chicago Defender*, July 30, 1949.

"Three States Seek Bar to Negro Vote," *Chicago Defender*, Jan. 1, 1949.

"To Hire Negroes in All N. Y. A&P Stores," *Chicago Defender*, Dec. 24, 1949.

"Unions Help Negro Switch from Farm to City Jobs," *Ebony*, Feb. 1949.

"Vet Lynched in Ga. Jail," *The Pittsburgh Courier*, Mar. 12, 1949.

"Vigilantes to Fight KKK with Own Methods; Churchman Fear Clashes," *Chicago Defender*, May 28, 1949.

"Wall Street of Negro America; Single Building in Durham Has More Million-Dollar Negro Businesses Than Anywhere Else in World," *Ebony*, Sept. 1949.

"Wellesley Adds Negro to Faculty," *Chicago Defender*, Aug. 20, 1949.

"What I told Kinsey About My Sex Life," *Ebony*, Dec. 1948.

"Why I Became a Catholic," *Ebony*, Mar. 1946.

"Why Negroes Buy Cadillacs," *Ebony*, Sept. 1949.

"Why Take Less . . . When Pepsi's Best!" Pepsi advertisement with Elizabeth Robinson, *Ebony*, Sept. 1949.

"Why Take Less . . . When Pepsi's Best!" Pepsi advertisement with Mary Lou Usher, *Ebony*, Aug. 1949.

"Why Take Less . . . When Pepsi's Best!" Pepsi advertisement with Miss Natalie Stuart, *Ebony*, July 1949.

"Why Take Less . . . When Pepsi's Best!" Pepsi advertisement with Yolande Stovall and Sherrill Luke, *Ebony*, Dec. 1949.

"With Vote Ban Lifted, Mobile Citizens Rush to Register," *Chicago Defender*, Feb. 12, 1949.

"You Might Be the Black If . . . Your Children Are Emotionally Disturbed, Say Psychologists; N.Y. Pair Probe Tot Troubles," *Chicago Defender*, May 14, 1949.

WEB SITES AND OTHER MEDIA

Answers.com, "1949," www.answers.com/main, Sept. 2004.

National Museum of American History, Smithsonian Institution, "America on the Move Exhibition," http://americanhistory.si.edu/onthemove/collection/object, Feb. 2006.

"The Negro Motorist Green Book, 1949," www.autolife.umd.umich.edu/Race/R_Casestudy/Negro_motorist_green_bk., Feb. 2006.

Chapter 6: The Cola Color Wars

BOOKS

Allen, Frederick. *Secret Formula: How Brilliant Marketing and Relentless Salesmanship Made Coca-Cola the Best-Known Product in the World*. New York: HarperBusiness, 1994.

Bibliography

NEWSPAPERS, PERIODICALS, AND BUSINESS EPHEMERA

"ABC Get 2 Top Television Programs from Competitors," *The Wall Street Journal*, Nov. 22, 1950, p. 11.

"Actors Hail Equity's Latest Move to Halt Discrimination," *Chicago Defender*, Mar. 25, 1950.

"Althea Gibson Uses Racket to Smash Color Bar," *Chicago Defender* magazine section, Sept. 9, 1950, p. 1.

Annual Report, for the year ended December 31, 1950, the Pepsi-Cola Company; released April 3, 1951, McKellar Collection.

"Award Bunche Nobel Prize," *Chicago Defender*, Sept. 30, 1950, p. 1.

" 'Be Happy, Go Lucky' Chosen New Lucky Strike Ad Slogan," *Chicago Defender*, Sept. 2, 1950.

"Be Happy, Go Lucky," advertisements for American Tobacco Company, *Chicago Defender*, Sept. 2, 23, 1950.

"Big Business Backs Talmadge Machine," *The Informer and Texas Freeman*, July 29, 1950.

"The Big Drink at the Big Game," Pepsi advertisement, likely point-of-purchase piece, Boyd Collection.

"Big Time Baseball Still Resents Negroes Despite Few Bright Spots," *Chicago Defender*, June 10, 1950.

" 'Billboard' Jackson Tells Strides Made in Business," *Chicago Defender*, Aug. 19, 1950.

"Bottle Coke Goes Up a Cent to Six Cents in Philadelphia Area," *The Wall Street Journal*, Sept. 9, 1950.

"Boycott Coca-Cola Until It Adopts FEPC, Says Toney," unidentified newspaper clipping, circa late 1950, Boyd Collection.

"Boycott Coca-Cola Until It Adopts FEPC," Press release, National Fair Play Committee.

"Brains and Business," *Ebony*, Feb. 1950.

"CBS Is Ready to Start Broadcasting Color Television Immediately," *The Wall Street Journal*, Mar. 23, 1950.

"Chase Bank Hires Negro," *Chicago Defender*, Feb. 25, 1950.

"Coca-Cola Advanced," *The Wall Street Journal*, Oct. 4, 1950.

"Coca-Cola Ban in Full Swing," New York *Amsterdam News*, Dec. 23, 1950.

"Coca-Cola Bottling Co. of Pennsylvania Shuts Plants in Pittsburgh," *The Wall Street Journal*, Jan. 4, 1950.

"Coca-Cola Co.'s Net in First Quarter Off from Like '49 Period," *The Wall Street Journal*, May 2, 1950.

"Coca-Cola Discriminates," flyer urging boycott distributed in Nebraska, Boyd Collection.

"Coca-Cola Foreign Sales Advance Cited by Farley," *The Wall Street Journal*, June 16, 1950.

"Corsi, Javits, Mack Top Mayoral List," *The New York Times*, Sept. 5, 1950.

"Cub Scouts Feted by Pepsi-Cola," n.d., clipping, *The Omaha Star*, Boyd Collection.

"Dr. Carter G. Woodson, Historian, Found Dead, Heart Attack Fatal to History Week Founder," *Chicago Defender*, Apr. 8, 1950.

"Draftees Mistreated, Ask Probe of Charge," *Chicago Defender*, Sept. 2, 1950.

"Dragon of Klan Asserts He Is on Talmadge Staff," *The New York Times*, June 29, 1949.

"End Stuyvesant Town Race Bank, Metropolitan Life Yields to Pressure," *Chicago Defender*, Sept. 2, 1950.

"Erskine Hawkins Discovers Cause of Slump in 'Name' Band Business," *Chicago Defender*, Mar. 4, 1950.

"Experts Say Decisions Scrap All Jim Crow as Dixie Bows to Supreme Court, Whole Racial Pattern of South Faces Change," *Chicago Defender*, June 17, 1950.

"Farley for Letting South Settle Rights," *The New York Times*, Nov. 22, 1950.

"Faye Emerson Says Race Hate Is U.S. Cancer," *Chicago Defender*, Nov. 27, 1948.

"5 Negroes on Toledo Daily Called Record," *Chicago Defender*, July 29, 1950.

"4 to Get Fusion Part Awards," *The New York Times*, Sept. 20, 1950.

"France Rejects Bid to Ban Coca-Cola, Sets Up New Standards for It," *The Wall Street Journal*, Mar. 2, 1950.

"Georgia, Pick the Winning Side," *Time*, June 26, 1950.

"Global Soft Drinks, American Pop Pours in a Swelling Flood Down Throats Abroad," *The Wall Street Journal*, May 23, 1950.

"Gordon Parks, Photojournalist Who Showed Dignity Amid Oppression, Dies at 93," *The New York Times*, Mar. 8, 2006.

"Herman Talmadge to Run," *The New York Times*, July 4, 1948.

"Hero of Battle, Two Others Dead," *Chicago Defender*, Sept. 16, 1950.

"Hits Rickey over Race Views," *Chicago Defender*, Jan. 28, 1950.

"Homemaker Needs to Be a Mechanic These Days," *Chicago Defender*, Feb. 18, 1950.

"How Business in Bay Area Has Progressed Since the War," *Chicago Defender*, Aug. 19, 1950.

"How Our Boys Took Yechon in First Major U.S. Victory of Korean War," *Chicago Defender,* July 29, 1950.

"Insurance Executive Urges Unity; Blistering Attack on Talmadge," unidentified newspaper clipping, circa July 1950, Boyd Collection.

"Integration at Work, Pepsi-Cola Personnel Here to Extol Drink," Baltimore *Afro American,* July 1, 1950.

Letter, "Dear Pepsi-Cola Bottler," sent by Edward F. Boyd from 3 West 57th Street headquarters, Apr. 1950, Boyd Collection.

Letter, "Dear Pepsi-Cola Bottler," sent by Edward F. Boyd from 3 West 57th Street headquarters, Aug. 3, 1950.

"Mack Severs Ties with Pepsi-Cola Co.," *The New York Times,* Sept. 28, 1950.

"Mammoth Farewell Party Held for Departing Troops," *The Courier,* n.d., Boyd Collection.

"Msgr. Sheen Dedicates New Hospital in Mobile," *The Pittsburgh Courier,* May 20, 1950.

"Name 2 to Tuskegee Board," *Chicago Defender,* Nov. 11, 1950

"Negro Ban Voted by Georgia House," *The New York Times,* Jan. 30, 1947.

"Negro General for M'Arthur," *Chicago Defender,* July 15, 1950.

"Negro GIs First Heroes," *The Pittsburgh Courier,* July 29, 1950.

"The Negro in the Next 50 years, 1950–2000, Dr. Benjamin Mays, Head of Morehouse College, Predicts," *Chicago Defender,* Aug. 19, 1950.

"The Negro in the Next 50 years, 1950–2000, Governor James E. Folsom of Alabama Predicts," *Chicago Defender,* Aug. 12, 1950.

"Negro Workers Crash Color Lines in Milwaukee's Brewing Industry," *Chicago Defender,* July 29, 1950.

"Negro's License Revoked in Sales of 'White' Homes," *The New York Times,* Mar. 24, 1949.

"Nickel Soda Pop, It Takes a Drubbing as High Costs Force Bottlers to Lift Prices," *The Wall Street Journal,* July 6, 1950.

"Nickel Soda Pop, It's Disappearing Fast as Costs Push Prices to Six to Ten Cents," *The Wall Street Journal,* Nov. 2, 1950.

Orientation and Training Program for Expanded Staff of National Sales Representatives . . . 1950, program signed by Edward F. Boyd for Pepsi-Cola seminar, Boyd Collection.

"Our Opinions: Rankin and Einstein," *Chicago Defender,* Feb. 25, 1950.

"Pepsi-Cola Board Chairman and President," *The New York Times,* Mar. 2, 1950.

"Pepsi-Cola Buys Raw Sugar at 6.30 Cents a Pound, New '50 High," *The Wall Street Journal,* Aug. 17, 1950.

"Pepsi-Cola Co., Reports 1949 Net of $2,135,238, Against $3,152,817 in '48, Steele, New President, Says Firm Plans Extensive Job of Rebuilding Profitable Markets," *The Wall Street Journal*, Apr. 12, 1950.

"Pepsi-Cola Co. Sells Its Cuban Subsidiary for About $6,300,200," *The Wall Street Journal*, Feb. 11, 1950.

Pepsi-Cola Dinner Dance menu and RSVP card for Waldorf Astoria dinner, Dec. 1, 1950, Allen L. McKellar Collection.

"Pepsi-Cola Elects Mack as Chairman of Board; Steele Named President," *The Wall Street Journal*, Mar. 2, 1950.

"Pepsi-Cola Employs 9 Negro Salesmen in LA Area," *The California Eagle*, Aug. 25, 1950.

"Pepsi-Cola Launching Promotion Campaigns to Build Up Markets," *The Wall Street Journal*, May 4, 1950.

"Pepsi-Cola Pushes Sales in Bay Area," *The Sun-Reporter*, July 29, 1950, Boyd Collection.

"The Public Pulse, Pollsters Rebound from Trouncing by Truman; Are Busier Than Ever," *The Wall Street Journal*, Mar. 23, 1950.

"Racial Bias Cracked as Althea Makes Tourney," *Chicago Defender*, Sept. 2, 1950.

"Racial Slur Angers Men in 24th Reg.," *Chicago Defender*, Aug. 28, 1950.

"RCA Boss Backs Fair Employment," Apr. 8, 1950.

"Realtors May Change Negro Bar Clause," *Chicago Defender*, Aug. 28, 1950.

"The Sales Bosses," *Fortune*, June 1950.

"Say Robeson Un-American, Stop Passport," *Chicago Defender*, Aug. 12, 1950.

"Says Negro Business Equals That of Canada," *Chicago Defender*, Sept. 16, 1950,

"Schlitz Brewing Co. Gives Organ to Milwaukee's St. Matthew Church," *Chicago Defender*, Aug. 19, 1950.

"Situations Wanted—Male," advertisement for Arnold Lewis, *The New York Times*, Jan. 10, 1950.

"Supreme Court Outlaws Dining Car Segregation, Sweatt, McLaurin Win," *The Pittsburgh Courier*, June 5, 1950.

"Talmadge Accused of Ousting Negroes," *The New York Times*, June 12, 1950.

"Talmadge Is Installed," *The New York Times*, Nov. 18, 1948.

"Talmadge Ousted in Georgia; Court Gives Thompson Reins," *The New York Times*, Mar. 20, 1979.

"Tan Yanks in Invasion, Wilson Watches Big Push on Two Fronts," *Chicago Defender*, Sept. 23, 1950.

"Teachers' Revolt in Georgia Grows," *The New York Times*, Apr. 10, 1949.

"They Made It, How 25 Young Men and Women Launched Their Careers," advertisement for book, *Chicago Defender*, Sept. 16, 1950.

"35 Liberals Told They Must Vacate," *Chicago Defender*, Aug. 19, 1950.

"Threaten 7 Brewers with Boycott in N.Y.," *Chicago Defender*, Aug. 19, 1950.

"Urge Harlemites Seek Jobs with Television," *Chicago Defender*, June 10, 1959.

"U. of Va. Balks at 2nd Negro, NAACP May Reopen Fight on Bias Policy," *Chicago Defender*, Sept. 23, 1950.

"U.S. Supreme Court Acts on Travel School Suits, Smashes Jim Crow Rule," June 19, 1950.

"Veterans of WWI Ridiculed as Beggars for Seeking a Bonus," *The Wall Street Journal*, p. B1.

"Vote 'Fraud' Confessed, Woman Tells F.B.I. of 'Pay' of $1 for Georgia Ballots," *The New York Times*, July 1, 1950.

"Walter S. Mack, Jr., Resigns as Chairman of Pepsi-Cola Board," *The Wall Street Journal*, Sept. 18, 1950.

"Walter White's Cousin [sic] Assails Talmadge Here," unidentified newspaper clipping, Boyd Collection.

"Washington Judge OKs Jim Crow in Restaurants," *Chicago Defender*, July 22, 1950.

"We're Glad You Won," *Chicago Defender*, June 17, 1970.

"What Is Hollywood's Real Attitude Toward Negroes?" *Chicago Defender*, May 20, 1950.

"Wide Drive for Carstairs," *The New York Times*, Sept. 12, 1950.

"Youngest Delegate," *The California Eagle*, July 21, 1950.

WEB SITES AND OTHER MEDIA

Answers.com, "1949," www.answers.com/main, Sept. 2004.

Chicago Public Library, "1779, Jean Baptiste Point du Sable," www.chipublib.org/004chicago/timeline/dusable/.

History Matters: The U.S. Survey Course on the Web, "The Problem" and "Family Histories": Charles Johnson Analyzes the Causes of the Chicago Race Riot," for characterization of Appomattox Clubs, http://historymatters.gmu.edu.

Chapter 7: The View from the Threshold

BOOKS

Martin, Milward W. *Twelve Full Ounces*, Holt, Rinehart and Winston, 1962.

Bibliography

NEWSPAPERS, PERIODICALS, AND BUSINESS EPHEMERA

"Annual Convention of Pepsi-Cola Bottlers, January 14–17, 1951," brochure distributed by the Pepsi-Cola Company, Boyd Collection.

"Be Happy-Go Lucky!" with Don Newcombe, advertisement for Lucky Strike cigarettes, *The Pittsburgh Courier,* Sept. 29, 1951.

"Be Happy-Go Lucky!" with Roy Campanella, advertisement for Lucky Strike cigarettes, *The Pittsburgh Courier,* Oct. 6, 1951.

"Billy Rowe's Notebook, Minor Notes," *The Pittsburgh Courier,* Sept. 1, 1951, p. 17.

"The Changing American Market," advertisement for *Fortune, The New York Times,* July 28, 1953, p. 44.

"Cicero Lynchers All Went Free! But Dr. DuBois Faces Jail," advertisement from the National Committee to Defend Dr. W. E. B. DuBois and Associates, *The Pittsburgh Courier,* Nov. 3, 1951.

"Coca-Cola, Chicago Unit Named Defendants in $750,000 Anti-Trust Suit," *The Wall Street Journal,* Jan. 26, 1951, p. 6.

"DuBois Trial Under Way," *The Pittsburgh Courier,* Nov. 3, 1951, p. 1.

"Durham-Raleigh Banquet for Pepsi National Sales Stuff Successful," *The Carolininan,* Mar. 24, 1951.

"Egyptian Eruption, U.S. Has a Big Stake in the Middle East's Newest, Hottest Row, British-Hating Egyptians Also Decry Americans' 'Pepsi-Cola Imperialism,' " *The Wall Street Journal.*

"The First Annual Press and Public Relations Conference and Newspaper Workshop," program from the Global New Syndicate, June 16, 1951.

"Former Pepsi-Cola Co. President Seeks to Acquire Nedick's Chain," *The New York Times,* May 31, 1951, p. 47.

"Good," first Coke ad in *Chicago Defender,* Jan. 20, 1951.

"Incident in Cicero," *The New York Times,* July 15, 1951.

"Klan Flogs Man, Wife," *The Pittsburgh Courier.*

"Leaders in Their Fields: Gordon Parks," Pepsi advertisement, *Ebony,* July 1951.

"Leaders in Their Fields: Ralph Bunche," Pepsi advertisement, *Ebony,* Aug. 1951.

Letter, "Attached Is a Proof," 1951, undated, sent by Edward F. Boyd from 3 West 57th Street headquarters, Boyd Collection.

Letter, "Dear Bottler," 1951, n.d., sent by Edward F. Boyd, Boyd Collection.

Letter, "Dear Editor," June 1, 1951, sent from Edward F. Boyd from 3 West 57th Street headquarters, Boyd Collection.

"Mack's Plans," *Business Week,* June 16, 1951, p. 153.

"Mexican 'Madness' Giveaway Epidemic Hits Below the Border, Prizes Run from Bottle-Openers to $30,000 Houses; Soft Drink Firms Show the Way, *The Wall Street Journal,* July 2, 1951, p. 1.

"Mobbed by Friends, DuBois in Tears After Acquittal, Federal Judge Halts 'Foreign Agent' Case, Frees Author and Four Others," *The Pittsburgh Courier,* Dec. 1, 1951, p. 1.

"More Than 400 Negroes Are over 100 Years Old," *Ebony,* Sept. 1952.

"National Pepsi-Cola Sales Force Includes Two Californians," unidentified newspaper clipping, 1951.

"Old Courses for Walter Mack," *Fortune,* Nov. 1951, p. 120.

"Pepsi-Cola in Ad Campaign," unidentified newspaper clipping, Boyd Collection.

"Pepsi-Cola Bottler Discusses Foreign Markets with Pepsi-Cola Parent Company officer," unidentified newspaper clipping, Boyd Collection.

"Pepsi-Cola (Finally) Hits the Spot," *Business Week,* July 5, 1952, p. 55.

"Pepsi-Cola Gifts at Cooking School," *Baltimore Afro American,* Apr. 28, 1951.

"Pepsi-Cola National Sales Staff Enjoys Respite in Miss.," unidentified clipping, Boyd Collection.

"Pepsi-Cola Pushes Sales in the Durham Area," unidentified newspaper clipping, Boyd Collection.

"Pepsi-Cola Reports Higher Sales; Result of Expansion Program," *The Wall Street Journal,* Apr. 2, 1951, p. 5.

"Pepsi-Cola Sales Representative in Dallas for Promotional Work," *The Dallas Star Post,* Oct. 13, 1951.

"Pepsi-Cola Salesmen Take to the Road," *The Carolinian,* Mar. 19, 1951.

"Pepsi-Cola Starts New Advertising Campaign in Newspapers, Magazines," *Omaha Star,* May 25, 1951.

"Pepsi-Cola Trains Race Employees," *New York Tribune,* Jan. 13, 1951.

"Pepsi-Cola's 4-Month Sales 12% Above 1950," *The Wall Street Journal,* May, 3, 1951, p. 3.

"Schlitz Salutes," advertisement for Schlitz beer, *The Pittsburgh Courier,* Sept. 29, 1951.

"Silent Salesmen, High Cost of Clerks Nourishes a Big Crop of Vending Machines," *The Wall Street Journal,* p. 1.

"Studies Medicine at University of Geneva," *Chicago Defender,* July 14, 1951.

"Succumbs to Injuries After 17 Months, Dies in Behalf of Vote Registration," *The Pittsburgh Courier,* Nov. 10, 1951.

WEB SITES AND OTHER MEDIA

The African American Registry, "Hilda Simms, Actress and Black Talent Supporter!" www.aaregistry.com/african_american_history/1765/Hilda_Simms, Oct. 2005.

Answers.com, "1951," www.answers.com/main, Sept. 2004.

Treasures of the University of Delaware Library, "Phillis Wheatley, (1753–1784)" www.lib.udel.edu/ud/spec/exhibits/treasures/american/wheatley, July 2006.

Chapter 8: *Crossing the Threshold*

NEWSPAPERS, PERIODICALS, AND BUSINESS EPHEMERA

"Ad Stepup: Stiffening Sales Battle Brings New Increases in Advertising Outlays," *The Wall Street Journal*, June 19, 1953.

"Adventures in Negro History II," Pepsi-Cola booklet accompanying record series, 1963, Harvey C. Russell Collection.

"Advertising: Agency Forms Unit in Paris; Pepsi-Cola Fills Post," *The New York Times*, June 22, 1964.

"Advertising: Battle for Minds?" *The New York Times*, May 22, 1959.

"Advertising: Pepsi Courts African Market," *The New York Times*, May 25, 1961.

"Advertising: Recognizing Negro Potential, Efforts Increasing to Tap the Vast Market in U.S.," *The New York Times*, Aug. 10, 1958.

"Advertising: Women Emancipated in Liquor Campaign," *The New York Times*, Oct. 18, 1963.

"African-American Institute Elects Wilkins a Trustee," *The New York Times*, Aug. 1, 1966.

"Alfred Steele, 57, of Pepsi-Cola Dies, Chairman and Chief Officer Had Been with Coca-Cola—Joan Crawford's Husband," *The New York Times*, Apr. 20, 1959.

"Alfred N. Steele Named Chairman of Pepsi-Cola; Barnet New President," *The Wall Street Journal*, Aug. 1, 1955.

"Amid the Ad Boom, One Firm Is in Tailspin," *The Wall Street Journal*, Oct. 26, 1955.

"Are Negro Models on Way Out?" New York *Amsterdam News*, June 3, 1950.

"Are You Getting Your Share of the 20 Billion Dollar Plus Negro Market," ad from Alexander Jackson Co., *The Wall Street Journal*, Mar. 4, 1963.

"Barnet Named Pepsi-Cola's Chief Executive Officer," *The Wall Street Journal*, May 8, 1959.

"BBDO Awarded Pepsi-Cola's Advertising Account Worth About $11 Million a Year," *The Wall Street Journal*, Apr. 7 1960.

"Below Picture of Negro Vice President of Pepsi-Cola, at Left, and His White Wife, in Center," flyer created by Ku Klux Klan, Harvey C. Russell Collection.

"Big Business Names a Veep," *Ebony*, July 1962, p. 25.

"Biow to Retire, Disband Agency, Big Advertising Organization Will Dissolve on June 30," *The New York Times*, Apr. 7, 1956.

"Blair Holdings Proxy Battle Looming Over Plan to Acquire Petri," *The Wall Street Journal*, Nov. 17, 1954.

"Books for Christmas Can Make Gifts of Immeasurable Value," Langston Hughes column, *Chicago Defender*, Dec. 13, 1952.

"Business: KKK Thinks Pepsi's Negro Veep's Wife Is White," *JET*, n.d., Harvey C. Russell Collection.

"Canned Beverages on Market in May, Cantrell & Cochrane to Offer Five Flavors at 7 and 10 cents for 6 and 12 Ounce Sizes," *The New York Times*, Apr. 21, 1953.

"Canned Soda Pop: Canada Dry, Dr. Pepper, Hoffman, Others Flock to Try New Packaging, 1954 Can Use by 'Bottlers' Expected to Be Six Times '53; Pioneers Expand, But Coke, Pepsi Stay Aloof," *The Wall Street Journal*, May 10, 1954.

"Canned Soda Pop: Wyoming Kids Sipping from 'Beer' Cans Hint Pop Packaging Change," *The Wall Street Journal*, Sept. 24, 1953.

"The Cardozo Family History, 1700s to 1979," by Neenah Payne, unpublished research, 56 pp.

"Check Big Business Link to Intimidation in Dixie," *Chicago Defender*, Oct. 15, 1955.

"Colored Customers, Civil Rights Push Alerts Companies to Potential of the Negro Market," *The Wall Street Journal*, Aug. 19, 1963.

"Conflict in Dixie, Whites Boycott Whites Thought to Support Integration of Schools, Alabama Ford Dealer Suffers from Foundation's Work," *The Wall Street Journal*, Mar. 9, 1956.

"Council Spurring Negro Businesses, Interracial Group Provides Guidance for Concerns," *The New York Times*, July 6, 1966.

"Court Allows Holder to Join in Suit Against Pepsi-Cola President," *The Wall Street Journal*, Oct. 19, 1954.

"Dignity, Respect Found in Ghana," *Chicago Defender*, April 19, 1958.

"Divorces in Advertising, Report on Recent Wave of 'Friendly' Separations of Clients and Agencies," *The New York Times*, Dec. 21, 1955.

"Follow the Champions, Have a Coke . . . for Quality You Can Trust," advertisement showing Larry Doby, *The Wilmington Journal*, June 5, 1954.

Bibliography

"Giveaways and Raffles Help Probe, Promote in the Negro Market," *The Wall Street Journal*, Mar. 29, 1956.

"Governor Orders Welfare Survey, He Says Sharp Rise in Cost in Time of Prosperity Is 'Economic Paradox,' " *The New York Times*, Dec. 17, 1964.

"A Hand Up Not a Handout," advertisement for the Office of Economic Opportunity, *The New York Times*, Sept. 25, 1967.

"Harvey Russell Is Named a Pepsi-Cola Executive," *Chicago Defender*, Jan. 30, 1962.

"H. Naylor Fitzhugh, 82, Educator and Pioneer in Target Marketing," *The New York Times*, July 29, 1992.

"Herbert L. Barnet of Pepsi-Cola, 61, Ex-Chairman, Who Assumed Post in 1963, Is Dead," *The New York Times*, Dec. 5, 1970.

"Highlights: Pepsi-Cola Declares 40 Cents in Dividends; Sales Gain Is Noted," *The Wall Street Journal*, Nov. 24, 1954.

"Joan Crawford to Aid Negro Troupe on Funds," *The New York Times*, Mar. 27, 1971.

"Joan Crawford, Widow of Chairman, Named to Pepsi-Cola Board, President Cites Actress' Knowledge of Firm's Business; April Sales Topped '58 and March," *The Wall Street Journal*, May 7, 1959.

"Kenyon & Eckhardt Is Awarded Pepsi-Cola Advertising Account," *The Wall Street Journal*, Dec. 15, 1955.

"Klan Jobs Called Bonanza for Two, They Bilked Other Members, House Investigators Say—Both Decline to Reply," *The New York Times*, Oct. 22, 1965.

"Labor Letter," *The Wall Street Journal*, July 15, 1969.

"Labor Letter, Job-Hopping Rises Among Negro Executives as They Seek Better Positions," *The Wall Street Journal*, Jan. 11, 1966.

Letter to Advertising Department, Pepsi-Cola Company, from J. W. Jackson, president and treasurer of Pepsi-Cola Bottling Co. of Wilmington, Inc., June 10, 1954, Harvey C. Russell Collection.

"Marketing Gold Mine!" by John Pepper and Bert Ferguson, advertisement for WDIA radio station, Memphis-Mid-South area, *The Wall Street Journal*, Apr. 14, 1955.

"Memo to American Business Re: Foreign and Domestic Trade, 'Cast Down Your Bucket Where You are!' " *Ebony* advertisement, *The Wall Street Journal*, Apr. 10, 1961.

"Most Negroes in Poll Say They Would Back Boycott of Concerns, Marketing Survey Indicates 89% Would Take Part If Their National Leaders Requested," *The Wall Street Journal*, Sept. 26, 1963.

"Negro Boycott Forces Till Killers to Sell Store Chain," New York *Amsterdam News,* Jan. 5, 1957.

"Negro Businesses to Receive Advice and Financial Aid, Group Formed Here to Guide and Encourage Enterprise—14 Banks Cooperate," *The New York Times,* June 18, 1964.

"The Negro Consumer, He Is Getting More Attention from Big National Advertisers, Negro Population Rises 57% Faster Than White; It's Concentrated in Big Cities, New Jobs from Buyers' Strike," *The Wall Street Journal,* June 30, 1961.

"Negro Executive Finds There Is Room at the Top, New Vice President at Pepsi-Cola Sees Gain for His Race," *The New York Times,* July 1, 1962.

"Negro Is Selected by Schenley for High Post in Its Sales Unit, Charles T. Williams Is First of His Race with a Title in Liquor Industry," *The New York Times,* Sept. 6, 1963.

"Negroes Earn Executive Posts in Sales and Technical Fields," *The New York Times,* Jan. 17, 1965.

"News of the Advertising and Marketing Fields," *The New York Times,* Oct. 30, 1955.

"News of Advertising and Marketing," *The New York Times,* Jan. 20, 1956.

"No Deposit: Soft Drinks Coming to Market in Throw-Away Cans," *The Wall Street Journal,* Apr. 21, 1953.

"Novelty Items 1952, Pepsi-Cola Company," brochure distributed to bottlers representing various vendors, Allen L. McKellar Collection.

"Pabst's Soft Drink Will Be Launched Monday in the New York Area, Tap-A-Cola Comes Extra-Dry and Non-Fattening; 6 More Plants May Be Needed to Produce It," *The Wall Street Journal,* May 21, 1954.

"Pepsi-Cola and Three Aces Go to Nigeria," *Chicago Defender,* March 19, 1960.

"Pepsi-Cola Buys Building," *The Wall Street Journal,* June 13, 1956.

"Pepsi-Cola Co. to Pay Widow of Chairman $300,000 over 5 Years, Joan Crawford to Get Payments Under Steele's Contract; She'll Also Receive Director's Fee," *The Wall Street Journal,* June 2, 1959.

"Pepsi-Cola Didn't Make Loan to Sen. McCarthy, President Steele Says," *The Wall Street Journal,* May 7, 1953.

"Pepsi-Cola Elevates Special Markets Aid," *The New York Times,* Jan. 30, 1962.

"Pepsi-Cola '51 Net More Than Doubled '50, Bottled Sales Rose 14%," *The Wall Street Journal,* Apr. 4, 1952.

"Pepsi-Cola Headquarters Opened," *The Wall Street Journal,* Feb. 2, 1960.

"Pepsi-Cola Nigerian Franchises," *The Wall Street Journal,* Aug. 4, 1959.

"Pepsi-Cola President Reports Current Sales 'At Accelerating Rate,' " *The Wall Street Journal,* Mar. 30, 1955.

"Pepsi-Cola Refreshes Without Filling," black-model advertisements, March 8, April 5, April 26, May 26, and June 14, 1958.

"Pepsi-Cola Says Net, Sales in '59 Set Records; to Market New Drinks, Fruit Flavors to Be Included in New Line; 16-Ounce Pepsi-Cola Bottle Planned," *The Wall Street Journal,* Feb. 3, 1960.

"Pepsi-Cola Seeks a New Ad Agency, Account Totals 10.5 Million—Toigo Stand on Contract Is Disclaimed by Biow," *The New York Times,* Dec. 6, 1955.

"Pepsi-Cola Stockholder Charges President Ran Firm for Personal Gain; Owner of 100 Shares Brings Suit in N.Y. Court; Steele's Lawyer Calls Claim Without Merit," *The Wall Street Journal,* June 6, 1953.

"Pepsi-Cola Unit Sales Set Record Last Year, Net Rose 41% over 1952," *The Wall Street Journal,* Mar. 31, 1954.

"Pepsico Picks Office of Community Affairs."

"Pepsi Keeps Close Check on Bottlers,' *Chicago Defender,* June 17, 1961.

"Pepsi, Vowing Diversity Isn't Just Image Polish, Seeks Inclusive Culture," *The Wall Street Journal,* April 19, 2005.

"Plan Awards for 6 Liberal Companies," *Chicago Defender,* Aug. 30, 1958.

"Refreshing—Not Filling—for Waistline Watchers," New York *Amsterdam News,* Mar. 8, 1958.

"Rose-Meta Campaigns Against Idea Negroid Hair Inferior," *Ebony,* May 1946.

"7 Negroes Cited as Businessmen, Executives Called Example of Hope for Youth," *The New York Times,* May 29, 1964.

"Show Men See Signs of Sales Resurgence in Downtown Centers, Some Switch Emphasis to Woo City Dwellers and Appeal to the Growing Negro Market," *The Wall Street Journal,* Nov. 23, 1962.

"Soda Pop: Soft Drink Companies Step Up Tests of Cans, Bigger Bottle Sizes, Firms Hope to Match Record Sales of 1953; Dietetic Drink Makers Optimistic, A Peek at Coca-Cola's Plans," *The Wall Street Journal,* Nov. 22, 1954.

"Southern Merchants Give More Attention to Negro Market, Tradesmen are Going Against Old Prejudices to Develop Big Potential," *The Wall Street Journal,* Jan. 4, 1954.

"10,882 yards for Cleveland . . .168,427 miles for Pepsi," advertisement for Pepsi featuring Jim Brown, *Sports Illustrated,* March 8, 1965.

"Thousands Here Pay Tribute to Whitney Young Jr.," *The New York Times,* Mar. 16, 1971.

"TV Tumble: Television Networks Are Hit by Big Wave of Ad Cancellations;

Esso, Toni, Admiral Drop Big Shows; Unemployment Stalks Faye Emerson," *The Wall Street Journal*, Apr. 4, 1952.

"Why not let Ebony Sell Your Negro Prospects?" *Ebony* ad, *The Wall Street Journal*, March 10, 1964.

WEB SITES AND OTHER MEDIA

All Souls Church, Unitarian, "A History of Social Justice at All Souls," Washington, D.C., http://www.all-souls.org/socialjustice/history.htm.

GlobalSecurity.org, "100th Battalion, 442nd Infantry," http://www.global security.org/military/agency/army/100-442in.htm, Oct. 2005.

Howard University School of Law, "Brown@50: Fulfilling the Promise," www.brownat50.org/brownBios/BioWmMing.html, for biographies of early civil-rights lawyers, June 2006.

"Moss Kendrix," Museum of Public Relations, http://www.prmuseum.com/kendrix/moss1.html, Mar. 2005.

Tuskegee Airmen, Inc.–National Web, www.tuskegeeairmen.org/history, June 2006.

Epilogue

NEWSPAPERS, PERIODICALS, AND BUSINESS EPHEMERA

The following were taken from the file on former employee Richard L. Hurt in the library of *The Boston Globe*, Boston.

"Book of the Day: A Long, Hard Look at Planning Urban America," by Richard L. Hurt, *The Boston Globe*, Feb. 19, 1969.

"Columbia Point II: City of Shame? Ridiculous Says 3-Year Dweller," by Richard L. Hurt, *The Boston Globe*, Sept. 10, 1962.

"Columbia Point IV: Does Unwritten Law Segregate Families," *The Boston Globe*, Sept. 12, 1962.

"Columbia Point VI: 1951 Prospects of Bright Future Mostly Unfulfilled," *The Boston Globe*, Sept. 14, 1962.

"Globe Reporter Wins Citation," unidentified and undated newspaper clipping, Hurt file, *The Boston Globe* library.

"Globe Reporters Forman, Hurt Receive National News Awards," *The Boston Globe*, Feb. 20, 1963.

"Morton Mintz' Thalidomide Series in Washington Post Wins Heywood Broun Award," press release, American Newspaper Guild, Feb. 18, 1963.

Bibliography

"Hold Key Posts in Advertising Agency," *The New York Times,* May 3, 1954.

"Kingdoms of Cola: The Conquests of Mr. Mack," *The New York Times,* Aug. 12, 1979.

"Lennen & Mitchell Names Executive Vice President," *The New York Times,* Feb. 14, 1949.

"Mack Bubbles over New Cola," *The New York Times,* Nov. 8, 1978.

Letter of Introduction of Allen L. McKellar from Ray Jordan, sales manager, Pepsi-Cola Bottlers of St. Louis, Jan. 26, 1953, Allen L. McKellar Collection.

"Negro Boycott Forces Till Killers to Sell Store Chain," *Amsterdam News,* Jan. 5, 1957.

Pope Visits America, *Time,* Oct. 15, 1965, clippings from Nicholas collection.

"Son of Boyd Family Takes Post with CARE," newspaper clipping, unidentified California weekly, Boyd Collection.

"There's Only One Coca-Cola," advertisement, New York *Amsterdam News,* Dec. 17, 1955.

"Two Old Cola Nuts," *Forbes,* Nov. 27, 1978.

WEB SITES AND OTHER MEDIA

Biographies, Walter Washington, www.exploredc.org/index, June 2006.

"Fish Wins Race, Voters OK DuBois Signs," *The Berkshire Eagle,* May 24, 2005.

"The Harvey C. Russell Inclusion Award," program brochure for Jan. 15, 2004, ceremony, PepsiCo., Frito-Lay North America Headquarters.

"History of Tuskegee University," www.tuskegee.edu/Global/story, June 2006.

"Nigerian Civil War," www.en.wikipedia.org/wiki/Nigeria_Civil_war, June 2006.

"PBS American Experience: The Murder of Emmett Till," Timeline, www.pbs.org/wgbh/amex/till/timeline/timeline2, June 2006.

"Years in Review: The IAEA Turns 40," www.iaea.org, July 2006.

Index

A&P, 13, 160
Abbott Laboratories, 9, 134
Actors Equity Association, 184
Adams, James W., 134
Admiral, 172
Advanced Space Engineering Division, 266
"Adventures in Negro History," 268
Adventures of a Bystander (Drucker), 9
Advertising Age, 62
Africa, 56, 263–64
African-Americans:
  in advertising, 78–81, 108–9, 114–19, 120–21, 125–26, 128–29, 142–43, 166, 226–27, 250, 253–54, 268–69
  at Algonquin Hotel, 64
  as baseball fans, 112
  at Coke, 59
  Coke boycotted by, 202, 204
  Coke consumed by, 7, 181
  and college, 16, 17
  and corporate America, xi, xv, 29–32, 41, 144, 283

  HUAC and, 121–22, 124
  in 1947, 90–95
  northward movement of, 19
  Pepsi boycotted by, 204
  Pepsi consumed by, xii, xiii–xiv, 2, 3, 7, 10, 14, 20, 36, 40, 72, 81, 98
  and Pepsi's corporate culture, xiv
  Pepsi's hiring of, xi–xii, xv, 15, 36–37
  and Pepsi's marketing, xiv, xvii, 21, 61–62, 63
  Philip Morris and, 79–80
  post–World War II improvements for, 41–42
  Rockwell and, 119–20
  service personnel canteens for, 34, 73, 105
  as soldiers, 6–7, 32–34, 41, 60, 61–62
  as voters, 23
  see also Negro market; press, African-American; PepsiCo Incorporated, African-American team at; segregation
Afro American, 63, 74, 178, 214, 258

bottles of, 54–55, 216
Boyd's desire for job at, 235
and Democratic Party, 15
Dr Pepper's lawsuit against, 237
and foreign markets, 236
franchises of, 54
history of, 56–57, 166
market capitalization of, xix
1939 sales of, 13
1949 sales of, 157
1950 net income of, 230
overseas plants of, 36
Pepsi's rivalry with, xi, 175–76
price of, 96, 196, 205, 237–38
production speed of, 98
rum and, 161
six-ounce bottles of, 10
sugar rationing and, 34
vending machines of, 136, 197, 202,
    215, 216, 244
see also Woodruff, Robert Win-
    ship
Coca-Cola Export, 35, 201
Colgate, 141, 172–73
Collier's, 11
Communism, 76, 163–64, 179, 260,
    268
Communist Party, 124, 165, 175
Community Relations Project, 89
Concept of the Corporation, The
    (Drucker), 229
Congress, U.S., 69–70, 103, 122, 124,
    182, 197
Congress of Industrial Organiza-
    tions, 192
Congress of Racial Equality
    (CORE), 140
Conoco, 7

Constitution, U.S., 170
    Fourteenth Amendment to, 183
Cooley, Isabelle, 173
Cornely, Paul B., 116
Cotton Club, 110
Cousins, Norman, 64–65
Crawford, Anthony, 23
Crawford, Joan, 136, 207, 262–63,
    264, 269
Cresta Blanca, 134
Croom, Austen Herbert, 12
Crosby, Bing, 94
Cry the Beloved Country (film), 123
Cuba, 35, 55, 65, 173, 230
Curry, Etta, 134
Curtis, William J., 237
Cushing, George H., 76

D'Arcy Advertising Company, 137
Davidson Brothers, Inc., 266
Davis, Bette, 86, 88
Davis, John W., 143
Davis, Paul D., 185, 199, 214, 229
    in Ghana, 263
    in move to New York, 237
    Pepsi's hiring of, xvi, 178
    as photographer, 207
    team's suspicion of, 233
Davis, Sammy, Jr., 269
Day, Robert, 11
Death of a Salesman (Miller), 132, 161
Dee, Frankie, 134
Deep Are the Roots, 41
Democratic Party, U.S., 15, 49, 50,
    148, 225
Denison, Franklin, 270
de Porres, Martin, 154
DePorres Club, 203

Index

About the Author

STEPHANIE CAPPARELL is the author of *Shackleton's Way: Leadership Lessons from the Great Antarctic Explorer*. She has worked at *The Wall Street Journal* since 1990 and is currently an editor for that paper's Marketplace page. She holds degrees from Boston University and Columbia University. She lives in New York City.

THE

REAL PEPSI CHALLENGE

How One Pioneering Company Broke Color
Barriers in 1940s American Business

Stephanie Capparell

Study Group Guide

ABOUT THIS GUIDE

The following study group guide is intended to help you find interesting
and rewarding approaches to your reading of *The Real Pepsi Challenge*.
We hope this enhances your enjoyment and appreciation of the book.

STUDY GROUP GUIDE

The Real Pepsi Challenge: **How One Pioneering Company Broke Color Barriers in 1940s American Business**

By Stephanie Capparell

Discussion Questions

1. "Above all, [Walter S. Mack] was motivated by the bottom line. When he looked at black, he also saw green" (p. xiii). In the introduction, and throughout the book, the author notes that Mack's hiring practices were due not only to his desire for social progress, but also to his wish to make money. Does this lessen your opinion of him as a social and business innovator? Meanwhile, Mack also set up an integrated scholarship program and had a reputation for being a "businessman of conscience" (p. 40). In business philanthropy, how do the merits of opportunity compare with those of charity?

2. In the introduction the author points to three main lessons in the book: (a) how to strive for personal excellence even when the rewards are distant, (b) how business can thrive only where diversity thrives, and (c) that the roadblocks to social progress are the same as those that hamper economic success (p. xvii). Which of these do you believe is the most important role of business leaders today as they face pressures to train and develop staffs, boost the corporate bottom line and make contributions to communities? Have you had a personal experience that highlights one of these lessons that is similar to one that the first African-American salesmen at Pepsi learned?

3. The author quotes Frank Wu, dean of Wayne State University Law School, "Diversity, like democracy, is a process; it never ends" (p. xix). What does this statement mean to you in terms of participation of various individuals? At what point in the process of diversity is today's workplace? What are the next steps to be completed?

4. Allen McKellar, winner of the essay contest and one-year job, noted that when he was traveling, the audiences found the Pepsi special-markets representatives infinitely more interesting than the free samples of the product they were handing out (p. 22). This implies that as a salesman he was selling himself, just as much, if not more, than the product. Do you think that this is still true for people working in corporations?

5. In 1942 *The Pittsburgh Courier* initiated the Double V Campaign: "Victory at home, Victory abroad" (p. 32). How influential was World War II to corporate hiring practices both during the war and in the postwar period? Give examples. What were some of the problems that surfaced as workforces were integrated?

6. Compare and contrast the backgrounds and personalities of Walter Mack of Pepsi (p. 45) and Robert Woodruff of Coca-Cola (p. 55). What were the key differences that led them to different business and diversity hiring practices? Were these differences only personality based, or rooted deeper in the social and corporate landscapes of the time?

7. The author lists a number of news snippets from 1947, highlighting notable gains by African-Americans in the workforce (p. 93). Just to name a few, the National Urban League placed twenty-five thousand blacks in white-collar jobs, and Jackie Robinson was

called up to play for the Dodgers at Ebbets Field. Which of the strides forward that she lists were the most crucial and the most lasting?

8. When Edward Boyd was hiring the first class of African-American sales representatives for Pepsi, he said he "wanted clean-cut guys with an education, youngish, well turned out, a certain personality" (p. 99). Looking at the men profiled in the book, pick two or three and describe what made each stand out as an excellent candidate.

9. Boyd's strategy to boost sales in 1948 was four-pronged, including public relations to boost orders and consumer awareness, a large newspaper and magazine ad campaign, a letter-writing campaign, and point-of-purchase ad pieces and packaging displays for stores (p. 113). How did each of these approaches contribute to the overall success of their campaigns?

10. Boyd began an ad campaign called "Leaders in Their Field," using notable, successful African-American achievers rather than celebrities of the moment. Is there a similar ad campaign out in the marketplace today? Why or why not might such a campaign work in advertising now?

11. When speaking of Arthur Miller's play, *Death of a Salesman*, a *Fortune* magazine article pointed to a *Harvard Business Review* survey showing that "A majority of the people believe that very few businessmen have the good of the nation in mind when they make their important business decisions" (p. 132). Do you believe that this sentiment is true today? If you believe that there has been a change, what was its catalyst? If there has not been a change, what does this reveal about the nature of business?

12. When Chuck Wilson was hired by Pepsi for national sales, he noted that he was "a little suspicious of the whole thing" (p. 145). How did the salesmen's expectations upon hiring meet with the reality of their jobs?

13. Throughout the 1940s, African-American publishers and civic leaders pushed hard to get corporations to pursue the so-called Negro market. What were their motives? What did the lack of recognition of African-American spending clout have on individuals, companies, and society as a whole?

14. Dr. Benjamin E. Mays, head of Morehouse College, predicted in a 1950 essay, "There will be no utopia for the Negro in the year 2000. . . . Even if discrimination became illegal, as with the Jews, discrimination would survive. So, as paradoxical as it may seem, the second half of the twentieth century holds for the Negro at least three things: larger opportunity, greater competition and continued discrimination. And I predict that he will meet all three with dignity, pride and success" (p. 171). Using examples from the book, discuss whether Dr. Mays was right or wrong in his prediction.

15. One of the salesmen said that he would use "the race bit" to sell Pepsi. What did he mean? How did the two biggest cola rivals use race in their campaigns in the 1940s and 1950s to sell their product? How did the public react? As consumers, do you base your purchasing decisions on known diversity practices within companies?

16. As the leadership of Pepsi changed hands from Walter Mack to Alfred Steele, there were many changes to the structure and strategy of the company. The author noted that the leadership

had gone from Mack's typical "Is there anything I should know?" to Steele's command, "Don't wear out the rug in my office" (p. 232). What were some of the lasting effects for the salesmen in the special-markets division?

17. While traveling, many of the special-market salesmen visited and spoke at African-American churches. Julian Nicholas noted that, "It wasn't the gospel singing that kept people going to service. It was a total social outlet" (p. 234). Do churches have the same social and economic influence today as they did in the late 1940s? If not, what social entities have taken its place, where businesses might market to a similar audience?

18. What groundbreaking move in advertising did Pepsi's vice president Harvey Russell make in 1965 (p. 268)? Describe the political climate at the time, in terms of race relations. How did companies react to that climate? Do you think the relationship between politics and corporate leadership has changed since then?

Enhance Your Study Group

1. Visit Pepsi.com and compare the diversity of the company's marketing and advertising campaigns today with those discussed in the book. Examine the use of images of African-Americans in selling PepsiCo brands such as Lay's Potato Chips, Gatorade, Doritos, Aunt Jemima Syrups & Mixes, Tropicana Juices, and Quaker Oats. To what degree have they changed?

2. Visit http://www.pepsico.com/PEP_Diversity/timeline /index.cfm for a timeline of diversity at PepsiCo that covers many years past the scope of *The Real Pepsi Challenge*. Explore and discuss Pepsi's

commitment to diversity and special markets and compare it with another major corporation, using current diversity lists and awards.

3. Using the Internet, find surveys that compare the buying habits of various ethnic groups. What are recent examples in which a group's spending on a product or product category, such as groceries, clothing, or movie tickets, is greater than its population share would suggest?

4. Research the need for diversity in today's workplace. Gather statistics on the representation of women, African-Americans, and other minorities in entry-level corporate positions and compare those with hiring profiles for upper-level jobs and for corporate boards.